Campus Ecology and University Affairs

History, Applications, and Future

A Scholarly Personal Narrative

James H. Banning

TerraCotta
Publishing

Campus Ecology and University Affairs

James H. Banning © 2016
Email: campusecologist@gmail.com
Website: http://www.campusecologist.com

All rights reserved. No part of this publication may be reproduced, stored in a retrieval system, or transmitted in any form or by any means—electronic, mechanical, photocopy, recording, or any other—without the prior permission of the author.

ISBN-13: 13:978-0-9863812-7-0

ISBN-10: 0-9863812-7-6

Library of Congress Control Number: 2016951921

Printed in the United States of America

Cover Designer and Typesetter:
Michelle Kenny, Westlake Village, CA

TerraCotta
Publishing

Table of Contents

Preface _____ ix

Acknowledgments _____ xv

PART 1: History of the Ecological Perspective and Campus Ecology _____ 1

Chapter 1: History of the Ecological Perspective: A Personal View _____ 3

Chapter 2: The Campus Ecology Model _____ 27

PART 2: The Applications of Campus Ecology to University Affairs_____ 67

Chapter 3: Institutional Affairs and Campus Ecology _____ 69

    Applications: Planning and Campus Ecology _____ 69

    Applications: Campus Assessment and the Campus Ecology _____ 71

    Applications: Campus Community/Culture and Campus Ecology_____ 76

    Applications: The Physical Environment and Campus Ecology _____ 80

    Applications: Campus Safety and Campus Ecology _____ 88

Chapter 4: Academic Affairs and Campus Ecology _____ 93

    Applications: Recruitment/Admissions/Orientation and Campus Ecology _ 93

    Applications: Retention and Campus Ecology _____ 96

    Applications: Academic Outcomes and Campus Ecology _____ 104

    Applications: Academic Advising and Campus Ecology _____ 109

    Applications: Alternative Academic Delivery and Campus Ecology ____ 112

    Applications: Academic Departments and Campus Ecology _____ 114

    Applications: Academic Classroom Issues and Campus Ecology _____ 117

Chapter 5: Student Affairs and Campus Ecology _____ 123

    Applications: Engagement/Involvement and Campus Ecology _____ 124

- Applications: Mattering and Campus Ecology 127
- Applications: Student Satisfaction and Campus Ecology 129
- Applications: Student Development and Campus Ecology 131
- Applications: Student Behavior and Campus Ecology 138
- Applications: Activism and Campus Ecology 141
- Applications: Student Affairs Theory and Practice and Campus Ecology _143
- Applications: Student Affairs Training and Campus Ecology 151
- Applications: Student Affairs Ethics and Campus Ecology 155
- Applications: Student Affairs Counseling and Campus Ecology .. 156
- Applications: Student Affairs Housing and Campus Ecology 162
- Applications: Student Affairs Recreation and Campus Ecology .. 170
- Applications: Student Affairs Unions and Campus Ecology 170
- Applications: Student Affairs Learning Communities and Campus Ecology 172
- Applications: Student Affairs Health and Campus Ecology 174
- Applications: Student Affairs First Year Programs and Campus Ecology __ 180
- Applications: Student Affairs Student Leadership and Campus Ecology __185
- Applications: Student Affairs Faith Programs and Campus Ecology 188
- Applications: Student Affairs Honors Activities and Campus Ecology ___190
- Applications: Student Affairs Athletics and Campus Ecology 192
- Applications: Student Affairs Greeks and Campus Ecology 194

Chapter 6: Diversity Affairs and Campus Ecology 197
- Applications: Diversity Policies/Programs and Campus Ecology .. 198
- Applications: African Americans and Campus Ecology 203
- Applications: Latinas/os and Campus Ecology 208
- Applications: Asian Americans and Campus Ecology 211
- Applications: Native Americans and Campus Ecology 212
- Applications: International Students/Programs and Campus Ecology ___ 212
- Applications: White and Campus Ecology 217

Table of Contents

Applications: Multicultural Groups and Campus Ecology _____ 218
Applications: Appalachian Students and Campus Ecology _____ 221
Applications: Disability and Campus Ecology _____ 221
Applications: Women and Campus Ecology _____ 223
Applications: LGBT and Campus Ecology _____ 227
Applications: Men and Campus Ecology _____ 231
Applications: Gender and Campus Ecology _____ 232
Applications: Commuters and Campus Ecology _____ 235
Applications: Low Income Students and Campus Ecology _____ 237
Applications: Adults, Non-Traditionals, Veterans and Campus Ecology _ 238
Applications: First Generation Students and Campus Ecology _____ 240
Applications: Geography and Campus Ecology _____ 241

Chapter 7: The Community College _____ 243
Applications: Planning and Campus Ecology _____ 243
Applications: Campus Community/Culture and Campus Ecology _____ 243
Applications: Retention and Campus Ecology _____ 244
Applications: Academic Advising and Campus Ecology _____ 245
Applications: Academic Programs and Campus Ecology _____ 245
Applications: Academic Outcomes and Campus Ecology _____ 246
Applications: Academic Classrooms and Campus Ecology _____ 247
Applications: Mattering and Campus Ecology _____ 247
Applications: Engagement/Involvement and Campus Ecology _____ 248
Applications: Student Satisfaction and Campus Ecology _____ 248
Applications: Student Development and Campus Ecology _____ 249
Applications: Student Affairs Theory and Practice and Campus Ecology 249
Applications: Counseling and Campus Ecology _____ 250
Applications: Learning Community and Campus Ecology _____ 250
Applications: First Year Programs and Campus Ecology _____ 251

Applications: Diversity Policies and Programs 251
Applications: African Americans and Campus Ecology 251
Applications: Native Americans and Campus Ecology 252
Applications: Asian Americans and Campus Ecology 252
Applications: Multicultural Students and Campus Ecology 252
Applications: International Students/Programs and Campus Ecology 253
Applications: Gender and Campus Ecology 253
Applications: Women and Campus Ecology 253
Applications: Adults, Non-Traditionals, Veterans and Campus Ecology 253
Applications: Low Income Students and Campus Ecology 253
Applications: First Generation Students and Campus Ecology 254
Applications: Geography and Campus Ecology 254

PART 3: The Future 257

Chapter 8: The Future: An Epilogue 259

About the Author 275

Appendix A: First Paper on Campus Ecology by Dr. Leland Kaiser 277

Preface

For the past number of years, I have tried to envision "retirement." This book is one of the projects that kept coming to the forefront. My idea was to look at what has happened to the concept of campus ecology since it was first introduced in the early 1970s, thus, the title: *Campus Ecology and University Affairs: History, Application, and Future*. The processes to fulfill the promise of the title are reasonably straightforward. You find all that you can that has been written about campus ecology, conceptualize the historical references, organize and index the references regarding application to the range of university affairs, and then, finally, speculate about the future of the concept. Not an easy task, but one that falls within the skills of most academics who have made a career out of reading, research, and writing. It is the subtitle "A Scholarly Personal Narrative" that became a major challenge.

Daniel White, in the Preface to his book *Postmodern Ecology*, makes the following statement in reference to his book: "This kind of endeavor requires a combination of intellectual humility and arrogance: the humility to know that you can't know it all and the arrogance to try" (1998, xiii). The significance of White's statement is quite applicable to this book. In my literature search, I found over 900 manuscripts, including books, book chapters, theses and dissertations, newsletters, and website materials that at least mention the concept of campus ecology in reference to university affairs. It does take a good dose of intellectual humility to know that after months of searching you may not have found it all. However, it is the second aspect of White's statement that I want to focus on in relation to the subtitle—A Scholarly Personal Narrative.

My own personal history of scholarship and professional activity constitutes a large and significant overlap with the history and application of the concept of campus ecology. I was present at the meeting where the concept was introduced within the context of student affairs and higher education, and, of the 900 manuscripts found, 130 carry my name as an author or co-author. I am often referred to, erroneously, as the "father of campus ecology," but it would perhaps be more accurate to think of me as a "pioneer in campus ecology." I have taught campus ecology at the graduate level for over 30 years, and while my engagement with the concept of campus ecology is certainly substantial, it stills assumes far more arrogance than I am comfortable with. The question, however, becomes how to present the purpose of this endeavor and to ensure the readers that they know they are exploring the text written from a single experience or perspective—mine. To answer this question and to meet this challenge, I have selected the genre of scholarly personal narrative as developed and presented by Nash (2004) and Nash & Bradley (2011) as the style for this book.

The scholarly personal narrative is a style of inquiry and writing that focuses on the personal experiences of the writer that can include "particular events, people, and critical incidents from the writer's life" (Nash, p. 30) and is intentionally written in an academic story like format in order to "carry larger, more universalizable meanings for the readers" (Nash, p. 30). Nash's foundation for the personal scholarly narrative is the postmodern notion that "truth is made, not discovered." He goes on to suggest that the personal scholarly narrative is "both concrete and abstract. It is down to earth and theoretical" (Nash, p. 12). Chang (2011) captures the sense of the personal scholarly narrative: "SPN is good at mixing two seemingly incompatible ingredients—self-reference and sound scholarship—to create a powerful recipe for academic writing. What SPN does remarkably well is to integrate scholarly discourse and content... into the self-narrative..." (Chang, p. ix).

For a writer and practitioner who was trained (forced) to write in third person, the SPN genre is not an easy format to implement. As often as it is possible and appropriate, I share experiences and information in a story or narrative format. Most often these personal anecdotes are found within a text box titled "On a Personal Note." I use the pronoun "I" throughout the book because using first person rather than the more typical third person is well supported for academic writing even outside the SPN genre (Webb, 1992). For example, Kelly (2006), in his book *The Basic Concepts of the Ecological Approach*, titles the introductory chapter "Being Autobiographical: Roots and the Varied Soils for Ecological Inquiry." He follows the title with a quote from Blee (2003): "We are more honest as scholars when we acknowledge the myriad of ways in which our personal lives and emotions are intertwined with who, what, and how we study" (p. 22).

The book is divided into three parts: History, Application, and Future followed by an appendix that presents the first paper on campus ecology authored by Leland Kaiser. Part 1 includes a chapter focusing on a brief history of my experiences with the ecological perspective and a second chapter outlining the history of the campus ecology model and its application to university affairs. Part 2 presents topical indexes of how the concept of campus ecology has been applied to university affairs including institutional, academic, student, and diversity affairs. In addition, Chapter 7 in part two indexes applications of campus ecology specific to the community college. These topical indexes of applications should be supportive to future writers and researchers of the ecological perspective and the campus ecology concept. Part 3 includes a chapter that speculates on the future of the concept. Finally, Appendix A presents the paper by Leland Kaiser that first introduced the concept of campus ecology to a small group of student affairs and higher education professionals in the early 1970s.

References:

Blee, K. (2003). Study the enemy. In B. Glasser & R. Hertz (Eds.), *Our studies, ourselves: Sociologists' lives and work* (pp. 13-23). Oxford: Oxford University Press.

Chang, H. (2011). Foreword. In R. J. Nash & D. L. Bradley, *Me-search and re-search: A guide for writing scholarly personal narrative manuscripts* (pp. ix-xi). Charlotte, NC: Information Age Publishing, Inc.

Kelly, J. G. (2006). *Becoming ecological: An introduction to community psychology.* New York: Oxford University Press.

Nash, R. J. (2004). *Liberating scholarly writing: The power of the personal narrative.* New York: Teacher College Press.

Nash, R. J., & Bradley, D. L. (2011). *Me-search and re-search: A guide for writing scholarly personal narrative manuscripts.* Charlotte, NC: Information Age Publishing, Inc.

Webb, C. (1992). The use of the first person in academic writing: Objectivity, language, and gatekeeping. *Journal of Advanced Nursing, 17,* 747-752.

White, D. R. (1998). *Postmodern ecology: Communications, evolutions, and play.* Albany, NY: State University of New York Press.

Acknowledgments

Although I write with the "I," this work has been much more of a "we" effort. I want to recognize the significant people in the "we" category.

First, I want to acknowledge the support and work of Sue Banning. Not only has she provided the encouragement and support needed for the effort of this book, but she has been doing so throughout my relationship with campus ecology. During the tenure of the *Campus Ecologist Newsletter*, she served as publisher, copy editor, bookkeeper, and production and distribution manager. These were all the difficult tasks.

Second, I want to acknowledge the hundreds of students who have enrolled and participated in my campus ecology classes over the past 30 years. They have taught me new lessons about campus ecology. I thank Colorado State University's Student Affairs in Higher Education (SAHE) for providing support and a home for the campus ecology class.

Third, I want to thank the many scholars and colleagues who have contributed to the study and application of campus ecology. I want to give special acknowledgment to Leland Kaiser, C. Carney Strange, Jim Hurst, Linda Kuk, Nancy Evans, Kristen Renn, Karen Arnold, Lori Patton, and Will Barratt. They have been significant contributors to the advancement of the ecological perspective. In addition, the importance of the initial role of Western Interstate

Commission for Higher Education in the development of the campus ecology is acknowledged and the continuing support of SAHE has provided a home for the teaching of campus ecology.

Finally, this book would not have been possible without the support and guidance of Andrea Sims, Ph.D., owner/publisher of TerraCotta Publishing.

Part 1

History of the Ecological Perspective and Campus Ecology

Part 1 includes a chapter focusing on a brief history of the ecological perspective and its emergence in the student affairs work in higher education. It includes a personal account of my interest in the ecological perspective as well as the roots and conditions supporting this perspective. A second chapter outlines the development and the structure of the ecological perspective within student affairs and higher education via the concept of campus ecology. These two chapters provide the background for Part 2 where the applications focus not only on student affairs, but on university affairs including institutional, academic, and diversity affairs as well as university affairs applications associated with the community college.

Chapter 1

History of the Ecological Perspective:
A Personal View

An introductory chapter attempting to cover the full and rich history of the ecological perspective is impossible. In keeping with the scholarly personal narrative approach, I am sharing the history from a personal perspective starting with a critical event, followed by several happenings both personal and national that set the stage for the impact of my critical event. While my critical event was clearly personal, it also occurred within the "zeitgeist" of the time. The chapter closes with a discussion of student development and the ecological perspective. The material in this chapter sets the stage for the development of the ecological perspective; the material in the next chapter explores the concept of the campus ecology model within this ecological perspective.

A quick fast-forward of the concept of ecology up to the experience that brought about my involvement in the concept is needed. The word ecology stems from the Greeks and means the "study of the house" (Kormonday & Brown, 1998). Later, the Greeks would use the notion to focus on the interaction of animals and their environment. But the word "ecology" was not defined within the scientific community until the mid-nineteenth century when German scientist Ernst Haeckel introduced the concept of ecology to focus on the links of ecology and evolution (Kormonday & Brown, 1998). The next stop in the "fast forward" is to the field of human ecology, where we find two Chicago sociologists, Albion Small and George Vincent, focused on the relationship of the social world and the material environment (Small & Vincent, 1894). Then came Ellen Richards who introduced the field of home economics and the concept of human ecology in the early 1990s (Merchant, 2007). It is the field of human ecology that serves as the immediate backdrop for the emersion of the concept of campus ecology. Human ecology is defined as the study of the relationships between people and their environment (Marten, 2001). Campus ecology takes the concept of human behavior in relation to the natural, social, and built environments and focuses on the college and university campus. For example, Banning and Kuk (2005) defined the concept of campus ecology as follows:

> Campus ecology as an ecological perspective for the work of student affairs was also introduced during this time period. The concept of campus ecology is defined as the study of the campus as an ecological system made up of three components. The first is the organism/inhabitants component which includes students, faculty, staff, visitors, and others associated with the campus. The second component is the settings/environments component, and it includes both the social environment (the curriculum, the co-curriculum, the extra-curricular, and other social functions) and the physical environment (buildings, landscapes, walkways, and other natural and constructed features of the environment). The third component is the activities/behaviors component (learning, research, personal development, and other outcomes specific to higher education). (p. 9)

History of the Ecological Perspective: A Personal View

In other words, campus ecology is the "study of the house" where the house is defined as the college and university environment. It was a critical event within the "house" that called me to the ecological perspective.

The Critical Event

A critical event, the story, is one "that reveals a change of understanding or worldview by the storyteller" (Webster & Mertova, 2007, p. 73). This story is an event that has impact and is "almost always a change experience" (Webster & Mertova, 2007, p. 75). The following story was a change experience for me. My worldview regarding mental health became far more clear, enough so as to bring about a career change from a practicing clinical psychologist to a researcher, administrator, and a faculty member. My new focus and purpose was to try to bring about the ecological perspective to higher education campuses via campus ecology. (See "On a Personal Note" #1.)

"On a Personal Note" #1-1: Critical Event Leading to My Ecological Perspective

It was a fall morning, in the late 1960s at the University of Colorado in Boulder. I was sitting in my counseling/therapy office in Willard Hall waiting for my first client of the day to show for his 9:00 a.m. therapy appointment. My feet were propped up on the corner of my desk, and I was skimming through the student newspaper, the *Colorado Daily*. I noticed they were covering a number of events on and off campus relating to the protest movement in the community regarding our nation's involvement in the Vietnam War. In fact, they had a few pictures of the previous evening's protest parade down Broadway. I looked at the photos carefully to see if they happened to capture my wife and I and our young daughter marching. They had not. My window was opened part way to capture the mountain fresh air of the season, but the air had a definite smell of smoke. I went to the window, and I could see that a group of students with their banners and placards protesting the Vietnam War had started a small fire on the lawn next to the Regents, the administrative building at the time, apparently to draw attention to their cause. I could also hear chanting and commotion coming from another larger group of students.

The phone on my desk rang. I picked up the phone: "Hello, this is Jim Banning."

"Jim, this is Glen." (Glen was the Vice President for Student Affairs at the time for the CU-Boulder campus.) "Jim, I am sure you have noticed that we have a number of students on campus—protesters and hippies—who are causing problems. What are the possibilities you and the Counseling Center might be able to start some group therapy programs that would include these students? We don't want this situation to get out of hand."

I'm not sure how I responded to the request. Probably found an administratively tactful way to indicate that we would discuss it. I put down the phone and, as I recall, my entire body seemed to shake with cold chills. This emotional reaction was not to the Vice President's request, per se. He was a good student affairs administrator and was concerned for the campus. My emotional reaction took me to my next thought—I remember it clearly: As a clinical psychologist, I have actually taught people to ask such a question. The idea that the causes of abnormal behavior reside within the individual and can be treated by mental health professions was the message that I was teaching. Activism for social change was being seen as "abnormal" and, therefore, psychotherapy was needed. One of the immediate outcomes of the introspective look was that this traditional perspective of mental health, the role of clinical psychology, and my practice of this perspective and role was no longer going to be acceptable to the way I wanted to proceed with my career. Within months, I resigned as Director of the Counseling Center and began my career with the Western Interstate Commission for Higher Education (WICHE). The goal of the WICHE project was to develop new ways to address mental health on Western campuses. The "new way" became the ecological perspective as a way to look at student affairs or "campus ecology."

Pre-Critical Events: Roots of an Ecological Perspective

Kelly (2006) writes about roots and soils in the development of his ecological perspective. While the critical event of the phone call occurred at a specific time and place, it is not without a preceding history or "roots." I present these previous experiences that paved the way for the outcome of the phone call from the SPN perspective. Most notable to me on reflections were cultural relativism, paradigm shift, the construction of reality, the myth of mental illness, and the person/environment unit.

In the fall of 1958 at William Jewell College in Liberty, Missouri, Professor Murry Hunt introduced me to the concept of "cultural relativism." I consider this concept an important root in my journey to the ecological perspective. My "take away" was the notion that there are different ways to view behaviors, values, and concepts depending upon where one "is standing." This simple take away, however, opens the door to new ways of thinking about "established thinking" and a safeguard against provincialism. For me, cultural relativity served as a basic foundation to understanding Kuhn's (1962) concept of paradigm shift capturing the nature of scientific revolutions where new paradigms or "ways of thinking" can bring about profound change in understanding the phenomenon. Finally, I owe a debt of thanks to Berger and Luckmann (1966) for underscoring the notion that reality and paradigms are socially constructed. The next step in my journey was carrying these concepts into the field of clinical psychology. These "root" concepts allowed me to discover, absorb, and be influenced by the key writings of Thomas Szasz (1961). Of particular importance was his book titled *The Myth of Mental Illness* in which he wrote about mental illness as human problems in living. For me, this opened the door to thinking about mental illness, not just about the characteristics of individuals, but also about being concerned with the environmental conditions in which individuals reside.

The foregoing concepts were all instrumental for me as a clinical psychologist as I visited the literature and thinking surrounding the person/environment interaction (Brunswick, 1956; Lewin, 1936). Of particular interest was the work of environmental and ecological psychologists (Barker, 1968; Bronfenbrenner, 1979; & Wicker, 1979). Walsh (1978) gives a succinct summary of this work. He also captures the heart of my journey: "To understand the behavior of a person, one must understand the environmental context or situation within which the behavior occurs" (p. 6).

Concurrent Events: Soils of My Ecological Perspective

Kelly (2006) points to the importance of "soils" in understanding one's professional biography. I interpret the concept of soils as a way to understand the concurrent conditions that foster and encourage a particular professional development. In graduate school we used the concept of "zeitgeist" to capture this notion of "the spirit of the times." (We also used the concept to "show off" our scholarly language.)

There are a number of "conditions of the soil" or "spirit of the times" that supported my adoption of the ecological perspective and the development of the concept of campus ecology. The soil conditions take two forms. One includes what was happening in the larger community: the community mental health movement, the civil rights movement, Vietnam War protests, and the women's movement. The second condition includes the academic scholarship of human ecology, environmental and ecological psychology, the applied arenas of health prevention, and community mental health. The following section closes with a discussion of the two key "root and soil" conditions to the ecological perspective of campus ecology. I call these key ingredients the "Outreach Movement in College Counseling" and "Student Affairs and the Ecological Perspective."

Soil Conditions: The Larger Community

The events in the larger community during this time period, from the early 1960s and ending in the early 1970s, are often referred to as the contributing factors to the culture of the sixties. This time period included a number of significant cultural and political events leading to what is often noted as a time of counterculture and revolution in social norms. It was also a time when significant protest emerged, as well (Sampson, 1967). These significant changes included the anti-war movement, a protest against the Vietnam War; the civil rights movement, a protest against the discrimination of, most notably, Black and Hispanic Americans; the feminist movement, a protest against the inequalities of opportunities and personal freedom; and the gay rights movement, a protest against the lack of full equality in American society. These protests were against the conditions of society and the pain and suffering these conditions inflicted on important segments of the population.

This is the larger community's linkage in support of the ecological perspective with conditions in the environment that needed to be addressed in order to improve the life of individuals. These movements led to major environmental/policy changes including the Civil Rights Act of 1964, the Voting Rights Act of 1965, and the 1968 Fair Housing Act. These legislative achievements were intended to improve the lives of individuals, not by changing the individuals, but by changing the negative and harmful conditions of American society, a clear ecological intervention.

In addition to the above legislative acts, the Community Mental Health Act signed by President John F. Kennedy in 1963 gave specific support to the ecological perspective within the mental health field with its new focus on the community. Conyne, Horne, and Raczynski (2013) point to the 1963 Community Mental Health Act (CMHA) as a part of the "dynamic activity" (p. 8) of the sixties in the field of mental health. The direct link to the ecological perspective was the emphasis and requirements regarding prevention services. This linkage is clearly seen in Caplan's (1964) focus on primary prevention with the intent to change conditions in the environment in order to prevent individual mental health problems from developing. The basic "soil" message from the activities of larger communities of the sixties was that societal conditions/environments need to change and toxic conditions/environments need to be prevented. These themes of change and prevention are key to understanding the ecological perspective and campus ecology. On a personal note, I often use the Cornish Test of Insanity as a way to highlight these themes. (See "On a Personal Note" #1-2.)

"On a Personal Note" #1-2: Cornish Test of Insanity

Eli Bowers (1964) reports the following story: "A telling model of the need for prevention is embodied in an old Cornish custom which was at the same time a simple and valid test of what might be called social insanity. In the 1600s a person suspected of being insane was put in a small room in front of a sink in which was placed a bucket. The faucet was turned on. The subject was given a ladle and was asked to empty the water from the bucket. If he tried desperately to bail the water out of the bucket without curtailing or attempting to reduce the flow at its source, he was considered insane." Bowers's point is, "Any society or community which attempts in this 20th century to provide bigger and better buckets of cure for behavior disorders without at the same time trying to reduce or stop the flow of their sources is equally suspect of insanity." He concludes by saying, "I urge all of us to examine the tap, and to look for tools and methods by which we can begin to turn it down or turn it off."

The direct question for the campus environment is—what is coming out of the "campus taps" and how do we make changes to turn the tap off. Some taps to consider—An education that does not "involve" or "engage" the whole student? Monolithic thinking for a growing multicultural society? Racist and sexist modeling? Perhaps we need a few more good plumbers and a smaller clean-up crew. Perhaps we need more designers focusing on the ecological relation between students and the campus environment.

> **Source for story:**
>
> Bowers, E. M. (1964). Primary Prevention of Mental and Emotional Disorders: A frame of reference. *Mental Health Monographs No. 5,* Washington, DC: U.S. Department of Health, Education, and Welfare.
>
> Adapted from: Banning, J. H. (1985). Cornish test of insanity. *The Campus Ecologist, 3*(2), 2.

Soil Conditions: Academic Disciplines and Scholarship

While the soil conditions of the larger community were calling for a change in conditions to improve the human condition, academic disciplines and related scholarship were also shifting the emphasis toward the environment. The discipline of psychology in the 1960s moved to a near universal acceptance of the interactionist model that behavior is a function of the person transacting with the environment. Behavior is not the result of nurture or nature, but behavioral outcomes are influenced by both. Acceptance of this foundational position helped give rise to the sub-discipline within psychology most related to campus ecology, the field of ecological/environmental psychology. Ecological/environmental psychology is a field focused on the study of living systems, their environment or surroundings, and the reciprocity between the two (Heft, 2001). Surroundings within a campus application refers not just to the physical environment (natural and/or built), but to social settings, and policy and informational environments, as well. The soil condition provided by ecological/environmental psychology was enriched by the writings of Bronfenbrenner (1979), Barker (1968), and Wicker (1979). Moving the person-environmental perspective and its importance to college student personnel work is well represented in the work of Walsh (1973, 1978), particularly the 1973 monograph titled *Theories of Person-Environment Interaction Implications for the College Student.* In addition, Conyne and Clack (1981) presented a firm foundation for the use of the ecological perspective in their work *Environmental Assessment and Design.*

Key Root and Soil Conditions for the Development of Campus Ecology

It is difficult to sort out and identify all the influencing roots and soil conditions for the growth and support of an idea like campus ecology, but two conditions in my journey with campus ecology are important: the outreach movement in college counseling centers which gave conceptual direction to the application of campus ecology and the uncertainty in the student personnel field regarding role and direction. The latter provided an opportunity for discussion and exposure of the campus ecology to a wider audience that was taking an introspective look at itself and was open to considering new ideas and nuances for its foundational base.

The Outreach movement in college counseling.

The closest and richest nutrient or influence on the growth of the ecological perspective on campus and the concept of campus ecology was the outreach movement of the sixties and seventies associated with campus counseling centers. One of the early writings that prompted the field of counseling to consider the campus environment as important to their work was provided by Oetting in 1967. (See "On a Personal Note" #1-3: Quotes from Gene Oetting.) The center for both the conceptualization and application of this outreach movement was the University Counseling Center at Colorado State University, specifically the work of Morrill, Oetting, and Hurst (1974) and their work regarding the cube model. The development of the "cube" contributed significantly to the acceptance of the campus ecology concept within the mainstream of student affairs activity. The cube defines the activity of a counseling center (and other sites of interventions, as well) by using a three dimensional cube built on these three dimensions: What is the target of the intervention?; What is the purpose of the intervention?; and What is the method of the intervention? The target dimension included individuals, primary groups, associational groups, and institutions or communities. The dimension of purpose included remediation, prevention, and development. The third dimension included methods of intervention: direct service, consultation, and training and media. The cube designed in these three dimensions, along with their categories, produced a 36-cell cube. Morrill, Oetting, and Hurst (1974) assigned the category of direct method of intervention focus on the institutional target for the purpose of its development as a cell where campus ecology could reside. This relationship between this cell of the cube and campus ecology provided the opportunity for Banning and Kaiser (1974) to publish their work on the ecological perspective and model for campus design in a major student affairs journal: *The Personnel and Guidance Journal*.

"On a Personal Note" #1-3: Quotes from Gene Oetting

Gene Oetting's quotes are presented within the personal note format due to the importance of his writing to the emergence of the ecological perspective and the fact that his influence was personal. His office was next to mine at one point in our careers.

His work clearly points to the need for counseling professionals to begin to consider their role in the environment. I have put these statements in italics for emphasis.

> "...The counseling psychologist is concerned with identifying the developmental inadequacies and *locating or providing experiences that remedy the environmental deficiency*.... The counseling psychologist is... concerned with identifying the capabilities of the student and *helping him find and locate an environment that will provide him with tasks he needs and can use*.... There might also be situations where the developmental task that would be appropriate for continuing personal growth may simply not be available. *Environmental deprivation of this kind would also be seen as a mental health problem, and the counseling psychologist would, perhaps, encourage faculty or others to provide the experience, or, in the absence of other resources, might develop a program in order to meet the need.*"
>
> Oetting, E. R. (1967). Developmental definition of counseling psychology. *Journal of Counseling Psychology, 14*(4), 382-385. Quotes found on page 383.

The connection made between the cube outreach model and the ecological perspective of campus ecology served as a solid foundation for the field of student personnel to consider the importance of the ecological perspective not only for counseling, but for student affairs work in general. The importance of the 1967 Oetting statement in providing ground work for future developments in the ecological perspective is captured by Hurst (1987): "Oetting proposed an interactive model wherein students would become active agents in shaping or modifying their environment to facilitate the actualization of their goals. Although he did not use the terminology of campus ecology, he was articulate in advocating an ecosystems approach" (p. 7). Pace, Stamier, Yarris, and June (1996) revisited the original cube and gave more emphasis to interactions within the campus with other student services and noted the campus ecology model gave support to interventions between individual students and the campus environment. In addition to the support from the field of counseling for an ecological approach, the field of student affairs was opening its door to new guiding frameworks.

Student Affairs and the Ecological Perspective.

A complete review of the history of student affairs is beyond the scope of this project, but I will highlight the events that I have found important to the relationship between this history and the ecological perspective. Nearly all historical accounts of the history of student affairs contribute its formal beginnings with the statement of the student personnel point of view in 1937. In his review of this statement and the restatement in 1949 (Carpenter, 2004), he states: "Confusion about the field of student affairs and its goals are reflected in the first and second statements" (p. 17). In summarizing the confusion, he points to the movement from student service only to student "enrichment and facilitation" (p. 18), as well. While this movement does not mention or endorse the ecological perspective, the door is opening to framing the work of student affairs to include activities outside the boundaries of service. This interest in enrichment and facilitation provided a foundation for the student development movement in student affairs. In a 1987 document authored by the National Association of Student Personnel Administrators (NASPA, 1987), the framework for student affairs continued its emphasis on the student, but also recognized the importance of the institution and its academic mission. The document directed little attention to the understanding of the environment. The ecological perspective regarding the environment and the concept of campus ecology were not mentioned. I find this omission notable given both the academic interest in the campus

History of the Ecological Perspective: A Personal View

environment during the sixties and work published by educational agencies in the early seventies. The major works concerning the campus environment of the sixties appeared to have little impact on the NASPA statement other than the general recognition of the importance of the campus environment. Examples of the major works of the sixties include Stern's (1965) *Student Ecology and the Campus Environment*, Michael and Boyer's (1965) article *Campus Environment*, which noted the work of Astin (1963), Pace (1961, 1963), and Pervin (1968). *Guidance: The Ecology of Students* by Danskin, Kennedy, and Friesen (1965) also underlined the importance of the ecological perspective when they noted: "… school counselors may be able greatly to enrich their services to students by investing themselves in a study of the interactions between a student and his learning environment" (p. 130).

Other documents regarding the ecological perspective even more central to student affairs appeared to have little impact. The NASPA document of 1987 was published 14 years after the introduction of the ecological perspective to the student affairs field (WICHE, 1973; Banning & Kaiser, 1974) and nearly 10 years after the publication by NASPA of the monograph *Campus Ecology: A Perspective for Student Affairs* (Banning, 1978). But despite these efforts, the focus remained primarily on student services and development. The statements of the student personnel perspective and the student development perspective with the focus on the individual as a framework for student affairs has been well accepted, but the field has been not without critical reviews (Bloland, 1991; Bloland, Stamakakos, & Rogers, 1994; Crookston, 1976; Bucci, 1993; Kuh, Whitt, & Shedd, 1987; Sandeen, 2011). Specifically, in regard to the ecological perspective, the lack of attention to the ecological approach was clearly noted in the following statement by Miller and Prince (1976, p. 166): "A telling argument for a shift to this approach is that the focus of much student personnel activity over the years has been helping people to adjust to present structure, rather than analyzing the nature of that environment."

Within the field of student affairs practice, the emphasis began to move from the "student development" or "the ecological perspective" to "student development and the ecological perspective." Both concepts were developing as important to the work of student affairs. Important to the effort of bringing together these two perspectives are the works of Hurst (1987) and Rogers (1990a & 1990b). Rodgers (1990a) makes the case as follows: "… student development efforts tacitly focused primarily on the person (P) often neglecting the environment (E) and the interaction (I). Similarly, in using the person-environment perspective without using developmental theories, campus ecology projects did not assess, redesign, or evaluate for development per se" (p. 28). The two approaches were seen as compatible and integration possible. Hurst (1987), in his efforts of developing a rapprochement to student development and campus ecology, concluded:

> The student affairs profession has taken giant strides over the past two decades in moving from an in loco parentis system that emphasized regulatory activities through a student and environmental phase, to the current status of managing a campus as an ecosystem. The intentional design or modification of an ecosystem, when well-constructed, facilitates the teaching/learning process in all dimensions of student development. (p. 16)

More recently, this vision of integration is seen in the works of Evans, Forney, Guido, Patton, and Renn (2010) and Stange and Banning (2001, 2015). The campus ecology movement is also placed in the evolution of student development theory by Jones and Stewart (2016).

History of the Ecological Perspective: A Personal View

This chapter has documented that the ecological perspective on human behavior has both a lengthy and rich history and a broad utility to a variety of disciplines and service agencies. The next chapter details one approach that moves the ecological perspective to a campus setting by the concept of campus ecology.

References:

Astin, A. W. (1963). Further validation of the environmental assessment technique. *Journal of Educational Psychology, 54,* 63-71.

Banning, J. H., (Ed.). (1978). *Campus ecology: A perspective for student affairs.* Cincinnati, OH: NASPA Monograph.

Banning, J. H., (1985). Cornish test of insanity. *The Campus Ecologist, 3*(2), 2.

Banning, J. H., & Kaiser, L. (1974). Ecological perspective and model for campus design. *The Personnel and Guidance Journal, 52*(6), 370-375.

Banning, J. H., & Kuk, L. (2005). Campus ecology and college student health. *Spectrum,* November, 9-15.

Barker, R. G. (1968*). Ecological psychology: Concepts and methods for studying the environment of human behavior.* Stanford, CA: Stanford University Press.

Berger, P. L., & Luckmann, T. (1966). *The social construction of reality: A treatise in the sociology of knowledge.* Garden City, NY: Doubleday & Company, Inc.

Bloland, P. A. (March 1991). *A brief history of student development.* Paper presented at the Annual Conference of the American College Personnel Association, Atlanta, GA.

Bloland, P. A., Stamatakos, L. C., & Rogers, R. (1994). *Reform in student affairs: A critique of student development.* Greensboro, NC: School of Education, University of North Carolina at Greensboro, NC.

Bowers, E. M. (1964). Primary prevention of mental and emotional disorders: A frame of reference. *Mental Health Monograph No. 5*. Washington, DC: U.S. Department of Health, Education, and Welfare.

Bronfenbrenner, U. (1979). *The ecology of human development: Experiments by nature and design*. Cambridge, MA: Harvard University Press.

Brunswik, E. (1956). *Perception and the representative design of psychological experiments*. Berkeley, CA: University of California Press.

Bucci, F. A. (1993). "Student personnel: All hail and farewell!" Revisited. *NASPA Journal, 30*(3), 169-75.

Caplan, G. (1964). *Principles of preventive psychiatry*. New York: Basic Books.

Carpenter, S. (2004). The philosophical heritage of student affairs. In F. J. D. MacKinnon, (Ed.), *Rentz's student affairs practice in higher education* (pp. 3-26). Springfield, IL: Charles C. Thomas Publisher.

Conyne, R. K., & Clack, R. J. (1981). *Environmental assessment and design*. New York: Praeger Publishers.

Conyne, R. K., Horne, A. M., & Raczynski, K. (2013). *Prevention in psychology: An introduction to the prevention practice kit*. Los Angeles: Sage Publications.

Crookston, B. B. (1976). Student personnel: All hail and farewell! *Personnel and Guidance Journal, 55*(1), 26-29.

Danskin, D. G., Kennedy Jr., C. E., & Friesen, W. S. (1965). Guidance: The ecology of students. *The Personnel and Guidance Journal, 44*(2), 130-134.

Evans, N. J., Forney, D. S., Guido, F. M., Patton, L. D. & Renn, K. A. (2010). *Student development in college: Theory, research, and practice.* San Francisco, CA: Jossey-Bass.

Heft, H. (2001). *Ecological psychology in context.* New York: Psychology Press.

Hurst, J. C. (1987). Student development and campus ecology. *NASPA Journal, 25*(1), 5-17.

Jones, S. R., & Stewart, D. E. (2016). Evolution of student development theory. *New Directions for Student Services, 154*, 17-28.

Kelly, J. G. (2006). *Becoming ecological: An expedition into community psychology.* New York: Oxford University Press.

Kormonday, E. J., & Brown, D. E. (1998). *Fundamentals of Human Ecology.* Upper Saddle River, NJ: Prentice-Hall.

Kuh, G. D., Whitt, E. J., & Shedd, J. D. (1987). *Student affairs work, 2001: A paradigmatic odyssey.* Alexandria, VA: American College Personnel Association.

Kuhn, T. S. (1962). *The structure of scientific revolutions.* Chicago: The University of Chicago Press.

Lewin, K. (1936). *Principles of topological psychology.* New York: McGraw Hill.

Marten, G. G. (2001). *Human ecology: Basic concepts for sustainable development.* Sterling, VA: Earthscan Publications Ltd.

Merchant, C. (2007). *American environmental history: An introduction.* New York: Columbia University Press.

Michael, W. B., & Boyer, E. L. (1965). Campus environment. *Review of Educational Research, 35*(4), 264-276.

Miller, T. K, & Prince, J. S. (1976). *The future of student affairs.* San Francisco, CA: Jossey-Bass.

Morrill, W. H., Oetting, E. R., & Hurst, J. C. (1974). Dimensions in counselor functioning. *The Personnel and Guidance Journal, 52*(6), 354-359.

National Association of Student Personnel Administrators (1987). *A perspective on student affairs: A statement issued on the 50th anniversary of the student personnel point of view.* Washington, DC: NASPA.

Oetting, E. R. (1967). Developmental definition of counseling psychology. *Journal of Counseling Psychology, 14*(4), 382-385.

Pace, C. R. (1961). Diversity of college environments. *Journal of the National Association of Women Deans and Counselors, 25,* 21-26.

Pace, C. R. (1963) *CUES: College and university environmental scales: Technical manual.* Princeton, NJ: Educational Testing Services.

Pace, D., Stamler, V. E., Yarris, E., & June, L. (1996). Rounding out the cube: Evolution to a global model for counseling centers. *Journal of Counseling & Development, 74,* 321-325.

Pervin, L. A. (1968). Performance and satisfaction as a function of individual-environmental fit. *Psychological Bulletin, 69,* 56-68.

Rogers, R. F. (1990a). Recent theories and research underlying student development. In D. Creamer (Ed.), *College student development: Theory and practice for the 1990s.* (27-79). Alexandria, VA: American College Personnel Association.

Rogers, R. F. (1990b). An integration of campus ecology and student development: The Olentangy project. In D. Creamer (Ed.), *College student development: Theory and practice for the 1990s*. (155-180). Alexandria, VA: American College Personnel Association.

Sampson, E. E. (1967). Student activism and the decade of protest. *Journal of Social Issues, 23*(3), 1-33.

Sandeen, A. (2011). Does Student Affairs Have an Enduring Mission? *Journal of College and Character, 12*(4), 1-8. Retrieved from http://journals.naspa.org/jcc

Small, A. W., & Vincent, G. E. (1894). *An introduction to the study of society*. New York: American Book Company.

Stern, G. G. (1965). Student ecology and the college environment. *Journal of Medical Education, 40*, 132-54.

Strange, C. C., & Banning, J. H. (2001). *Educating by design: Creating campus environments that work*. San Francisco, CA: Jossey-Bass.

Strange, C. C., & Banning, J. H. (2015). Designing for learning: Creating campus environments for student success. San Francisco, CA: Jossey-Bass.

Szasz, T. (1961). *The myth of mental illness: Foundations of a theory of personal conduct*. New York: Harper & Row.

Walsh, W. B. (1973). Theories of person-environment interaction: Implications for the college student. Iowa City, IA: American College Testing Program.

Walsh, W. B. (1978). Person/Environment Interaction. In J. H. Banning (Ed.), *Campus ecology: A Perspective for Student Affairs*. Cincinnati, OH: National Student Personnel Association.

Webster, L., & Mertova, P. (2007). *Using narrative inquiry as a research method: An Introduction to using critical event narrative analysis in research on learning and teaching.* London: Routledge.

Western Interstate Commission for Higher Education (1973). *The ecosystem model: Designing campus environments.* Boulder, CO: WICHE.

Wicker, A. W. (1979). *An introduction to ecological psychology.* Monterey, CA: Brooks/Cole.

Chapter 2

The Campus Ecology Model

In Chapter 1, I chronicled my personal experience and societal background events and influences that were instrumental in bringing about the ecological perspective. It is from this general ecological perspective that the concept of campus ecology emerged from a group effort of a Western Interstate Commission for Higher Education task force. It was within this task force that Dr. Leland Kaiser presented the first paper (to my knowledge) on campus ecology as a model for higher education, particularly student services. (See "On a Personal Note" #2-1: In the Beginning.)

> **"On a Personal Note" #2-1: In the Beginning**
>
> In 1970 I became the Project Director at the Western Interstate Commission for Higher Education in Boulder, Colorado, having recently resigned from the position of Director of Counseling Center at the University of Colorado, Boulder, Colorado. **(See "On a Personal Note" #1-1: Critical Events Leading to the Ecological Perspective.)** The title of the WICHE project was *Improving Mental Health Services Campuses*. This was a NIMH Experimental and Special Training Branch Grant (No. MH 12419-01). The purpose

of the grant was to develop models to improve mental health on the college campus using the perspective of community psychology, or more specifically, the community mental health model.

Dr. Bernard Bloom of the University of Colorado's Psychology Department was the author of the grant. I was hired by WICHE to implement the grant. I interpreted or reduced this perspective to a rather simple question: How can we improve mental health on the college campus without hiring more counselors, psychologists, psychotherapists, and psychiatrists? Following the wisdom of the community mental health model and the societal cry for "power to the people," I formed a group of task forces made up of diverse people including legislators, university administrators, student affairs professionals, faculty, students, and community members. Each task force was given a topical area from which they were to develop models for improving mental health on college and university campuses. The group that was given the charge of looking at the campus environments represented, in part, this diversity. The task force represented four persons of color, four women, faculty, students, deans of students, psychologists, psychiatrists, public health workers, social workers, campus physicians, and equal opportunity administrators. At our meeting in about 1971 at the Los Posada Hotel in Santa Fe, NM, Leland Kaiser, a health planner and psychologist, presented a draft paper to the group regarding the use of the concept of campus ecology as a way to view campus environments. (See Appendix A.) In 1973, the group published a task force monograph titled: *The Ecosystem Model: Designing Campus Environments*, and in 1974, Leland Kaiser and I published an article in *The Personnel and Guidance Journal* titled "An Ecological Perspective and

Model for Campus Design." These efforts and documents were the vehicles that brought the concept and term "campus ecology" to the student affairs activities of higher education. The notion of the ecological perspective and the importance of the environment in higher education were well established prior to these efforts. The notion of building a campus model using the term "campus ecology" was new to the literature, although the concept of "student ecology" had appeared on a few occasions (Danskin, Kennedy, Jr., & Friesen, 1965; & Stern, 1965).

Campus ecology was introduced in contrast to the more prevalent perspectives at the time. These were termed by Banning and Kaiser (1974) as the unenlightened perspective, the adjustment perspective, and the developmental perspective. The unenlightened perspective, also referred to as the removal perspective, is built on the assumption that not all students belong in college or are expected to have success. Finding interventions to help remove students from their current environment or moving students on to other opportunities is needed. In other words, if the ecological fit between student and institution is not working, you assist the student in leaving. The adjustment perspective is more forgiving and focuses attention on helping the students manage the adjustment to campus, typically through personal counseling. The assumption is that the student-institution fit can be improved by helping the student adjust and change. The developmental perspective also focuses on the student changing, but does not assume a need for a personal psychological adjustment to make the fit to the institution a better one. It assumes the issue of adjustment falls more within the transition experience to the campus, issues of maturity, or deficits in skills needed to be successful. There may be an array of additional areas of functioning that indicate student need of developmental assistance.

Banning and Kaiser (1974) also note, however, that all three of these perspectives have efficacy. Students who are an immediate danger to themselves or the campus community need to be removed for their safety, as well as the campus community. The usefulness and importance of counseling and development programs on campus has been historically well established. These are needed perspectives. However, the issue raised by Banning and Kaiser (1974) focused on the lack of attention to how the institution could change in order to bring about a better ecological fit between the student and the campus. This is seen as a critical shortcoming of non-ecological perspectives. Banning and Kaiser (1974, p. 371) summarize:

> An ecological perspective overcomes the one-sidedness of the other perspectives. The essence of the ecological perspective is the transaction between the student and his or her environment. This perspective, therefore, incorporates the influence of environments on persons and persons on environments. The focus of concern is not solely on the student characteristics or environmental characteristics but on the transactional relationship between students and their environment.

The shift of focus to the transactional relationship between students and their environment can be viewed as a paradigm shift (Kuhn, 1962) that occurred in the field of college student personnel work. The shift is basically from viewing students as individuals to viewing students as part of an ecology. Older paradigms that focused on the students' intra-psychic concerns were no longer adequate given the increasing student diversity. Student personnel, as well as other human service delivery systems, have been involved in this "shift struggle." For example, referring to the field of psychological services, Ralph Catalano (1979) states:

The Campus Ecology Model

The fault in this is that psychology's basic assumptions, analogies, conventions, and exemplars are concerned with measuring and explaining individual behavior as a function of internal, or very immediate influences. This 'person' oriented paradigm is of little help in measuring or explaining the economic and political forces which shape the larger environmental determinants of emotional stability. (p. 10)

Similarly, Banning and Kaiser (1974) were voicing a need for this basic shift by suggesting the need to take an ecological perspective toward college student personnel work rather than the more traditional student removal, student adjustment, and student development perspective. The contrast in the traditional approach to student problems versus the campus ecology approach was outlined in the 1973 WICHE (p. 17) document *The Ecosystem Model: Designing Campus Environments* as follows:

Traditional

- Follows the medical model. Student is defined as ill and treated.

- Primarily concerned with aiding student to cope with environment or transition to another environment.

- System is generally passive. Action is initiated only after someone outside the mental health facility, i.e., the patient (student) or the person

Ecosystem

- Considers not only characteristics of student, but also characteristics of environment and transactional relationship between student and environment. Environment can be defined as ill and treated.

- Concerned not only with aiding student to cope with environment, but also with modifying environment

- making a referral, makes a problem known.

- Requires a problem to develop and become symptomatic before any action can be initiated, often after it is too late to salvage the educational experience. Is relatively less concerned with prevention than with treatment.

- Tends to be isolated from the rest of the institution. Limited efforts to inform students of resources available. Limited participation with other elements of institution in sharing information. Limited participation in decision making.

- Reaches a limited proportion of the population (primarily students who define themselves or are defined as needing help).

to encourage student development.

- System is active. It attempts to identify students and institution characteristics and works on designing appropriate student/environment fit.

- Attempts to anticipate problems and initiate remedial action before the situation is beyond salvage. It is relatively more concerned with prevention than with treatment.

- Encourages active participation with rest of institution through gathering and disseminating information and becoming involved in the decision making process.

- Has potential to influence a larger percentage of the population (unnecessary for students to be defined as patients or clients).

"On a Personal Note" #2-2: Case Study: A Matter of Perspective

I often use the following case study in my campus ecology course to help students distinguish the four perspectives: unenlightened, adjustment, developmental, and ecological.

The Case Study: A counseling service within the Division of Student Affairs, at a large western university which had a history of providing one of the best undergraduate experiences to the academic "elite" of the country, found that more and more adult women were coming to the counseling center for help. The women were generally over 25 years of age, were spouses, and had small children. Upon arrival at the counseling center, they reported the following symptoms: anxiety, depression, confusion over their roles in life, and they often questioned whether a university education was worth all the trouble. The president of this university hears about the situation of the "women going to the counseling center" and asks you, as the Director of Student Services, to prepare four responses for her consideration. She would like these four responses to correspond to the following perspectives: the unenlightened perspective; the counseling perspective; the developmental perspective; and the ecological perspective. Using each of the above four perspectives, please give a brief short description of your response.

Typically, the student's responses highlight the essences of each of the perspective. Responses from the unenlightened/ removal perspective usually focus on the notion that the group of women in the scenario are probably not prepared for an "elite" institution, and they should be given advice to transfer to a less rigorous institution. The students use the adjustment

> perspective to suggest more in-depth counseling to explore the need to be at the institution as well as the associated stress. The developmental perspective is often presented from a student programming approach and suggestions include "brown bag" discussion groups, time management workshops, and study skills programs. In the responses from the ecological perspective, students raise questions regarding the institution's responsibility, including the institutional policies that might impact the situation, academic advising, and often the notion of changing the environment by adding support systems like a daycare center.

The campus ecology model was developed as a vehicle to bring the ecological perspective to campus work. While the early efforts in campus ecology focused on the work of student affairs, the concept now is being used within institutional, academic, and diversity affairs as well. (See Part 2.) Campus ecology has become the behavioral study of the complex transactional relationships among the social and physical dimensions of campus environments and those who inhabit them, including students, staff, faculty, and visitors.

Campus Ecology as a Model

While there is not uniform agreement on the differences between a theory and a model, most scholars see models as involving concepts and relationships among the concepts (Jaccard & Jacoby, 2010). There are a number of definitions associated with the concept of model, but the *McMillard Dictionary* provides a useful addition to the standard concepts and relationship definition by adding that a model relates to statements on how something works. To follow the path of how something works, there are several important concept areas of the campus ecology model that need to be presented: (a) the nature of the transactional relationship and influence among behaviors, persons, and environments; (b) conceptions of the structure and dynamics of the environment; (c) the design/programmatic features of campus ecology (eco-system design process); (d) ecological intervention strategies; and (e) the important ethical considerations associated with the model.

"On a Personal Note" #2-3: Key Campus Ecology Readings

Aulepp, L., & Delworth, U. (1976). *Training manual for an ecosystem model.* Boulder, CO: Western Interstate Commission for Higher Education.

Banning, J. H. (Ed.). (1978). *Campus ecology: A perspective for student affairs.* Cincinnati, OH: NASPA Monograph.

Banning, J. H. (1980). Campus ecology: Its impact on college student personnel work. In D. G. Creamer, (Ed.), *Student development in higher education: Theories, practices, and future directions,* (pp. 129-138). Cincinnati, OH: ACPA Media.

Banning, J. H. (1980). The campus ecology manager role. In U. Delworth & G. Hanson (Eds.), *Student services: A handbook for the profession* (pp. 209-227). San Francisco: Jossey-Bass.

Banning, J. H. (1989). Creating a climate for successful student development: The campus ecology manager role. In U. Delworth and G. Hanson (Eds.), *Student Services: A handbook for the profession, 2nd. ed.* (209-227). San Francisco: Jossey-Bass.

Banning, J. H., & Bryner, C. E. (2001). A framework for organizing the scholarship of campus ecology. *Journal of Student Affairs, 10*, 9-20.

Banning, J., & Kaiser, L. (1974). An Ecological Perspective and Model for Campus Design. *The Personnel and Guidance Journal, 52*(6), 370-375.

Evans, N. J., Forney, D. S., Guido, F. M., Patton, L. D., & Renn, K. A. (2009). Ecological approaches to college student development. *Student development in college: Theory, research, and practice.* (pp. 157-175). San Francisco, CA: Jossey-Bass.

Evans, N. J., Forney, D. S., Guido, F. M., Patton, L. D. & Renn, K. A. (2010). *Student development in college: Theory, research, and practice.* San Francisco, CA: Jossey-Bass.

Gonzales, G. M. (1989). Understanding the campus community: An ecological paradigm. *New Directions for Student services, 48*, 17-26.

Huebner, L. A. (Ed.). (1979). *Redesigning campus environments. New directions for student services. No. 8.* San Francisco, CA: Jossey-Bass.

Hurst, J. C. (1987). Student development and campus ecology. *NASPA Journal, 25*(1), 5-17.

Kaiser, L. (1975). Designing campus environments. *NASPA Journal, 13*(1), 33-39.

Kaiser, L. R. (1978). Campus ecology and campus design. In J. H. Banning (Ed.), *Campus ecology: A Perspective for student affairs* (24- 31) Cincinnati, OH: National Association of Student Personnel Administrators.

Kaiser, L. R., & Sherretz, L. (1978). Designing campus environments: A review of selected literature. In J. H. Banning (Ed.), *Campus Ecology: A perspective for student affairs* (pp. 77-126). Cincinnati, OH: National Association of Student Personnel Administrators.

Kuk, L., & Banning, J. H. (2016). *Student affairs leadership: Defining the role through an ecological framework.* Sterling, VA: Stylus Publishing.

Moore, M., & Delworth, U. (1976). *Training manual for student services program development.* Boulder, CO: Western Interstate Commission for Higher Education.

Renn, K. A., & Arnold, K. D. (2003). Reconceptualizing research on college student peer culture. *The Journal of Higher Education, 74*(3), 261-291.

Renn, K. A., & Patton, L. A. (2011). Campus ecology and environments. In J. H. Schuh, S. R. Jones, S. R. Harper, and Associates, *Student services: A handbook for the profession* (pp. 242-256). San Francisco, CA: Jossey-Bass.

Renn, K. A., & Reason, R. D. (2012). *College students in the United States: Characteristics, experiences, and outcomes.* San Francisco, CA: Jossey-Bass.

Strange, C. C. (1996). Dynamics of campus environments. In S. R. Komives, D. B. Woodard, and Associates, *Student services: A handbook for the profession (3rd Ed.)* (pp. 244-268). San Francisco, CA: Jossey-Bass.

> Strange, C. C., & Banning, J. H. (2001). *Educating by design: Creating campus environments that work.* San Francisco, CA: Jossey-Bass.
>
> Strange, C. C., & Banning, *environments for student success.* San Francisco, CA: Jossey-Bass.
>
> Tierno, S. (2012). Campus ecology. *Place and Space*, Sept. Retrieved from http://scotttierno.com/place-space/campus-ecology/
>
> Western Interstate Commission for Higher Education (WICHE). (1973). *The ecosystem model: Designing campus environments.* Boulder, Colorado: WICHE.

The Nature of the Transactions: Persons, Environment, and Behavior in the Campus Ecology Model

The nature of the transaction among the person, environment, and behavior has been conceptualized by many authors. In the early work of campus ecology (Banning & Kaiser, 1974), the relationship was noted simply as the student impacts the environment and the environment impacts the student. More complex statements of this mutual transactional relationship were introduced by Bandura (1986) with the concept of reciprocal determinism. This concept maintains that behavior is determined by the mutual influence of three factors: internal factors associated with the person, environmental factors, and behavioral outcomes (Fetsco & McLure, 2005). Similarly, Danford (1983) described the relationship among these three factors as "a dynamic reciprocal determinism" (p. 19).

Of particular interest to the campus ecology model is the nature of the influence exerted by the environmental factors within the dynamic reciprocal determinism, since influence of the environment

The Campus Ecology Model

is the aspect of the model that distinguishes it as being different from the earlier person focused frameworks. In the WICHE (1973) document, the campus environment was defined as consisting of "all the stimuli that impinge upon the students' sensory modalities and includes physical, chemical, biological, and social stimuli" (p. 5). Key to understanding the nature of the influences of these campus stimuli are the concepts of environmental possibilism, environmental possibilism, and environmental determinism (Bell, Fisher, Baum, & Green, 1990; Porteus, 1977). Environmental possibilism suggests the influence of the environment is based on what possibilities it provides. For example, if a campus has a swimming pool, then it is possible for students to swim on campus. Environmental possibilism suggests the environment not only provides the influence of opportunity (possibilism), but the nature or design of the opportunity can increase its probability of influence. Again, using our campus swimming pool example, if the pool is well designed and is an indoor heated pool, then the probability for its use is increased in the winter over a poorly designed and unheated pool. In other words, if the environmental influence can be more than providing possibilities, then a probabilistic influence can be present. Environmental determinism suggests that the environment can determine individual behavior. Using our simple example, not having a swimming pool on campus determines it will not be used. On the other hand, if the policy environment of the campus includes the passing of a swimming test prior to graduation, then student use of an existing pool is pretty well determined. These concepts of degree of influence give additional understanding to the model's third philosophical assumption: "For the purpose of environmental design, the influencing properties of the campus environment are focused upon: however, the students are still viewed as active, choice-making agents who may resist, transform, or nullify environmental influences" (WICHE, 1973, p.

6). Within the campus ecology model, designing possibilities and possibilities with probabilities within the campus ecology model are embraced over any notion of strict determinism.

"On a Personal Note" #2-4: Environmental Influence: A Student Puzzle Exercise

The following is a student exercise using behavior outside of higher education in order to explore the influence of the environment in another setting.

AN ECOLOGICAL PUZZLE!
Free Throw Shooting in Basketball

Develop an ecological explanation of the following facts regarding free throw shooting in basketball. Why are two of the four players less skilled in free throw shooting even though all four players are exceptionally talented?

(1) Wilt Chamberlain (Overbrook High School in Philadelphia, Pennsylvania) in 1959-1960 averaged 37.6 points per game in the National Basketball Association (NBA), but his free throw shooting percentage was only .582.

(2) Bill Russel (McClymonds High School, Oakland, California) in 1959-1960 averaged 18.2 points per game in the NBA, but his free throw percentage was only .612.

(3) Bill Sharman (Porterville High School, Porterville, California) in 1959-1960 averaged 19.3 points per game in the NBA, but his free throw shooting percentage was .866.

(4) Cliff Hagen (Owensboro High School, Owensboro, Kentucky) in 1959-1960 averaged 24.8 points per game in the NBA, but his free throw shooting percentage was .803.

Additional facts

(1) As of 1973, the all-time NCAA season free throw percentage record was held by Jim Sutton, a native of South Dakota State in the 1957 season.

(2) Wilt Chamberlain, the greatest NBA player, holds records for the most free throws missed in one game, one season, and in a playoff game.

What is the explanation?

Answer to the Puzzle

Free throw shooting is a skill that is influenced by practice. The ecological explanation of the difference between the players is based on the variable of rural vs. urban. The players of rural background (Sharman and Hagen) develop their skills in an environment where the number of basketball hoops per youth-player was nearly one to one. Every rural home and/or barn seems to have a hoop attached. The urban players' (Chamberlain and Russel) ratio of hoops per youth-player was, on the other hand, much less than one to one. Urban youth play basketball in school yards, YMCAs, and recreation centers. Due to the number of youth wanting to play, time is usually not allotted for free throw shooting. On the other hand, in the rural setting, many afternoons are spent in one-person per hoop shooting free throws.

This explanation is based on the concept of over-manned vs. under-manned settings. (See Barker, R. G., & Gump, P.B. (Eds., 1964). Big School, Small School. Stanford, CA: Stanford University Press.) Also due to the difference between rural and urban on this variable, different rules of play develop, e.g., "make it-take it" or "winner's ball." Again, under the "winner's ball" rule, no time is devoted to free throw practice because the intent of the rule is to move the game along in a populated setting.

Conceptions of the Environmental Properties

Exploring the ways in which the campus environment can be conceptualized is critical to the campus ecology model. The history of the emphasis on the students and their individual characteristics is well documented. Persons are often described by the demographic variables of age, race, and gender. In addition, there is an abundance of "personality" variables such as attitudes, values, and traits. On the other hand, we are much less accustomed to describing environments. What are the variables or the ways to conceptualize environments? Do taxonomies for campus environments exist? A number of conceptual frameworks from which to view campus environments do exist. Here are brief descriptions along with the basic references for the social ecology, the physical setting, and the ecology of student development approaches, among others.

Every environment possesses properties by which it may be described. Leland Kaiser, in personal communications in the early seventies, outlined two approaches. One focuses on possible properties of a campus environment ("On a Personal Note" #2-5: Properties of an Environment) and the other ("On a Personal Note" #2-6: Dynamics of an Environment) presents a number of possible properties in a more dynamic format.

"On a Personal Note" #2-5: Properties of an Environment

Over the years, I have found this early communication from Kaiser (Leland Kaiser, personal communication) very helpful. He notes that a properly structured environment provides for a full range of dynamic processes which may be built in for the accomplishment of specific purposes. These environmental mechanisms can be consciously designed to influence specified behavior changes in students who reside within them. The following are examples of these properties:

Involves
Provokes or calls for interaction. It appeals to the student's curiosity and natural interest. Movement, color, sound, and light capture attention and invite manipulation. It is appropriate for the bored student.

Manages
Provides a highly structured routine and sequence of activities. The time is tightly scheduled leaving little opportunity for disruptive random activity. The teacher is a manager and the student is a worker. It is appropriate for the student who needs close supervision.

Enriches
Provides a diversity of learning opportunities. Emphasis is upon variety of approach and generalization of learning across situations. Facts are not taught in isolation, but are examined in a many-faceted reality. It is appropriate for potentiating creativity and remediating learning disabilities, as well as reaching the "normal" child.

Reorganizes
Provides incentives for the student to alter his/her behavior patterns. The old environment supports for maladaptive behavior are discontinued and payoffs are arranged for the desired new behavior. A behavior modification approach is suggested. It is appropriate for any student whose behavior you wish to reorganize.

Suppresses
Provides punishment for undesirable student behavior or eliminates emotionally disturbing stimuli from the pupil's external sensory input. Once "trigger stimuli" are identified, they are eliminated or neutralized. It is appropriate for destructive behavior (punishment) or rage (elimination of trigger stimuli).

Augments
Amplifies any desirable quality possessed by the student. Existing strengths are focused upon and expanded to the limit of the student's potential. Since skills and abilities are interrelated, any competence that is expanded sufficiently will cut across several disciplines. It may thus be possible to move a student from an existing area of high interest into areas of low interest as these become involved. It is useful for the "nonacademic" student.

Prompts
Provides repetition and drill. Teaching machines may develop the student's mastery of rote material. It is useful for students who need constant repetition, and it frees the teacher from this task. If the teaching machine is "fun," learning takes place as an artifact of play.

Facilitates
Provides the necessary vehicles for the expression of developed qualities in the student. A profile of student interests and abilities is matched with environmental facilitation. Often students have developed abilities for which the environment provides no possibility of expression. These abilities then lie dormant or may atrophy. It is appropriate for all students.

Potentiates
Makes possible the development of unknown qualities which exist only as potentials in the student. These may be uncovered in a process of systematic exploration. Once discovered they may be augmented and facilitated. This is appropriate for all students. Its goal is attainment of the limits set by heredity and early environment.

Stresses
Subjects the student to anxiety-provoking stimuli. It is useful for mobilization of a student and may facilitate performance if kept at low levels.

Isolates
Reduces the interpersonal or inter-object relationships of the student. The range or intensity of external stimuli may be lowered to any desirable level. It may be useful for the easily distractible student.

Compensates
Makes up for a deficit in student functioning. With proper environmental compensation, a student disability will not become a handicap. It is appropriate for any student who deviates markedly from the range of normal functioning on any dimension.

Monitors
Provides continuing feedback on a student's behavior, particularly his/her reactions to environmental stimuli. In this way an individual program may be designed and adjusted as necessary for the accomplishment of predetermined goals. A monitoring process is necessary for all students.

"On a Personal Note" #2-6: Dynamics of an Environment

In addition to the properties of the environment presented in the "On a Personal Note" #2-3: Environmental Properties, I have found this personal communication from Leland Kaiser extremely helpful in thinking about the dynamic nature of the campus environment. The document outlines a way to describe the dynamic properties of an environment.

Static – Dynamic

A static environment maintains a relatively fixed structure over a period of time. It may be either stable or stagnant. A dynamic environment manifests a rapidly changing structure. It may be innovative or chaotic.

Laissez-Faire – Programmed

In a laissez-faire environment, there is a lack of overall approach or consensus. The objectives are poorly delineated or inadequately operationalized. In a programmed environment, there is evidence of a consistent approach—a deliberate attempt to attain specified objectives. Objectives are translated into program activities.

Impoverished – Rich

An impoverished environment provides few opportunities for person-to-person, or person-to-object interactions. A rich environment provides many opportunities for such interactions. Learning is viewed as a function of the quantity and quality of such interactions.

Low Intensity – High Intensity

Sensory stimulation is high in a high-impact environment and low in a low-impact environment. A child's attention and involvement is a function of the stimulus levels of his environment. If a child has a high level of internal stimulation ("noise"-fantasy), he may fail to respond to low levels of environmental stimulation.

Closed – Open
An environment that is closed is isolated or buffered from the "outside world." It becomes an island in the larger social system. An open environment, by contrast, is receptive to outside stimulation and keeps in tune with it.

Broad Rope – Narrow Scope
Scope refers to the range of student behaviors that the environment is designed to influence. A broad scope environment is holistic, a narrow scope environment focuses upon a narrow range of behaviors and is quite selective in its effect upon the students.

Conforming – Nonconforming
A conforming environment is plastic. It may readily be modified by its inhabitants. A nonconforming environment resists any efforts at inner-directed change. It is rigid and unyielding.

Deviation Amplifying – Deviation Correcting
In a deviation amplifying environment, any irregularity introduced tends to be magnified out of proportion to its importance. This environment is unstable. A deviation correcting environment is stable; it corrects any introduced irregularity and easily regains balance.

High Load – Low Load
A high load environment is extremely demanding of the student and pushes him toward peak production. A low load environment is relaxed and the student is seldom required to

put forth strong continuous effort. Frequent leisure, rest, and relaxation are indicative of low loading.

Primitive – Technologized

A primitive environment has few tools, equipment, or modern conveniences. It is often found in a camp or natural setting. A technologized environment is mechanized, automated, and modern. It is often in a suburban or urban setting.

Social – Asocial

A social environment maximizes interpersonal relationships and social groupings. An asocial environment minimizes human contacts and tends to isolate individuals.

Original – Imposed

An original environment is what exists before people self-consciously set about to alter it. An imposed environment is a restructured environment that is a product of conscious intervention.

Efficient – Inefficient

An efficient environment is a high-yield environment—the output compares favorably with the cost involved. An inefficient environment has an unfavorable cost-benefit analysis. It is effective, but too expensive.

Effective – Ineffective

An effective environment is valid, i.e., it produces the product for which it is designed. An ineffective environment is not valid. It fails to produce the product for which it is designed, i.e., the objectives are not operationalized. An environment may be effective (valid) but inefficient (costly). It cannot be efficient unless it is effective.

Benign – Noxious
This is a summary judgment. An environment is benign that has a positive effect on the student. An environment is noxious that has a negative effect on the student.

Additional Conceptual Frameworks for Understanding the Environment

In addition to Kaiser's work on the structure and dynamics of the environment, notable theorists and scholars have also contributed important frameworks for understanding environments. The following are examples:

Walsh's campus environment approach.

Walsh, in his 1973 ACT monograph, outlines a number of ways to approach the person-environment interaction that is applicable to the campus ecology framework. He reviews six approaches.

- Barker's (1968) theory of behavior setting
- Clark and Trow's (1966) subculture approach
- Holland's (1966) theory of personality types and model environments
- Stern's (1970) need/press-culture theory
- Moos's (1974) social climate dimensions
- Pervin's (1967) transactional approach

Steele's physical setting approach.

Steele's (1973) approach focuses on the role that the dimensions of the physical setting play in organization development. Every physical setting can be viewed in terms of the relationship between and among the elements of the setting and the functions performed by the elements. Elements are those aspects of the physical setting that are likely to influence the functioning of individuals or groups in the setting. For example, an element could be a particular thing (a piece of furniture) or a pattern of things (the arrangement of furniture). Steele's taxonomy for the dimensions of the physical setting is as follows (p. 25):

- Security and Shelter refer to protection from harmful or unwanted stimuli in one's surroundings
- Social Contact refers to the arrangements of facilities and spaces that permit or promote social interaction
- Symbolic Identification refers to the messages sent by settings that tell someone what a person, group, or organization is like
- Task Instrumentality refers to the facilities and layouts appropriate for carrying out tasks in a particular setting
- Pleasure refers to the pleasure or gratification the place gives to those who use it
- Growth refers to the stimulus for growth the setting gives the user

Moos's social ecology approach.

The social ecology approach is best illustrated by the work of Moos (1974) in the chapter entitled "Systems for the Assessment and Classification of Human Environments: An Overview." In this chapter, Moos suggests the environment could be viewed in terms of the following six dimensions:

- Ecological Dimensions

    a. Geographical and Meteorological variables

    b. Architectural and Physical Design variables

The Campus Ecology Model

- Behavior Settings
- Dimensions of Organizational Structure
- Personal and Behavioral Characteristics of the Milieu Inhabitants
- Psychosocial Characteristics and Organizational Climate
- Functional or Reinforcement Analyses of Environments

Blocher's ecology of student development approach.

Blocher's work (1974, 1978) best exemplifies an ecology approach to student development. He conceptualizes the environment that is necessary for the development of students as containing three basic subsystems along with each subsystem containing specific conditions. Blocher's taxonomy is as follows:

- Opportunity subsystem refers to the problems or situations available in the environment that stimulate the person to address a particular task. The opportunity subsystem includes the conditions of involvement, challenge, and integration.

- Support subsystem refers to the pattern of resources available to the person for coping with the tasks or problems in the opportunity structure of the environment. The support subsystem includes the conditions of structure and support.

- Reward subsystem refers to the reinforcements for effort expended that are contained in the environment. The reward subsystem includes the conditions of feedback and application.

Rappaport's community psychology approach.

Writing from a perspective of community psychology, Rappaport (1977) outlines a framework to view environments. Within this framework are the following eight approaches:

- Identification of the reinforcement contingencies in the environment
- Environment as an aggregate of person characteristics
- An organizational development approach focusing on environmental intervention strategies
- Assessment of geographical, physical, and architectural environment
- Behavior setting approach
- Organizational climate approach
- Systematic properties of the environment
- Social ecology approach

Thomas F. Gilbert's behavior engineering model.

The following example was adapted from Gilbert's (1978) work titled *Human Competence: Engineering Worthy Performance*. In Gilbert's (1978) words: "The behavior engineering model serves one purpose only: it helps us to observe behavior in an orderly fashion, and to ask the 'obvious' questions (the ones we so often forget to ask) toward the single end of improving human competence" (p. 95).

- Is the institutional/environmental data available?
- Are the students aware of this information (institutional/environmental data)?

- Has the institution/environment provided the necessary tools (instruments)?
- Do the students have the capacity to use the tools?
- Does the institution/environment provide the incentives?
- What are the students' motives?

The above model can be a useful assessment and redesign tool for the campus. To illustrate its usefulness, the behavior of academic dishonesty can be examined by the model. For example, is the high incidence of academic dishonesty due to a student information vs. a campus data problem, and/or student capacity vs. campus testing arrangements, and/or student motivation vs. campus incentives for not being dishonest? Depending upon the analysis, corrective actions can be designed to help eliminate academic dishonesty and promote academic integrity. For example, plagiarism may be reduced by giving students a clear statement of how the institution defines plagiarism. The environmental data becomes student information.

Strange's dynamic components of campus environments.

Strange (2003), also presented in Strange and Banning (2015), describes the components of campus environments as follows:

- Physical—natural and synthetic features and designs (such as landscapes, terrain, placement of buildings, internal lighting).
- Human Aggregate—collective characteristics of participants (such as arrangements of people in relation to common traits)
- Organizational—organized structures that serve specific goals (such as decision making, rules, rewards, complexity)

- Constructed—collective perceptions of people in a setting (such as attributions of campus press, climate, culture) (p. 299)

The above conceptual systems or taxonomies of the environment are examples of ways to view campus environments. Banning and McKinley (1980) have applied several of these frameworks directed to the everyday working environment of the student affairs professional. By exploring the utility of these and other approaches, not only may a more useful taxonomy emerge, but we may also gain a better understanding of the role the campus environment plays in university affairs.

The Design/Programmatic Features (Ecosystem Design Process) of the Campus Ecology Model

The design process associated with the campus ecology model provides the opportunity to better fit campus environments to students. The eco-system design process aims to design and/or redesign a campus environment to support and encourage the behavioral outcomes desired by students and the institution, in other words, student success.

Assumptions of the ecosystem design process.

The ecosystem design process has a number of assumptions. The following are basic to campus design and first presented in the 1973 WICHE document:

1. The campus environment consists of all the stimuli that impinge upon the students' sensory modalities and includes physical, chemical, biological, and social stimuli.

2. A transactional relationship exists between college students and their campus environment, i.e., the students shape the environment and are shaped by it.

The Campus Ecology Model

3. For purposes of environmental design, the shaping properties of the campus environment are focused upon; however, the students are still viewed as active, choice-making agents who may resist, transform, or nullify environmental influences.

4. Every student possesses capacity for a wide spectrum of possible behaviors. A given campus environment may facilitate or inhibit any one or more of these behaviors. The campus should be intentionally designed to offer opportunities, incentives, and reinforcements for growth and development.

5. Students will attempt to cope with any educational environment in which they are placed. If the environment is not compatible with the students, the students may react negatively or fail to develop desirable qualities.

6. Because of the wide range of individual differences among students, fitting the campus environment to the students requires the creation of a variety of campus sub-environments. There must be an attempt to design for the wide range of individual characteristics found among students.

7. Every campus has a design, even if the administration, faculty, and students have not planned it or are not consciously aware of it. A design technology for campus environments, therefore, is useful both for the analysis of existing campus environments and the design of new ones.

8. Successful campus design is dependent upon participation of all campus members including students, faculty, staff, administration, and trustees or regents (WICHE, 1973, p. 6).

Ecosystem design process.

A design philosophy must be paralleled with a design methodology before the construction of intentional campus environments is a reality. The ecosystem design process is the design component of the campus ecology perspective (Banning & Kaiser, 1974; Kaiser, 1975). There are seven basic steps in the ecosystem design processes. The steps to this process were outlined in the 1973 WICHE document:

Step 1. Designers, in conjunction with community members, select values.

Step 2. Values are then translated into specific goals.

Step 3. Environments are designed that contain mechanisms to reach the stated goals.

Step 4. Environments are fitted to the participants in the environment.

Step 5. Participant perceptions of the environment are measured.

Step 6. Participant behavior resulting from environmental perceptions is monitored.

Step 7. Data on the environmental design's success and failures, as indicated by the participant perception and behavior, is fed back to the designers in order that they may continue to learn about person/environment fit and design better environments (WICHE, 1973, page 7).

The design steps are interdependent and design work typically begins with Step 1 or Step 5. If one were designing a new environment, the ecosystem process would start with the selection of educational values (Step 1) and follow the next steps in the process. However, if the current environment is not providing a good student-environment fit, then the campus designers would start the process at Step 5, measuring participant perceptions of the environments, and then work through the remaining Steps of 6 thru 4.These steps apply to the process whether the environmental design is intended for the entire campus (macro level), groups within the campus community (micro level), or individuals on campus (life space). Aulepp and Delworth (1976) provide a full training manual for the implementation of the ecosystem design process.

Ecological Interventions

Early in the development of the campus ecology model, the main intervention strategy focused on the redesign of the environment using the ecosystem design process (Banning & Kaiser, 1974, & WICHE, 1973). More recently (Banning & Kuk, 2005; Kuk, Banning, & Amey, 2010; Kuk & Banning, 2016), the campus ecology model has embraced the work of Felner and Felner (1989). Their work gives a practical guidance to campus interventions through the implementation of ecological intervention strategies (Felner & Felner, 1989).

The Felner and Felner (1989) ecological intervention model contains three components that are key to the interventions compatible with the campus ecology model. The first component is the person-focused intervention designed to intervene at the person level. Within a campus health model, Banning and Kuk (2005) defined the person focused health issues as including "biological vulnerabilities, genetic risks, and physical trauma" (p. 11). A second component to the ecological intervention model is the transactional-focused interaction, which is designed to address both the person variable and the associated environmental conditions. The transactional-interventions are often focused on unique combinations of persons and environments. Banning and Kuk (2005, p. 12) give the following example:

Given traditional student ages, their developmental status, and their perceived sense of freedom from parental control, as well as daily interactions with a campus environment made up of similar inhabitants of both genders, this transaction of persons and environment increases the likelihood of sexual activities. An effective transactional intervention would focus on both sides of the environment-person equation. Educational programming regard STDs could occur at the same time efforts were made within the campus environment to ensure that there are opportunities for obtaining condoms and other STD prevention tools.

The third component of the ecological intervention model is the environmental focused intervention, which focuses directly on the physical and/or social environment. To continue with the health example, an environmentally focused intervention, could include the development of opportunities for exercise. This could include bike paths, increased bike parking adjacent to classroom buildings, and policy incentives, for example, reducing campus fees by not bringing a vehicle to campus. By embracing the Felner and Felner intervention model, the campus ecology model becomes not only an environmental look at student behavior and development, but a tool for a wide range of university tasks and opportunities.

Ethical Considerations of the Campus Ecology Model

In his 1978 work, Kaiser presents the design ethic of campus ecology and notes the importance of inhabitant participation by stating a design ethic of campus ecology: "It is immoral to design for people. It is a moral right to design with people. Students affected by any campus space have a moral right to participate in its design or redesign" (1978, p. 29). Huebner and Banning (1987) expanded the ethical considerations of the campus ecology model by including the following ethical issues that need to be considered when implementing the campus ecology model: freedom and control, privacy, informed consent, competency, political positioning, and values. They conclude the discussion of these issues by presenting participation as the safeguard against a select few determining the design of a campus environment. Full participation also provides for a broad source of ideas when implementing new designs. The critical importance of participation is also advanced in the work of Kelman and Warwick (1978) when they underscored the importance of the following questions: (a) Who will participate in the intervention? (b) Who will benefit and who will not from the intervention? (c) What methods will be used to bring about the change associated with the intervention? and (d) Who will monitor the process and outcomes of the intervention? The foregoing issues, questions, and the importance of full participation in addressing help to ensure the campus ecology model becomes an ethical framework for community and campus change and does not fall victim to the charge of social engineering by the few and powerful.

Summary of the Campus Ecology Model

The essence of the campus ecology model is to bring about a better fit among the inhabitants of a campus and the campus environment. The ecological perspective of the model directs attention to both person and environmental change. Key to the campus ecology model is understanding the mutual dynamic nature of the transaction between persons and environments. This understanding is enhanced by examining the variety of ways in which campus environments can be conceptualized and how they can influence behavior. Change is an inherent feature of the campus ecology model. The model supports intentional environmental design, ecological intervention strategies, and the adherence to ethical practices that are built on the foundation of full participation of all inhabitants of the environment.

The chapters in Part 2 contain topical indexes that organize how the campus ecology model has been used to influence conceptual understanding of campus issues as well as the implementation of programs and activities related to these issues.

References

Aulepp, L., & Delworth, U. (1976). *Training manual for an ecosystem model.* Boulder, CO: Western Interstate Commission for Higher Education.

Bandura, A. (1986). *Social foundations of thought and action: A social cognitive theory.* Englewood Cliffs, NJ: Prentice-Hall.

Banning, J., & Kaiser, L. (1974). An Ecological Perspective and Model for Campus Design. *The Personnel and Guidance Journal, 52*(6), 370-375.

Banning, J. H., & Kuk, L. (2005). Campus ecology and college student health. *Spectrum*, November, 9-15.

Banning, J. H., and McKinley, D. (1980). Conceptions of the Campus Environment. In W. Morrill, J. Hurst, and E. Oetting (Eds.), *Dimensions of Intervention for Student Development* (pp. 39-57). New York: John Wiley and Sons.

Barker, R. G. (1968). *Ecological Psychology.* Stanford, CA: Stanford Press.

Barker, R. G., & Gump, P. B. (Eds.). (1964). *Big School, Small School.* Stanford, CA: Stanford University Press.

Bell, P. A., Fisher, J. D., Baum, A., & Green, T. G. (1990). *Environmental psychology.* Austin, TX: Holt, Rinehart, and Winston.

Blocher, D. H. (1974). Toward an Ecology of Student Development. *Personnel and Guidance Journal, 52,* 360-365.

Blocher, D. H. (1978). Campus Learning Environment and the Ecology of Student Development. In J. H. Banning (Ed.),

Campus Ecology: A Perspective for Student Affairs (pp. 17-23). Cincinnati, OH: NASPA.

Bloom, B. L. (1975). *Psychological stress in the campus community.* New York: Behavioral Publications, Inc.

Catalano, R. (1979). *Health behavior and the community.* New York: Pergamon Press, Inc.

Clark, B. R., & Trow, M. (1966). The organizational context. In T. M. Newcomb and E. K. Wilson (Eds.), *College peer groups: Problems and prospects for research* (pp. 17-70). Chicago, IL: Aldine.

Danford, G. (1983). Dynamic reciprocal determinism: A synthetic transactional model of person-behavior-environment relations. In D. Amedeo, J. Griffin, & J. Potter (Eds.), *EDRA 1983: Proceedings of the Fourteenth International Conference of Environmental Research Design Association* (pp.19-28). Washington, DC: EDRA.

Danskin, D. G., Kennedy Jr., C. E., & Friesen, W. S. (1965). Guidance: The ecology of students. *The Personnel and Guidance Journal, 44*(2), 130-134.

Felner, R. D., & Felner, T. V. (1989). Primary prevention programs in the educational context: A transactional ecological framework and analysis. In L. A. Bond & B. C. Compas (Eds.), *Primary prevention and promotion in the schools* (pp. 13-49). Newbury Park, CA: Sage.

Fetsco, T. A., & McClure, J. (2005). *Educational psychology: An integrated approach to classroom decisions.* Boston, MA: Allyn & Bacon.

Gilbert, Thomas F. (1978). *Human competence: Engineering worthy performance.* New York: McGraw-Hill Book Company.

Holland, J. L. (1966). *The Psychology of Vocational Choice: A Theory of Personality Types and Model Environments.* Waltham, MA: Blaisdell.

Huebner, L., & Banning, J. H. (1987). Ethics of intentional design. *NASPA Journal, 25*(1), 29-37.

Jaccard, J., & Jacoby, J. (2010). *Theory construction and model-building skills: A practical guide for social scientists.* New York: The Guilford Press.

Kaiser, L. (1975). Designing campus environments. *NASPA Journal, 13*(1), 33-39.

Kaiser, L. (1978). Campus ecology and campus design. In Banning, J. H. (Ed.), *Campus ecology: A perspective for student affairs.* Cincinnati, OH: NASPA.

Kelman, H., & Warwick, D. (1978). The ethics of social intervention: Goals, means, consequences. In G. Bermant, H. Kelman, & D. Warwick (Eds.), *The ethics of social intervention* (pp. 3-33). New York: Wiley and Sons.

Kuhn, T. S. (1962). *The structure of scientific revolutions.* Chicago, IL: The University of Chicago Press.

Kuk, L., & Banning, J. H. (2016). *Student affairs leadership: Defining the role through an ecological framework.* Sterling, VA: Stylus.

Kuk, L., Bannng, J. H., & Amey, M. J. (2008). *Positioning student affairs for sustainable change: Achieving organizational effectiveness through multiple perspectives.* Sterling, VA: Stylus.

Moos, R. H. (1974). Systems for the Assessment and Classification of Human Environments: An Overview. In R. H. Moos and P. M. Inset (Eds.), *Issues in Social Ecology* (pp. 5-28). Palo Alto, CA: National Press Books.

Pervin, L. A. (1967). A twenty-college study of student x college interaction use TAPE (Transactional Analysis of Personality and Environment): Rationale, reliability, and validity. *Journal of Educational Psychology, 58*(5), 290-302.

Porteus, J. (1977). *Environment and behavior.* Reading, MA: Addison-Wesley.

Rappaport, J. (1977). *Community psychology: Values, research and action.* New York: Holt, Rinehart and Winston.

Steele, F. (1973). *Physical Settings and Organization Development.* Reading, MA: Addison-Wesley Publishing Company.

Stern, G. G. (1965). Student ecology and the college environment. *Journal of Medical Education, 40,* 132-54.

Stern, G. G. (1970). *People in context.* New York: Wiley.

Strange, C. C. (1996). Dynamics of campus environments. In S. R. Komives, D. B. Woodard, and Associates, *Student services: A handbook for the profession.* (3rd ed.) (pp. 244-268). San Francisco, CA: Jossey-Bass.

Strange, C. C., & Banning, J. H. (2001). *Educating by design: Creating campus environments that work.* San Francisco, CA: Jossey-Bass.

Strange, C. C. (2003). In S. R. Komives, D.B. Woodard, and Associates, *Student services: A Handbook for the profession.* (4th Ed.). (pp. 297-316). San Francisco, CA: Jossey-Bass.

Strange, C. C., & Banning, J. H. (2015). Designing for learning: Creating campus environments for student success. San Francisco, CA: Jossey-Bass.

Walsh, W. B. (1973). *Theories of Person-Environment Interaction: Implications for the College Student.* Iowa City. IA, The American College Testing Program.

Walsh, W. B. (1978). Person/environment interaction. In J. Banning (Ed.), Campus Ecology: A Perspective for Student Affairs (pp. 6-16). Cincinnati, OH: NASPA.

Western Interstate Commission for Higher Education (WICHE). (1973). *The ecosystem model: Designing campus environments.* Boulder, Colorado: Western Interstate Commission for Higher Education.

Part 2

The Applications of Campus Ecology to University Affairs

Part 2 presents topical indexes of how the concept of campus ecology has been applied to the conceptual understanding of campus affairs as well as to interventions and programs addressing campus issues. The five chapters include institutional affairs, academic affairs, student affairs, diversity affairs, and the community college. Each of the manuscripts indexed in the chapters and their sub-categories mention, reference, and/or use the concept of campus ecology within the manuscript. Even though some documents only mention the concept of campus ecology in a very generic manner, they were included in the index on the rationale that the concept of "campus ecology" was present in the thinking and writing of the authors.

Chapter 3

Institutional Affairs and Campus Ecology

Introduction

Despite the arbitrariness of dividing up the campus into administrative sectors particularly within the presentation of an ecological perspective where a basic tenet is that all aspects of an environment are connected and have dynamic mutual influence, such a division allows for the presentation of campus environment's complexity. This sector on institutional affairs focuses on the broad issues of campus planning and campus assessment, and three issues that have important links to the campus ecology model. These three issues are assessing campus community/culture, the physical environment, and the concern of campus safety.

Institutional Affairs

Applications: Planning and Campus Ecology

Banning, J. H. (1989). Using the ecosystem design process as a planning process. *The Campus Ecologist, 7*(4), 2-3.

Banning, J. H. (1993). Dober's Campus Design: A book review. *The Campus Ecologist, 11*(3), 1-2.

Banning, J. H. (1993). Quotes From: Dober's campus design. *The Campus Ecologist, 11*(3), 3.

Banning, J. H. (1995). Feng Shui goes to college? *The Campus Ecologist, 13*(1), 1-3.

Banning, J. H. (1996). The role of campus ecology in the designing of campus architecture. *The Campus Ecologist, 14*(1), 3.

Chapman, M. P. (1994). Social change and American campus design. *Planning for Higher Education, 22*(3), 1-12.

Chapman, M. P. (2006). *American places: In search of the twenty-first century campus.* Portsmouth, NH: Greenwood Publishing Group.

Demonica, D., & Ogurek, D. (2002). A new approach to community college master planning. *College Planning & Management, 5*(6), 42-44.

Doshi, A., Kumar, S., & Whitmer, S. (2014). Does space matter? Assessing the undergraduate "lived experience" to enhance learning. *Planning for Higher Education, 43*(1), 1-20.

Ellis, S. E. (2010). Introduction to strategic planning in student affairs: A model for process and elements of a plan. *New Directions for Student Services, 132,* 5-16.

Jamison, B. A. (1996). *Guidelines for developing a campus master plan document for small colleges and universities* (Doctoral Dissertation). Retrieved from ProQuest Dissertation and Theses Global database. (UMI No. 9638062)

Kenney, D., Dumont, R., & Kenney, G. (2005). *Mission and place: Strengthening learning and community through campus design.* Westport, CT: American Council on Education and Praeger Publishers.

Salahu-Din, H. A. (1987). *An investigation of campus perceptions of first-year, undergraduate students in arts and science at a Midwestern, land-grant University: Considerations in strategic planning* (Doctoral Dissertation). Retrieved from ProQuest Dissertation and Theses Global database. (UMI No. 8724699)

Stigall, S. W. (2007). Recommendations to improve space projection models and university space usage. *New Directions for Institutional Research, 2007*(135), 29-36.

Applications: Campus Assessment and the Campus Ecology

Aulepp, L., & Delworth, U. (1978). A team approach to environmental assessment. In J. H. Banning (Ed.), *Campus Ecology: A perspective for student affairs* (pp. 53-76). Cincinnati, OH: National Association of Student Personnel Administrators.

Banning, J. H. (1983). A book review: Environment Assessment and Design. *The Campus Ecologist, 1*(3), 3.

Banning, J. H. (1984). Ways to observe the campus environment. *The Campus Ecologist, 2*(1), 3.

Banning, J. H. (1988). Behavioral traces: A concept for campus ecologists. *The Campus Ecologist, 6*(2), 1,3.

Banning, J. H. (1988). New resources: Environmental Assessment. *Campus Ecologist, 6*(1), 2.

Banning, J. H. (1989). Environmental scanning: A tool for campus ecologist. *The Campus Ecologist, 7*(4), 1-2,4.

Banning, J. H. (1991). Ethnography: A promising method of inquiry for the study of campus ecology. *The Campus Ecologist, 9*(3), 1,3.

Banning, J. H. (1992). Campus photographs of posters and cartoons: Images of women. *The Campus Ecologist, 10*(3), 2-3.

Banning, J. H. (1992). Visual anthropology: Viewing the campus ecology for messages of sexism. *The Campus Ecologist, 10*(1), 1-4.

Banning, J. H. (1993). The pedestrian's visual experience on campus: Informal learning of cultural messages. *The Campus Ecologist, 11*(1), 1-4.

Banning, J. H. (1993). A taxonomy for classroom understanding. *The Campus Ecologist, 11*(3), 3-4.

Banning, J. H. (1994). The use of nonverbal cues of the physical environment in campus consultation. *The Campus Ecologist, 12*(4), 1-4.

Banning, J. H. (1995). Campus images: Homopredjudice. *The Campus Ecologist, 13*(3), 3.

Banning, J. H. (1996). Bumper sticker ethnography: Another way to view the campus ecology. *The Campus Ecologist, 14*(3), 1-4.

Banning, J. H. (1997). Assessing the campus' ethical climate: A multidimensional approach. *New Directions for Student Services* (77), 95-105. Retrieved from https://ezproxy2.library.colostate.edu/login?url=http://search.ebscohost.com/login.aspx?direct=true&AuthType=cookie,ip,url,cpid&custid=s4640792&db=aph&AN=9708242960&site=ehost-live

Banning, J. H. (2000). Bumper sticker ethnography: A study of campus culture. *Journal of Student Affairs, 9*, 11-17.

Banning, J. H., & Luna, F. C. (1992). Viewing the campus ecology for messages about Hispanic/Latino culture. *The Campus Ecologist, 10*(4), 1-4.

Barr, M. J., & Keating, L. A. (1985). Introduction: Elements of program development. In M. J. Barr & L. A. Keating (Eds.), *Developing Effective Student Services Programs: Systematic Approaches for Practitioners* (pp. 1-12). San Francisco , CA: Jossey-Bass.

Choice, T. L. (1998). *An analysis of the assessment of general education outcomes in Illinois community colleges* (Doctoral Dissertation). Retrieved from ProQuest Dissertation and Theses Global database. (UMI No. 9918701)

Evans, N. J. (1983). Environmental assessment: Current practices and future directions. *Journal of College Student Personnel, 24*(4), 293-99.

Guido, F. M., & Birnbaum, M. (2010). 21st Century Data: Using Photography as a Method in Student Affairs Assessment. *Journal of Student Affairs, 20*, 14-26.

Harrington, C. E., & Schibik, T. J. (2003). Reflexive photography as an alternative method for the study of the freshman year experience. *NASPA Journal, 41*(1), 23-40.

Hellyer, S. J. (2005). *Diverse perceptions of a midwest university* (Doctoral Dissertation). Retrieved from ProQuest Dissertation and Theses Global database. (UMI No. 3178424)

Huebner, L., & Lawson, J. M. (1990). Understanding and assessing college environments. In D. G. Creamer (Ed.), *College student development* (pp. 127-151). Alexandria, VA: American College Personnel Association.

Jolly, C. J. (2001). *The relationship between the "official" and "operative" identities of a private liberal arts college* (Doctoral Dissertation). Retrieved from ProQuest Dissertation and Theses Global database. (UMI No. 3010616)

Knezevich, P. (2000). *A comparison of campus cultures between Ball State University and Lincoln Land Community College as seen through the ecological perspective* (Unpublished Master's Thesis). Ball State University, Muncie, IN.

Kuh, G. (1993). Assessing campus environments. In M. J. Barr (Ed.), *The handbook of student affairs administration* (pp. 30-48). San Francisco, CA: Jossey-Bass.

Kuh, G. D. (2009). Understanding campus environments. In G. S. McClellan & J. Stringer (Eds.), *The Handbook of Student Affairs Administration* (pp. 65-88). San Francisco, CA: Jossey-Bass.

Lion, B. (2015). *Catholic student experiences and perceptions at a non-Catholic Christion institution* (Doctoral Dissertation). Retrieved from ProQuest Dissertation and Theses Global database. (UMI No. 3726095)

Maier, S. (2010). *Assessing school climate using a sequential transformative design* (Doctoral Dissertation). Retrieved from ProQuest Dissertation and Theses Global database. (UMI No. 3419061)

Mitchell, A. A., Sergent, M. T., & Sedlacek, W. E. (1994). *Mapping the university learning environment.* Retrieved from http://files.eric.ed.gov/fulltext/ED372668.pdf

Mourtzanos, E. G. (2005). *Exploring the relationship between collegiate environment and residential satisfaction: A cross-institutional comparison and a psychometric evaluation of the Resident Survey* (Doctoral Dissertation). Retrieved from ProQuest Dissertation and Theses Global database. (UMI No.3166874)

Neal, I. L. (1992). *Comparisons of perceptions of college campus environment by undergraduate students at eleven Illinois universities* (Doctoral Dissertation). Retrieved from ProQuest Dissertation and Theses Global database. (UMI No.9311286)

Paterson, J. W. (2000). *Development of an assessment instrument to determine the maturity level of student organizations* (Doctoral Dissertation). Retrieved from ProQuest Dissertation and Theses Global database. (UMI No. 9968982)

Paul, S. C., & Morrill, W. H. (1979). Applying the ecosystem perspective to the ecosystem perspective. *New Directions for Student Services, 8,* 85-98.

Pizzuti-Ashby, J. G., & Alary, D. G. (2008, May). *Campus Snapshot: Assessing the Campus Environment through a Student Lens.* Paper presented at the Association for Institutional Research Conference, Seattle, WA. Retrieved from http://files.eric.ed.gov/fulltext/ED507068.pdf

Salter, D. W., Junco, R., & Irvin, S. D. (2004). Campus social climate correlates of environmental type dimensions. *NASPA Journal, 41*(4), 742-759.

Schuh, J. H. (1990). Streamlining the ecosystem approach to residence hall environmental assessment. *NASPA Journal, 27*(3), 185-191.

Thomas, M. (2014). *Outsourcing Technology and Support in Higher Education* (Doctoral Dissertation). Retrieved from ProQuest Dissertation and Theses Global database. (UMI No. 3643190)

Tisdale, J. (1991). The college catalog: A barometer of campus ecology. *The Campus Ecologist, 9*(4), 3.

Upcraft, M. L., & Schuh, J. H. (1996). *Assessment in Student Affairs: A guide for practitioners.* San Francisco, CA: Jossey-Bass.

Webber, S. N. (2002). *Development of the Community Assessment Scale: Operationalizing Boyer's six principles for a vital learning community* (Doctoral Dissertation). Retrieved from ProQuest Dissertation and Theses Global database. (UMI No. 3074451)

Younge, S. L., Oetting, E. R., Banning, J. H., & Younge, K. A. (1991). Psychological messages from the physical environment: The drug and alcohol treatment center environment. *Substance Use & Misuse, 25*(S7-S8), 905-955.

Zingales, J. A. (2001). *Mission statement values and behavioral outcomes at seven Benedictine colleges and universities* (Doctoral Dissertation). Retrieved from ProQuest Dissertation and Theses Global database. (UMI No. 3019330)

Applications: Campus Community/Culture and Campus Ecology

Banning, J. H. (1988). Barriers to the development of community on campus. *The Campus Ecologist, 6*(4), 2, 3.

Banning, J. H. (1988). Building community: A macro and micro approach. *The Campus Ecologist, 6*(3), 1, 3.

Banning, J. H. (1989). Participation: The road to an ethical community. *The Campus Ecologist, 7*(1), 1-2.

Banning, J. H. (1990). Campus ecology: Recent publications of interest. *The Campus Ecologist, 8*(3), 3.

Banning, J. H. (1991). Student affairs: Are we helping in the search for community. *The Campus Ecologist, 9*(2), 1-2.

Banning, J. H. (1997). Assessing the campus' ethical climate: A multidimensional approach. *New Directions for Student Services* (77), 95-105.

Bauer, K. W. (1998). Editor's note. In K. W. Bauer (Ed.), *Campus climate: Understanding the critical components of today's colleges and universities* (pp. 1-5). San Francisco, CA: Jossey-Bass.

Chiang, C. H. (2012). *Commercialization of Higher Education: MBA Students' Experience and Expectations* (Doctoral Dissertation). Retrieved from ProQuest Dissertation and Theses Global database. (UMI No.NR79413)

Hoblet, K. L. (2014). *Analysis of Perceived Integration of Six Principles of Community and Determination of Relationship to Crime* (Doctoral Dissertation). Retrieved from ProQuest Dissertation and Theses Global database. (UMI No. 3631434)

Horton, G. S. (2015). *The impact of college campus shooting incidents: An exploration of student perceptions* (Doctoral Dissertation). Retrieved from ProQuest Dissertation and Theses Global database. (UMI No. 3734048)

Huesca, R. (1996). Diversity in communication for social change. *Peace Review, 8*(1), 69-73.

Jacobson, J. K. (1984). *An assessment of critical factors in measuring the quality of learning environments* (Doctoral Dissertation). Retrieved from ProQuest Dissertation and Theses Global database. (UMI No. 8418778)

Jolly, C. J. (2001). *The relationship between the "official" and "operative" identities of a private liberal arts college* (Doctoral Dissertation). Retrieved from ProQuest Dissertation and Theses Global database. (UMI No. 3010616)

Kuk, L., Banning, J. H., & Thomas, D. (2009). Enhancing Student Organizations as Agents for community development and civic engagement. *Journal of Student Affairs, 18,* 98-107.

Maier, S. (2010). *Assessing school climate using a sequential transformative design* (Doctoral Dissertation). Retrieved from ProQuest Dissertation and Theses Global database. (UMI No. 3419061)

Mourtzanos, E. G. (2005). *Exploring the relationship between collegiate environment and residential satisfaction: A cross-institutional comparison and a psychometric evaluation of the Resident Survey* (Doctoral Dissertation). Retrieved from ProQuest Dissertation and Theses Global database. (UMI No. 3166874)

Neal, I. L. (1992). *Comparisons of perceptions of college campus environment by undergraduate students at eleven Illinois universities* (Doctoral Dissertation). Retrieved from ProQuest Dissertation and Theses Global database. (UMI No. 9311286)

Paulson, M. (1996). We're building a campus and creating a community. *The Campus Ecologist, 14*(1), 1-3.

Price, J. M. (1992). *Community and campus culture: Out-of-class involvement at a midwest liberal arts college* (Doctoral Dissertation). Retrieved from ProQuest Dissertation and Theses Global database. (UMI No. 9335044)

Reading, G. D. (2000). *Using a campus compact to transmit values and create a sense of community: A case study* (Doctoral Dissertation). Retrieved from ProQuest Dissertation and Theses Global database. (UMI No. 9975325)

Renn, K. A., & Arnold, K. D. (2003). Reconceptualizing research on college student peer culture. *The Journal of Higher Education, 74*(3), 261-291.

Rogers, K. L. (2000). *Student services in bible colleges and universities accredited by the Accrediting Association of Bible Colleges (AABC)* (Doctoral Dissertation). Retrieved from ProQuest Dissertation and Theses Global database. (UMI No. 3064417)

Rose, C. A. (2007). *Civic visions: An exploration of university students' perceptions of the civic commitment of their campus community* (Master's Thesis). Retrieved from ProQuest Dissertation and Theses Global database. (UMI No. MR30613)

Rue, H. E. (1988). *The identification of components of community on the college campus* (Doctoral Dissertation). Retrieved from ProQuest Dissertation and Theses Global database. (UMI No. 8818207)

Simpson, J. L. (2001). *The making of multivocal culture: (Re)constructing community on a university campus* (Doctoral Dissertation). Retrieved from ProQuest Dissertation and Theses Global database. (UMI No. 3005100)

Shupp, M. R. (2016). Creating healthy climates through intentionality of practice. In S. T. Gregory & J. Edwards, *Invitational education and practice in higher education: An international perspective* (pp. 179-192). Lexington, KY: Lexington Books.

Talboys, W. M. (1995). *Using financial ratios in the analysis of four private universities in the southwest United States: A case study* (Doctoral Dissertation). Retrieved from ProQuest Dissertation and Theses Global database. (UMI No. 9615638)

Tuttle, J. K. (2006). *The effects of a commuter collegium on Christian college commuter students' sense of community* (Doctoral Dissertation). Retrieved from ProQuest Dissertation and Theses Global database. (UMI No. 3228566)

Webber, S. N. (2002). *Development of the Community Assessment Scale: Operationalizing Boyer's six principles for a vital learning community* (Doctoral Dissertation). Retrieved from ProQuest Dissertation and Theses Global database. (UMI No. 3074451)

Wilson, H. L. (2015). Campus climate for trans* students. *Journal of Student Affairs, 25*, 37-44.

Young, R. B. (1993). The essence of aesthetics. *New Directions for Student Services, 61*, 47-59.

Zingales, J. A. (2001). *Mission statement values and behavioral outcomes at seven Benedictine colleges and universities* (Doctoral Dissertation). Retrieved from ProQuest Dissertation and Theses Global database. (UMI No. 3019330)

Applications: The Physical Environment and Campus Ecology

Andreas, R., & Kubik, J. (1985). Redesigning our campuses to meet the needs of our commuting students: Study lounges. *The Campus Ecologist, 3*(1), 2.

Banning, J. H. (1983). The built environment: Do ivy walls have memories? *The Campus Ecologist, 1*(2), 1-3.

Banning, J. H. (1983). People's Park: Revisited from an ecological perspective. *The Campus Ecologist, 1*(3), 1.

Banning, J. H. (1985). "Participatory Architecture". *The Campus Ecologist, 3*(3), 2.

Banning, J. H. (1986). The classroom environment. *The Campus Ecologist, 4*(4), 3.

Banning, J. H. (1987). Quotes on Ecology. *The Campus Ecologist, 5*(2), 3.

Banning, J. H. (1988). Behavioral traces: A concept for campus ecologists. *The Campus Ecologist, 6*(2), 1, 3.

Banning, J. H. (1991). Campus buildings and behavior. *The Campus Ecologist, 9*(1), 3.

Banning, J. H. (1992). The connection between learning and the learning environment. In E. Herbert & A. Meek (Eds.), *Children, Learning, & School design* (pp. 19-29). Winnetka, IL: Winnetka Public Schools.

Banning, J. H. (1993). Dober's Campus Design: A book review. *The Campus Ecologist, 11*(3), 1-2.

Banning, J. H. (1993). The pedestrian's visual experience on campus: Informal learning of cultural messages. *The Campus Ecologist, 11*(1), 1-4.

Banning, J. H. (1993). The physical environment of the college classroom: An instructional aid. *The Campus Ecologist, 11*(4), 1-4.

Banning, J. H. (1993). Quotes From: Dober's campus design. *The Campus Ecologist, 11*(3), 3.

Banning, J. H. (1993). Learning and the physical environment. *The Campus Ecologist, 11*(4), 3.

Banning, J. H. (1994). The use of nonverbal cues of the physical environment in campus consultation. *The Campus Ecologist, 12*(4), 1-4.

Banning, J. H. (1995). Feng Shui goes to college? *The Campus Ecologist, 13*(1), 1-3.

Banning, J. H. (1995). Where do I sit? The landscape of informal learning. *The Campus Ecologist, 13*(4), 1-4.

Banning, J. H. (1996). The role of campus ecology in the designing of campus architecture. *The Campus Ecologist, 14*(1), 3.

Banning, J. H. (1996). Wayfinding: Welcoming? Or a sign of the two ecology problem. *The Campus Ecologist, 14*(4), 3-4.

Banning, J. H. (1999). Facility Design: Lessons from the 20th century. *College Services Administration, 22*(4), 16-19.

Banning, J. H. (2000). Bricks and Mortarboards: How Student union buildings learn and teach. *College Services, 23*(6), 16-19.

Banning, J. H. (2001). Developing the environmental program. In Bartley-Taylor (Ed.), *Higher Education housing facilities: Options for construction, renovation, privatization, and financing* (pp. 38-43). Columbus, OH: The National Association of College Auxiliary Services.

Banning, J. H. (2002). Student development: In-between buildings. *Journal of Student Affairs, 11*, 21-25.

Banning, J. H., & Bartels, S. (1997). A Taxonomy: Campus physical artifacts as communicators of campus multiculturalism. *NASPA Journal, 35*(1), 29-37.

Banning, J. H., Clemons, S., McKelfresh, D., & Gibbs, R. W. (2010). Special places for students: Third place and restorative place. *College Student Journal, 44*(4), 906-912.

Banning, J. H., Clemons, S., McKelfresh, D., & Waxman, L. (2006). Designing the third place. *College Services, 6*(3), 42-47.

Banning, J. H., & Cunard, M. R. (1986). Environment supports student development. *ACU-I Bulletin, 54*(1), 8-10.

Banning, J. H., & Cunard, M. R. (1986). The physical environment supports student development. *The Campus Ecologist, 4*(1), 1-3.

Banning, J. H., & Cunard, M. R. (1996). Assessment and design of the physical environment in support of student development. In N. Metz (Ed.), *ACUI Classics: Student Development* (pp. 131-135). Bloomington, IN: Association of College Unions-International.

Banning, J. H., & Cunard, M. R. (1996). An ecological perspective of buildings and behavior. *College Services Administration, 19*(4), 38-41.

Beck, S., Berson, J., Hagan, A., Pontius, J., & Umschied, D. (2000). Where do students study? An analysis of preferred study environments. *Journal of the Indiana University Student Personnel Association, (2001 Edition)*, 33-48.

Bennett, M. A., & Benton, S. L. (2001). What are the buildings saying? A study of first-year undergraduate students' attributions about college campus architecture. *NASPA Journal, 38*(2), 159-177.

Bott, S., Banning, J., Wells, M., Haas, G., & Lakey, J. (2006). A sense of place: A framework and its application to campus ecology. *College Services, 6*, 42-47.

Clemons, S. A., Banning, J. H., & McKelfresh, D. A. (2004). The importance of sense of place and sense of self in residence hall room design. *Journal of Student Affairs, 13*, 8-15.

Compton, T. R. (2000). *Students' expectations of the college experience based on their perceptions of the physical environment* (Doctoral Dissertation). Retrieved from ProQuest Dissertation and Theses Global database. (UMI No. 9988336)

Doshi, A., Kumar, S., & Whitmer, S. (2014). Does space matter? Assessing the undergraduate "lived experience" to enhance learning. *Planning for Higher Education, 43*(1), 1-20.

Eckert, E. (2012). *Examining the environment: The development of a survey instrument to assess student perceptions of the university outdoor physical campus* (Doctoral Dissertation). Retrieved from ProQuest Dissertation and Theses Global database. (UMI No. 3510753)

Gordon, J. H. (1980). *The identification and importance of physical symbols by selected institutions of higher education in Indiana* (Doctoral Dissertation). Retrieved from ProQuest Dissertation and Theses Global database. (UMI No. 8022695)

Greene, T. (1996). Mapping campus landscapes. *The Campus Ecologist, 14*(2), 1-4.

Griffin, T. D. (1990). The physical environment of the college classroom and its affects on students. *The Campus Ecologist, 8*(1), 1-3.

Haque, M. T., Miller, A., Miller, S., Tai, L. (2003). Sacred by design: Shifting to higher ground through the design of meditation and memorial gardens. *Garden History (Jan.-June), 56*, 68.

Harrell, K. L. (2012). *Green student centers' influence on the campus environment* (Doctoral Dissertation). Retrieved from ProQuest Dissertation and Theses Global database. (UMI No. 3535753)

Harrington, K. D. (2013). *Community on campus: The role of physical space* (Doctoral Dissertation). Retrieved from ProQuest Dissertation and Theses Global database. (UMI No. 3583648)

Heiss, J. K. (2006). *Moving into students' spaces: The impact of location of academic advising on student engagement among undecided students* (Doctoral Dissertation). Retrieved from ProQuest Dissertation and Theses Global database. (UMI No. 3222783)

Hotard, J. B. (1993). *Student pathways on campus* (Doctoral Dissertation). Retrieved from ProQuest Dissertation and Theses Global database. (UMI No. 9414432)

Hubiak, W., & Banning, J. H. (1994). The implications of place attachment for campus workplaces. *The Campus Ecologist, 12*(3), 1-4.

Johnson, A. D. (2000). *Campus ecology and the functions of physical settings: a review of Ball State University's current Student Center* (Unpublished Master's Thesis). Ball State University, Muncie, IN.

Kenney, D., Dumont, R., & Kenney, G. (2005). *Mission and place: Strengthening learning and community through campus design*. Westport, CT: American Council on Education and Praeger Publishers.

Kleberg, J. (1987). Academics and campus architecture linked. *The Campus Ecologist, 5*(1), 3.

Love, C. T., Banning, J. H., & Kotsiopulos, A. (1998). Visual diversity for a faculty consumer science higher education facility. *Journal of Family and Consumer Sciences, 90*(3), 52-54.

Lozano, A. (2010). Latina/o culture centers: Providing a sense of belonging and promoting student success. In L. Patton (Ed.), *Culture centers in higher education: Perspectives on identity, theory, and practice* (pp. 3-25). Sterling, VA: Stylus Publishing.

McClellan, G. S., & Stringer, J. (Eds.). (2009). *Handbook of Student Affairs Administration*. San Fransico, CA: Jossey-Bass.

McDowell, A. M., & Higbee, J. L. (2014). Responding to the concerns of student cultural groups: Redesigning spaces for cultural centers. *Contemporary Issues in Education Research, 7*(3), 227-236.

Miller, M., & Banning, J. H. (1992). Campus design: Guidance from the past. *The Campus Ecologist, 10*(2), 1-4.

Morrison, N. J. (2007). *The meaning of place in an urban context for the under-represented minority student experience at NYU* (Doctoral Dissertation). Retrieved from ProQuest Dissertation and Theses Global database. (UMI No. 3255856)

O'Guinn, M. D., Farley, M., Supple, M., & Sabatino, J. (1994). Playing in the front yard. *Journal of the Indiana University Student Personnel Association, (Fall 1994 Edition)*, 1-11.

Okoli, D. T. (2013). *Sense of place and student engagement among undergraduate students at a major public research university* (Doctoral Dissertation). Retrieved from ProQuest Dissertation and Theses Global database. (UMI No. 3608379)

Ortiz, J. M. (1990). Music as sound campus ecology. *The Campus Ecologist, 8*(4), 1-3.

Peoples, L. (2014). Designing a Law Library to Encourage Learning. *Journal of Legal Education, 63*(4), 612-639.

Price, I., Matzdorf, F., Smith, L., & Agahi, H. (2003). The impact of facilities on student choice of university. *Facilities, 21*(10), 212-222.

Price, J. (2009). Facilities planning and development. In G. S. McClellan & J. Stringer (Eds.), *The handbook of student affairs administration* (pp. 608-629). San Francisco, CA: Jossey-Bass.

Roecks, A. L. (1973). A comparative study of the non-cognitive, cognitive and demographic characteristics of undergraduates who resided in double rooms with undergraduates who resided in single rooms at Gonzaga University (Unpublished Master's Thesis). Gonzaga University, Spokane, WA. Retrieved from https://eric.ed.gov/?q=Roecks&id=ED119087

Ryan, M. A. (2008). *Women who build buildings: The experiences of student affairs professionals in constructing student-focused space on university campuses* (Doctoral Dissertation). Retrieved from ProQuest Dissertation and Theses Global database. (UMI No. 3303431)

Semken, S., & Freeman, C. B. (2008). Sense of place in the practice and assessment of place based science teaching. *Science Education, 92*(6), 1042-1057.

Seplow, S. L. (2001). *Students' perceptions of the impacts of construction and environmental influences on their participation, experience and learning in their residence hall community* (Doctoral Dissertation). Retrieved from ProQuest Dissertation and Theses Global database. (UMI No. 3024087)

Stigall, S. W. (2007). Recommendations to improve space projection models and university space usage. *New Directions for Institutional Research, 135*, 29-36.

Theroux, R. D. (2008). *Communicating the meanings of cultural artifacts: An exploratory study of orientation units* (Doctoral Dissertation). Retrieved from ProQuest Dissertation and Theses Global database. (UMI No. 3338258)

Troxell, A. R. (2010). *Campus Architecture and Student Culture in American Higher Education* (Honors Thesis). Bucknell University, Lewisberg, PA. Retrieved from http://digitalcommons.bucknell.edu/honors_thesis

Walch, D. (2010). *Physical environments and their influence on student utilization of public spaces in the Texas Tech*

University Student Union facility (Unpublished Master's Thesis). Texas Tech University, Lubbock, TX. Retrieved from https://repositories.tdl.org/ttu-ir/handle/2346/ETD-TTU-2010-12-1103

Wonnett, R. (2010). *A place apart: The judicial interpretation of campus place as a public forum* (Doctoral Dissertation). Retrieved from ProQuest Dissertation and Theses Global database. (UMI No. 3441285)

Zandvliet, D. B. (2012). Development and validation of the Place-Based Learning and Constructivist Environment Survey (PLACES). *Learning Environments Research, 15*(2), 125-140.

Zandvliet, D. B. (2013). PLACES and SPACES: Case studies in the evaluation of post-secondary, place-based learning environments. *Studies in Educational Evaluation, 41*, 18-28.

Zimring, C., Joseph, A., Nicoll, G., & Tespas, S. (2005). Influences of building design and site design on physical activity. *American Journal of Preventive Medicine, 28*(2S2), 186-193.

Applications: Campus Safety and Campus Ecology

Banning, J. H. (1989). The ecology of vandalism. *The Campus Ecologist, 7*(2), 3.

Cooper, M. B. A. (1997). *The relationship of student perceptions and behaviors regarding personal safety: A comparative study of two small, private colleges* (Doctoral Dissertation). Retrieved from ProQuest Dissertation and Theses Global database. (UMI No. 9808053)

Dongarra, P. (2014). *Policing the campus: Perceptions of campus police among the university population* (Master's Thesis).

Retrieved from ProQuest Dissertation and Theses Global database. (UMI No. 1573423)

Evans, N. J., & Rankin, S. (1998). Heterosexism and Campus Violence: Assessment and Intervention Strategies. In R. Fenske, A. Hoffman, & J. H. Schuh (Eds.), *Violence on campus: Defining the problems, strategies for action* (pp. 169-186). Gaithersburg, MD: Aspen.

Fazari, G. M. (2003). *Patterns of on-campus theft victimization among undergraduate students and their impact on satisfaction at a higher education institution* (Doctoral Dissertation). Retrieved from ProQuest Dissertation and Theses Global database. (UMI No. 3081014)

Hall, A. L. (2014). *Incredi-bull-ly inclusive?: Assessing the climate on a college campus (Doctoral Dissertation).* Retrieved from ProQuest Dissertation and Theses Global database. (UMI No. 1563192)

Hoblet, K. L. (2014). *Analysis of Perceived Integration of Six Principles of Community and Determination of Relationship to Crime* (Doctoral Dissertation). Retrieved from ProQuest Dissertation and Theses Global database. (UMI No. 3631434)

Horton, G. S. (2015). *The impact of college campus shooting incidents: An exploration of student perceptions* (Doctoral Dissertation). Retrieved from ProQuest Dissertation and Theses Global database. (UMI No. 3734048)

Hummer, D. C., II. (1998). *The impact of campus public safety operations and crime prevention program implementation upon serious criminality at United States colleges and universities: An application of the situational perspective* (Doctoral Dissertation).

Retrieved from ProQuest Dissertation and Theses Global database. (UMI No. 9909320)

Roark, M. L. (1987). Preventing violence on college campuses. *Journal of Counseling & Development, 65*(7), 367-371.

Rund, J. A. (2002). The changing context of campus safety. *New Directions for Student Services, 99*, 3-10.

Siegel, D. G., & Raymond, C. H. (1992). An ecological approach to violent crime on campus. *Journal of Security Administration, 15*(2), 19-29.

Chapter 4

Academic Affairs and Campus Ecology

The campus ecology and its relation to academic affairs is organized around two themes: the student's academic journey and academic programs and issues. The student's academic journey focuses on the relationship between campus ecology and the journey paths that include coming to campus, especially recruiting, admissions, and orientation. This journey structure will also include the topics of retention and academic outcomes. All these paths are influenced by other organizational structures on campus as well, but the references are listed here as a part of the students' academic journey. The second theme of academic programs and issues captures how campus ecology has been noted in faculty advising, alternative delivery programs, academic departments, and academic classroom issues.

Student's Academic Journey

Applications: Recruitment/Admissions/Orientation and Campus Ecology

Banning, J. H. (1989). Impact of college environments on freshman students. In M. L. Upcraft & J. N. Gardner (Eds.),

The Freshman year experience (pp. 53-62). San Francisco, CA: Jossey-Bass.

Banning, J. H. (1989). Transitions Update. *The Campus Ecologist, 7*(1), 3.

Browning, M. C. (2000). *Graduate student enrollment management: Toward a model that predicts student enrollment. A case study at Phillips Graduate Institute* (Doctoral Dissertation). Retrieved from ProQuest Dissertation and Theses Global database. (UMI No. 3054852)

Cook, T., & Rushton, S. B. (2009). *How to recruit and retain higher education students: A handbook of good practice.* New York: Routledge.

Cowart, C. V. (1990). *The contribution of freshman orientation programs to academic and social integration of sophomore students* (Doctoral Dissertation). Retrieved from ProQuest Dissertation and Theses Global database. (UMI No. 9116728)

Gillis, M. E. (1993). *The effects of a continuous orientation course on the academic and social integration of college freshmen* (Doctoral Dissertation). Retrieved from ProQuest Dissertation and Theses Global database. (UMI No. 9329777)

Greenough, A. S. (2003). *In search of the "right place": Institutional image, person-environment fit and college choice* (Doctoral Dissertation). Retrieved from ProQuest Dissertation and Theses Global database. (UMI No. 3107812)

Holmes, M. L. (1990). *The analysis of enrollment patterns and student profile characteristics at a small rural New England university, 1978-1988* (Doctoral Dissertation). Retrieved from ProQuest Dissertation and Theses Global database. (UMI No. 9110072)

Johnson, B. D. (2002). *Preparing students for the university: What is the effect of community college accommodation on students who transfer to state universities?* (Doctoral Dissertation). Retrieved from ProQuest Dissertation and Theses Global database. (UMI No. 3056242)

Logan, S. G. (1989). *A comparative study of student retention and academic success based on participation in orientation and support programs* (Doctoral Dissertation). Retrieved from ProQuest Dissertation and Theses Global database. (UMI No. 8920970)

Louis, J. (1989). Getting In. *The Journal of Higher Education, 60*(3), 247-277.

O'Beirne, B. (1991). The role of residential programs in the recruitment and orientation of new students. In W. Zeller (Ed.), *Residence Life programs and the first-year experience* (pp. 21-28). Columbia, SC: National Resource Center for the Freshman Year Experience.

Price, I., Matzdorf, F., Smith, L., & Agahi, H. (2002). The Impact of Facilities on Student Choice of University. *Facilities, 21*(10), 212-222.

Sanford, M. R. (1990). *The effectiveness of summer orientation programs on retention and subsequent academic performance of minority students: A follow-up study* (Doctoral Dissertation). Retrieved from ProQuest Dissertation and Theses Global database. (UMI No. 9100501)

Tankersley, C. J. (2013). *Becoming an orientation leader: A catalyst for self-authorship development* (Doctoral Dissertation). Retrieved from ProQuest Dissertation and Theses Global database. (UMI No. 3671167)

Wapner, S. (1981). Transactions of persons-environments: Some critical transactions. *Journal of Environmental Psychology, 1*(3), 223-229.

Webber, W. J. (1988). *Admissions directors' perceptions of the enrollment management model at selected four-year public institutions of higher education* (Doctoral Dissertation). Retrieved from ProQuest Dissertation and Theses Global database. (UMI No. 8814755)

Wiese, M. D. (1994). College choice cognitive dissonance: Managing student/institution fit. *Journal of Marketing for Higher Education, 5*(1), 35-48.

William, T. E. (1986). Student-institution fit: Linking campus ecology to enrollment management. *The Campus Ecologist, 4*(4), 1-2.

Williams, T. E. (1986). Optimizing student institution fit. *New Directions for Higher Education, (53),* 14(1), 35-46.

Williams, V. M., Jr. (1996). *Motivational orientations of reentry adult male graduate students to participate in higher education* (Doctoral Dissertation). Retrieved from ProQuest Dissertation and Theses Global database. (UMI No. 9622874)

Applications: Retention and Campus Ecology

Attinasi Jr, L. C. (1989). Getting in: Mexican Americans' perceptions of university attendance and the implications for freshman year persistence. *The Journal of Higher Education, 60*(3), 247-277.

Banning, J. H. (1986). Lemmings to the sea: Student attrition. *The Campus Ecologist, 4*(2), 1-2.

Bilsky, J. H. (2000). *Student satisfaction among select demographic groups at a Florida community college* (Doctoral Dissertation). Retrieved from ProQuest Dissertation and Theses Global database. (UMI No. 9984391)

Boone, C. A. (2003). *Person-environment fit and college freshmen retention: Effects of congruence between the pre-collegiate and collegiate settings* (Doctoral Dissertation). Retrieved from ProQuest Dissertation and Theses Global database. (UMI No. 3101153)

Braxton, J. M. (2000). Introduction. In J. Braxton (Ed.), *Reworking the student departure puzzle* (pp. 1-10). Nashville, TN: Vanderbilt University Press.

Brown, M. C. (1998). African American college student retention and the ecological psychology of historically black colleges. *National Association of Student Professional Journal, 1*, 50-66.

Brown-Weinstock, P. (2009). *Adjustment and persistence of students from an urban environment to a rural community college* (Doctoral Dissertation). Retrieved from ProQuest Dissertation and Theses Global database. (UMI No. 3410791)

Butcher, J. L. (1997). *Involvement and persistence: Nontraditional student perceptions of the student-college relationship* (Doctoral Dissertation). Retrieved from ProQuest Dissertation and Theses Global database. (UMI No. 9819077)

Clark, S. B., & Crawford, S. L. (1992). An analysis of African-American first-year college student attitudes and attrition rates. *Urban education, 27*(1), 59-79.

Cook, A., & Rushton, S. B. (2008). *Student transition: Practices and policies to promote retention.* Coleraine, IR: Staff and Educational Development Association.

Cook, T., & Rushton, S. B. (2009). *How to recruit and retain higher education students: A handbook of good practice.* New York: Routledge.

Cuseo, J. (2008). *The "BIG PICTURE": Key causes of student attrition & key components of a comprehensive student retention plan.* Retrieved from http://web.ysu.edu/gen/ysu_generated_bin/documents/basic_module/Key_Causes_of_Student_AttritionComprehensive_Retention_Plan.pdf

Engs, M. S. (1996). *Factors affecting the retention of Native American students at a southwestern community college* (Doctoral Dissertation). Retrieved from ProQuest Dissertation and Theses Global database. (UMI No. 9710193)

Engstrom, Z. B. (2008). *The impact of learning community involvement and campus climate on student satisfaction and the retention of Latino students at a highly selective private institution* (Doctoral Dissertation). Retrieved from ProQuest Dissertation and Theses Global database. (UMI No. 3311110)

Estrada, L. J. (1990). *A comparative assessment of persistence factors impacting Anglo and Hispanic students at a predominantly Anglo institution of higher education* (Doctoral Dissertation). Retrieved from ProQuest Dissertation and Theses Global database. (UMI No. 9115273)

Forbes, G. D. (1998). *The concept of religious fit and student retention at Christian colleges* (Doctoral Dissertation). Retrieved from ProQuest Dissertation and Theses Global database. (UMI No. 9918363)

Fortune, E. P. (1984). IV A model for recruiting and retaining minority students in criminal justice majors. *Journal of Crime and Justice, 7*(1), 43-62.

Fremont, R. H., II. (2002). *College graduation rates and the elite student-athlete* (Doctoral Dissertation). Retrieved from ProQuest Dissertation and Theses Global database. (UMI No. 3045678)

Furr, S. R., & Elling, T. W. (2002). African American students in a predominately – White University. Factors associated with retention. *College Student Journal, 36*(2), 188-203.

Harrison, J. T. (2003). *Residence life and programming as a contributing factor to student success and retention* (Master's Thesis). Retrieved from ProQuest Dissertation and Theses Global database. (UMI No. MQ82413)

Hecker, M. J. (1994). *Assessing the effectiveness of a developmental educational program using GPA attainment, student retention, and student involvement as measurement variables* (Doctoral Dissertation). Retrieved from ProQuest Dissertation and Theses Global database. (UMI No. 9503712)

Herchmer, J. L. (2013). *A Self-Success Plan and Student Persistence in College: A Case Study* (Doctoral Dissertation). Retrieved from ProQuest Dissertation and Theses Global database. (UMI No. 3571471)

Hernandez, J. C. (1999). *En sus voces (in their voices): Understanding the retention of Latino/a college students* (Doctoral Dissertation). Retrieved from ProQuest Dissertation and Theses Global database. (UMI No. 9957158)

Hillard, M. K. (1996). *An assessment of persistence and mattering among nontraditional, community college students* (Doctoral Dissertation). Retrieved from ProQuest Dissertation and Theses Global database. (UMI No. 9628684)

Kent, S. E. (2004). *Persistence of adult undergraduate students and their perceptions of how they matter to a public institution* (Doctoral Dissertation). Retrieved from ProQuest Dissertation and Theses Global database. (UMI No. 3130530)

Kuh, G. D., & Love, P. G. (2000). A cultural perspective on student departure. In J. Braxton (Ed.), *Reworking the student departure puzzle* (pp. 196-212). Nashville, TN: Vanderbilt.

Lee, Y. (2005). *Effects of multiple group involvement on identifying and interpreting perceived needs* (Doctoral Dissertation). Retrieved from ProQuest Dissertation and Theses Global database. (UMI No. 3177181)

Lemley, E. Y. (1990). *Effects of selected extracurricular involvement on persistence in a church-related university* (Doctoral Dissertation). Retrieved from ProQuest Dissertation and Theses Global database. (UMI No. 9104815)

Leonard, M. Q. (2002). An Outreach Framework for Retaining Nontraditional Students at Open Admissions Institutions. *Journal of College Counseling, 5*(1), 60-73.

Logan, S. G. (1989). *A comparative study of student retention and academic success based on participation in orientation and support programs* (Doctoral Dissertation). Retrieved from ProQuest Dissertation and Theses Global database. (UMI No. 8920970)

Martinson Zunkel, K. A. (2002). *Relationships among learning community participation, student self-efficacy, confidence, outcome expectations, and commitment* (Doctoral Dissertation). Retrieved from ProQuest Dissertation and Theses Global database. (UMI No. 3061881)

McMillion, S. S. (1999). *Campus environment factors of two small, rural community colleges and their influences on persistence behaviors of African-American students in the college transfer program* (Doctoral Dissertation). Retrieved from ProQuest Dissertation and Theses Global database. (UMI No. 9922697)

Miller, G. D., III. (1998). *Predicting freshmen persistence and voluntary withdrawal from Heath's model of maturing* (Doctoral Dissertation). Retrieved from ProQuest Dissertation and Theses Global database. (UMI No. 9842415)

Morales, L. (2000). *Institutional and organizational attributes influencing the retention of transfer students at a California state university* (Doctoral Dissertation). Retrieved from ProQuest Dissertation and Theses Global database. (UMI No. 9964030)

Pascarella, E. T., & Terenzini, P. T. (2005). *How College affects students: A third decade of research*. San Francisco, CA: Jossey-Bass.

Payne, R. W. (1995). *Predicting voluntary student departure from Northern Arizona University* (Doctoral Dissertation). Retrieved from ProQuest Dissertation and Theses Global database. (UMI No. 9529989)

Sanford, M. R. (1990). *The effectiveness of summer orientation programs on retention and subsequent academic performance of minority students: A follow-up study* (Doctoral Dissertation). Retrieved from ProQuest Dissertation and Theses Global database. (UMI No. 9100501)

Schroeder, C. C. (2013). Reframing Retention Strategy: A Focus on Process. *New Directions for Higher Education No. 161*, 39-47.

Schuetz, P. (2005). UCLA Community college review: Campus environment: A missing link in studies of community college attrition. *Community College Review, 32*(4), 60-80.

Sjoberg, C. E. (1999). *The relationship of environmental predictors and institutional characteristics to student persistence* (Doctoral Dissertation). Retrieved from ProQuest Dissertation and Theses Global database. (UMI No. (9942471)

Smith, J. S. (2004). The effects of student receptivity on college achievement and retention. *Journal of College Student Retention: Research, Theory and Practice, 6*(3), 273-288.

Steele, J. R. (2014). *Housing and residential life: Determining the connection between theme communities and student's retention rates* (Master's Thesis). Retrieved from http://csus-dspace.calstate.edu/bitstream/handle/10211.3/122158/Joan%20R%20Steele%20Thesis%20Edited%205-11-14%20FINAL.pdf?sequence=2

Stryker, J. C. (1999). *Retention planning for the future: Challenges facing the rural land-grant university in the twenty-first century* (Doctoral Dissertation). Retrieved from ProQuest Dissertation and Theses Global database. (UMI No. 9927877)

Sykes, R. P. (1996). *Staying power: Independent schools and retention* (Doctoral Dissertation). Retrieved from ProQuest Dissertation and Theses Global database. (UMI No. 9701360)

Villanueva, V. A. (2015). *A study of Latino student persistence in emerging adulthood: A grounded theory study* (Doctoral Dissertation). Retrieved from ProQuest Dissertation and Theses Global database. (UMI No. 3689250)

Whiston, S. C. (1986). *An examination of college student retention and attrition utilizing a campus ecological assessment (student services)* (Doctoral Dissertation). Retrieved from ProQuest Dissertation and Theses Global database. (UMI No. 8623114)

White, J. L. (2005). *Persistence of interest in science, technology, engineering and mathematics: An analysis of persisting and non-persisting students* (Doctoral Dissertation). Retrieved from ProQuest Dissertation and Theses Global database. (UMI No. 3169266)

Wilburn, B. S. (1999). *An examination of college persistence and Hispanic students' perceptions of academic and social integration at a two-year campus of a doctoral degree-granting university* (Doctoral Dissertation). Retrieved from ProQuest Dissertation and Theses Global database. (UMI No. 9963702)

Williamson-Ashe, S. R. (2008). *The influence of academic and social integration, educational objectives, and intent on community college student persistence* (Doctoral Dissertation). Retrieved from ProQuest Dissertation and Theses Global database. (UMI No. 3325445)

Wilson, D. J. (1998). *Visionary leadership of chief student affairs officers and its impact on partnership initiatives with Academic Affairs and student retention* (Doctoral Dissertation). Retrieved from ProQuest Dissertation and Theses Global database. (UMI No. 9908700)

Wilson-Cook, C. M. (1990). *A quantitative and qualitative investigation of the persistence of a select group of reinstated students at a four-year institution of higher education* (Doctoral Dissertation). Retrieved from ProQuest Dissertation and Theses Global database. (UMI No. 9114940)

Yang, H. W. (2001). *A comparison of academic achievement, continuous full-time enrollment, and persistency rate between first-semester freshman students who participated in one of the two types of freshman orientation programs at Fresno City College*

(Doctoral Dissertation). Retrieved from ProQuest Dissertation and Theses Global database. (UMI No. 3022946)

Applications: Academic Outcomes and Campus Ecology

Ahren, C. S. (2009). *Disentangling the unique effects of co-curricular engagement on self-reported student learning outcomes* (Doctoral Dissertation). Retrieved from ProQuest Dissertation and Theses Global database. (UMI No. 3354894)

Aldridge, H. M., Jr. (2005). *Analysis of the perceptions of learning-centered changes in community college student affairs* (Doctoral Dissertation). Retrieved from ProQuest Dissertation and Theses Global database. (UMI No. 3174967)

Austin, L. (1992). *Factors influencing the academic success of adult college students after initial academic suspension* (Doctoral Dissertation). Retrieved from ProQuest Dissertation and Theses Global database. (UMI No. 9303216)

Baird, L. L. (1996). Learning from research on student outcomes. In S. Komives & D. B. Woodward (Eds.), *Student services: A handbook for the profession* 3rd ed. (pp. 515-535). San Francisco, CA: Jossey-Bass.

Baird, L. L. (2003). New lessons from research on student outcomes. In S. Komives & D. B. Woodward (Eds.), *Student services: A handbook for the profession* (pp. 595-617). San Francisco, CA: Jossey-Bass.

Banning, J. H. (1987). The ecology of outcomes. *The Campus Ecologist, 5*(2), 1-3.

Boyd, K. D. (2010). *The nature of the student-institution relationship and behavioral indicators of personal and social responsibility: An exploration of the association between relational quality outcomes, alcohol use, and academic honesty* (Unpublished Doctoral Dissertation). University of Georgia, Athens, GA.

Brown, S. C. (1999). *Learning across the campus: How college facilitates the development of wisdom* (Doctoral Dissertation). Retrieved from ProQuest Dissertation and Theses Global database. (UMI No. 9942950)

Choice, T. L. (1998). *An analysis of the assessment of general education outcomes in Illinois community colleges* (Doctoral Dissertation). Retrieved from ProQuest Dissertation and Theses Global database. (UMI No. 9918701)

Conrady, L. L. (2008). *A phenomenological case study of mentoring outcomes: Benefiting the mentor in student development, self-esteem, and identity formation* (Doctoral Dissertation). Retrieved from ProQuest Dissertation and Theses Global database. (UMI No. 3324703)

Czupryn, K. A. (1989). *Academic achievement and academic satisfaction as a function of person-environment fit* (Doctoral Dissertation). Retrieved from ProQuest Dissertation and Theses Global database. (UMI No. 9004671)

Dale, P., & Shoenhair, C. (2000). *Learning-Centered Practices in Student Services*. A Paradise Valley Community College Report. Retrieved from ERIC Database (ED445732).

Dale, P. A. (2013). Establishing a learning center culture. In M. M. Gardner, K. A. Kline, & M. J. Bresciani (Eds.), *Assessing Student Learning in the Community and Two-Year College: Successful Strategies and Tools Developed by Practitioners in Student and Academic Affairs* (pp. 18-38). Sterling, VA: Stylus Publishing.

Destinon, M. v., Ganz, B., & Engs, M. (1993). Outcomes assessment and minority students in community colleges. *Community College Journal of Research and Practice, 17*(6), 497-508.

Flores, A. L. A. (2012). *Dual enrollment programs: A comparative study of high school students' college academic achievement at different settings* (Doctoral Dissertation). Retrieved from ProQuest Dissertation and Theses Global database. (UMI No. 3540784)

Fremont, R. H., II. (2002). *College graduation rates and the elite student-athlete* (Doctoral Dissertation). Retrieved from ProQuest Dissertation and Theses Global database. (UMI No. 3045678)

Fuller, B. E. (1998). *Understanding the transition into college: An exploration of the psychosocial and environmental factors that predict successful academic outcome* (Doctoral Dissertation). Retrieved from ProQuest Dissertation and Theses Global database. (UMI No. 9924882)

Gerber, C. (1988, October). Preserving a Quality Environment for Learning. *International Symposium Proceedings*, Columbus, OH. Retrieved from http://www.ericed.gov/contentdelivery/serlet/ERICServlet?accno=ED356523

Harrison, T. C., Maples, M. F., Testa, A. M., & Jones, P. (1993). Academic self concept of university students: implications for counseling. *The Journal of Humanistic Education and Development, 32*(2), 69-75.

Hecker, M. J. (1994). *Assessing the effectiveness of a developmental educational program using GPA attainment, student retention, and student involvement as measurement variables* (Doctoral

Dissertation). Retrieved from ProQuest Dissertation and Theses Global database. (UMI No. 9503712)

John, H., & Grizzell, J. (2014). *Low Grades and Student Health: At the Core of the University Mission (Part II)*. Retrieved from http://scholar.google.com/scholar?q=Low+Grades+and+Student+Health%3A+At+the+Core+of+the+University+Mission+%28Part+II%29&btnG=&hl=en&as_sdt=0%2C6

Layman, R. W. (2005). *Exploring differences in level of involvement, educational outcomes, and satisfaction of resident students and commuter students at a rural community college* (Doctoral Dissertation). Retrieved from ProQuest Dissertation and Theses Global database. (UMI No. 3191233)

Martinson Zunkel, K. A. (2002). *Relationships among learning community participation, student self-efficacy, confidence, outcome expectations, and commitment* (Doctoral Dissertation). Retrieved from ProQuest Dissertation and Theses Global database. (UMI No. 3061881)

May, D. J. (1997). *Improving retention among Native Americans through enhanced understanding of critical academic pathways: Exploring the relationships among GPA, acculturation status, campus climate, age, gender and urbanicity* (Doctoral Dissertation). Retrieved from ProQuest Dissertation and Theses Global database. (UMI No. 9827966)

McGuire, J. J. (1993). *The effect of deferring fraternity and sorority rush upon scholastic achievement, satisfaction, and quality and quantity of involvement among students at a small, private liberal arts university* (Doctoral Dissertation). Retrieved from ProQuest Dissertation and Theses Global database. (UMI No. 9318033)

Nelson, S., & McHugh Engstrom, C. (2013). Fraternity influences on binge drinking and grade point averages. *Journal of Student Affairs Research and Practice, 50*(4), 393-415.

Peglow-Hoch, M. A. (1997). *Counselor intervention with academically low achieving community college students: Does it make a difference?* (Doctoral Dissertation). Retrieved from ProQuest Dissertation and Theses Global database. (UMI No. 9805291)

Reynolds, A. L., & Weigard, M. J. (2010). The relationship among academic attitudes, psychological attitudes, and the first-semester academic achievement of first-year college students. *Journal of Student Affairs Research and Practice, 47*(2), 175-195.

Schimek, G. P. (2016). *Visual expression of liberal education mission* (Doctoral dissertation). Retrieved from http://hdl.handle.net/10217/173345

Shipes, J. F. (2002). *They did not teach: Veterans' experiences in a mid-career transition program at an urban university* (Doctoral Dissertation). Retrieved from ProQuest Dissertation and Theses Global database. (UMI No. 3068665)

Smith, J. S. (2006). Examining the long-term impact of achievement loss during the transition to high school. *Prufrock Journal, 17*(4), 211-221.

Stage, F., Watson, L., & Terrell, M. C. (Eds.). (1999). *Enhancing Student Learning.* Washington, DC: American College Personnel Association.

Strayhorn, T. L. (2014). What role does grit play in the academic success of black male collegians at predominantly white institutions? *Journal of African American Studies, 18,* 1-10. doi: 10.1007/s12111-012-9243-0

Tinney, T. M. (2012). *Factors influencing successful student outcomes between transfer and native populations in a postsecondary environment* (Doctoral Dissertation). Retrieved from ProQuest Dissertation and Theses Global database. (UMI No. 3546044)

Upcraft, M. L. (1999). Assessing student learning. In F. Stage, L. Watson, & M. C. Terrell (Eds.), *Enhancing student learning: setting the campus context* (pp. 123-138). Lanham, MD: University Press of America, Inc.

Walts, R. A. (1998). *Nonacademic institutional variables related to degree completion of nontraditional-age undergraduate students* (Doctoral Dissertation). Retrieved from ProQuest Dissertation and Theses Global database. (UMI No. 9841464)

Williams, R. A. M. (1996). *Assessing students' gains from the college experience at East Tennessee State University* (Doctoral Dissertation). Retrieved from ProQuest Dissertation and Theses Global database. (UMI No. 9623479)

Wilson, B. D. (2006). *Contextual student differences and scoring patterns of the Motivated Strategies for Learning Questionnaire (MSQL)* (Doctoral Dissertation). Retrieved from ProQuest Dissertation and Theses Global database. (UMI No. 3221791)

Academic Programs
Applications: Academic Advising and Campus Ecology

Beatty, J. (1991). The national academic advising association: a brief narrative history. *NACADA Journal, 11*(1), 5-25.

Conrady, L. L. (2008). *A phenomenological case study of mentoring outcomes: Benefiting the mentor in student development, self-esteem, and identity formation* (Doctoral Dissertation).

Retrieved from ProQuest Dissertation and Theses Global database. (UMI No.3324703)

Creamer, D. G., & Creamer, E. G. (1994). Practicing developmental advising: Theoretical contexts and functional applications. *NACADA Journal, 14*(2), 17-24.

Cuyjet, M. J. (1996). Program Development and Group advising. In S. Komives & D. B. Woodward (Eds.), *Student services: A handbook for the profession* (pp. 397-414). San Francisco, CA: Jossey-Bass.

DiNoto, D. M. (1991). *A study of variations in undergraduate academic advising processes by academic discipline and organizational structure of departments* (Doctoral Dissertation). Retrieved from ProQuest Dissertation and Theses Global database. (UMI No. 9208150)

Gordon, V. N. (1992). Annotated Bibliography of Recent Research Related to Academic Advising. *NACADA Journal, 12*(2), 87-92.

Hartsell, J. L. (1999). *The relationship between academic advising preferences, career decidedness and certain demographic characteristics of community college students* (Doctoral Dissertation). Retrieved from ProQuest Dissertation and Theses Global database. (UMI No. 9960178)

Heiss, J. K. (2006). *Moving into students' spaces: The impact of location of academic advising on student engagement among undecided students* (Doctoral Dissertation). Retrieved from ProQuest Dissertation and Theses Global database. (UMI No. 3222783)

Johnson-Dedeaux, V. M. (2011). *An investigation of students' satisfaction with academic advising and students' impressions of academic advisors at a rural community college* (Doctoral Dissertation). Retrieved from ProQuest Dissertation and Theses Global database. (UMI No. 3487153)

Lenning, O. T., & Nayman, R. L. (1980). The past, present, and future for learning centers. *New Directions for college Learning Assistance,* (2), 93-99.

Moore, K. E. (2014). *Differences in undergraduate adult student satisfaction with full-time faculty advisors and full-time non-faculty academic advisors* (Doctoral Dissertation). Retrieved from ProQuest Dissertation and Theses Global database. (UMI No. 3624094)

Posa, K. L. (2011). *A Study of Satisfaction and Perceived Learning and Development of Peer Mentors in Higher Education* (Doctoral Dissertation). Retrieved from ProQuest Dissertation and Theses Global database. (UMI No. 3486693)

Raushi, T. M. (1993). Developmental academic advising. *New Directions for Community Colleges,* (82), 5-19.

Royer, C. M. (1997). *Holism in advising: Implications for design* (Doctoral Dissertation). Retrieved from ProQuest Dissertation and Theses Global database. (UMI No. 9734653)

Schultz, R. A. (1989). *Differences between academically successful and unsuccessful students in an intrusive academic advising program* (Doctoral Dissertation). Retrieved from ProQuest Dissertation and Theses Global database. (UMI No. 9019517)

Sloan, D. (1989). Advising adults from the commuter perspective. *NACADA Journal, 9*(2), 67-75.

Swager, S. L. (1997). *Faculty/student interaction in an undergraduate research program: Task and interpersonal elements*

(Doctoral Dissertation). Retrieved from ProQuest Dissertation and Theses Global database. (UMI No. 9722103)

Tennant, A. (2013). *Intrusive advising and its implementation in residence halls* (Unpublished Master's Thesis). Kansas State University, Manhattan, KS.

Thompson, D. W. (2002). *The relationship between mentoring functions and personality temperaments of seminarians called into vocational ministry* (Doctoral Dissertation). Retrieved from ProQuest Dissertation and Theses Global database. (UMI No. 3050701)

Upcraft, M. L. (1995). Insights from theory: Understanding first-year student development. In M. L. Upcraft & G. L. Kramer (Eds.), *First-Year Academic Advising: Patterns in the Present, Pathways to the Future* (Monograph Series No. 18, pp. 15-24). Columbia, SC: National Center for the Freshman Year Experience and Students in Transition.

Applications: Alternative Academic Delivery and Campus Ecology

Axelson, S. L. (2007). *The use and value of student support services: A survey of undergraduate students in online classes* (Doctoral Dissertation). Retrieved from ProQuest Dissertation and Theses Global database. (UMI No. 3259798)

Brady, L. (2003). Distance Education and the First-Year Writing Curriculum. *WPA: Writing Program Administration, 26*(3), 132-148.

Brindley, J. E. (2014). Learner support in online education: Essential and evolving. In O. Zawacki-Richter & T. Anderson (Eds.), *Online distance education: Towards a research agenda* (pp. 287-310). Edmonton, Canada: Athabasca University Press.

Brown, J. T. (2004). *Student service satisfaction: Differences between traditional and distance learning students* (Master's Thesis). Retrieved from ProQuest Dissertation and Theses Global database. (UMI No. 1425242)

Folkestad, J. E., & Banning, J. H. (2010). The ecology model of learning: Evaluating digital media applications (DMAS) using established ecological subsystems of learning. *i-Manager's Journal of Educational Technology, 7*(2), 41-51.

Jackson, K. P. (2000). *Determining student support services for distance learners in American higher education* (Doctoral Dissertation). Retrieved from ProQuest Dissertation and Theses Global database. (UMI No. 9968935)

Kretovics, M. (2003). The role of student affairs in distance education: Cyber-services or virtual communities. *Online Journal of Distance Learning Administration, 6*(3), 1-15. Retrieved from http://www.westga.edu/~distance/ojdla/fall63/kretovics63.html

Kuk, L., & Banning, J. H. (2014). A Higher Education Leadership Distance Ph.D. Program: An Assessment Using Blocher's Ecological Learning Theory. *Creative Education, 5*, 701-712.

Lohsandt, M. C. (2005). *Online or in line: Perceptions of online learners in South Dakota regarding online student services* (Doctoral Dissertation). Retrieved from ProQuest Dissertation and Theses Global database. (UMI No. 3206234)

Rodrigues, D. (1998). *Models of distance education for composition: The role of interactive video conferencing.* Paper presented at the 1989 Computers and Writing Conference, Gainesville, FL.

Walsh North, R. (2003). *Fostering inclusive online learning environments for students with disabilities in higher education* (Master's Thesis). Retrieved from ProQuest Dissertation and Theses Global database. (UMI No. MQ89680)

Wehrle, M. L. (2007). *An assessment of alternative delivery doctoral programs in the Foodservice and Lodging Management and Family and Consumer Sciences Education at Iowa State University* (Doctoral Dissertation). Retrieved from ProQuest Dissertation and Theses Global database. (UMI No. 3274863)

Applications: Academic Departments and Campus Ecology

Archibeque-Engle, S. L. (2015). The intersection of agriculture, Latinas/os, and higher education in the land grant system: A mixed methods study (Doctoral Dissertation). Retrieved from ProQuest Dissertation and Theses Global database. (UMI No. 3746139)

Archibeque-Engle, S. (2015). Visual ethnography assessment of departments of animal sciences at three land grant universities: Who is welcome? *Journal of Critical Thought and Praxis, 4*(1), 1-31.

Brady, L. (2003). Distance Education and the First-Year Writing Curriculum. *WPA: Writing Program Administration, 26*(3), 132-148.

Connor, E. (2006). *An introduction to reference services in academic libraries*. New York: Routledge.

Davis, D. Z. (1979). The effect of person-environment interaction on anxiety, depression, and subjective distress of optometry students (Doctoral Dissertation). Retrieved from

ProQuest Dissertation and Theses Global database. (UMI No. 8112520)

DiNoto, D. M. (1991). *A study of variations in undergraduate academic advising processes by academic discipline and organizational structure of departments* (Doctoral Dissertation). Retrieved from ProQuest Dissertation and Theses Global database. (UMI No. 9208150)

Folkestad, J. E., & Banning, J. H. (2008). Ecology of the computer laboratory. *i-Manager's Journal of Educational Technology, 5*(1), 38-48.

Han, L., Wang, Y., & Luo, L. (2014). Student deep participation in library work: A Chinese academic library's experience. *The Journal of Academic Librarianship.* Retrieved from http://dx.doi.org/10.1016/j.acalib.2014.06005

Hobson-Panico, P., & Hobson-Panico, S. (1985). Can ombudsmen influence organizational effectiveness through the practice of campus ecology? *The Campus Ecologist, 3*(4), 1-2.

Johnson, M. L. (2003). *Differential analysis of student and teacher instructional expectations* (Doctoral Dissertation). Retrieved from ProQuest Dissertation and Theses Global database. (UMI No. 3114682)

Kuh, G., & Schuh, J. H. (1991). The ecology of involving colleges. *The Campus Ecologist, 9*(4), 1-3.

Kuk, L., & Banning, J. H. (2014). A Higher Education Leadership Distance Ph.D. Program: An Assessment Using Blocher's Ecological Learning Theory. *Creative Education, 5,* 701-712.

Larson, L., Stone, J., & Garcia, M. (2016). Starting from square one: Library communications from the ground up. *OLA Quarterly, 21*(4), 27-35.

Liu, J. (1992). *Investigation of the status of international education in colleges of education at land-grant and state universities* (Doctoral Dissertation). Retrieved from ProQuest Dissertation and Theses Global database. (UMI No. 9311509)

Love, C. T., Banning, J. H., & Kotsiopulos, A. (1998). Visual diversity for a faculty consumer science higher education facility. *Journal of Family and Consumer Sciences, 90*(3), 52-54.

Monty, R. W. (2013). *Theoretical communities of praxis: The university writing center as cultural contact zone* (Doctoral Dissertation). Retrieved from ProQuest Dissertation and Theses Global database. (UMI No. 3565925)

Mouritsen, M. M., & Quick, T, M. (1987). A curricular approach to ethical issues in student leadership development. *NASPA Journal, 25*(1) 63-78.

Oldham, B. E. (2005). *Organizational behavior and faculty motivation in higher education* (Doctoral Dissertation). Retrieved from ProQuest Dissertation and Theses Global database. (UMI No. 3197057)

Peoples, L. (2014). Designing a law library to encourage learning. *Journal of Legal Education, 63*(4), 612-639.

Smith, A. R. (2014). *Making their own way: The experiences of gay male students in STEM fields.* (Unpublished Master's Thesis). University of Nebraska.

Smith, P. R. (1993). *A meeting of cultures: Faculty and part-time doctoral students in an Ed program* (Doctoral Dissertation).

Retrieved from ProQuest Dissertation and Theses Global database. (UMI No. 9420290)

Wade, S. (2010). *True stories: Narrative ecologies in revolutionary fiction and college composition* (Doctoral Dissertation). Retrieved from ProQuest Dissertation and Theses Global database. (UMI No. 3432518)

Wehrle, M. L. (2007). *An assessment of alternative delivery doctoral programs in the Foodservice and Lodging Management and Family and Consumer Sciences Education at Iowa State University* (Doctoral Dissertation). Retrieved from ProQuest Dissertation and Theses Global database. (UMI No. 3274863)

Weinberg, G. R. (2001). *A unified model for teaching first-year writing at the college level* (Doctoral Dissertation). Retrieved from ProQuest Dissertation and Theses Global database. (UMI No. 3002940)

Applications: Academic Classroom Issues and Campus Ecology

Banning, J. H. (1984). The ecology of academic integrity in the classroom. *The Campus Ecologist, 2*(4), 1.

Banning, J. H. (1986). The classroom environment. *The Campus Ecologist, 4*(4), 3.

Banning, J. H. (1992). The connection between learning and the learning environment. In E. Herbert & A. Meek (Eds.), *Children, Learning, & School design* (pp. 19-29). Winnetka, IL: Winnetka Public Schools.

Banning, J. H. (1993). The physical environment of the college classroom: An instructional aid. *The Campus Ecologist, 11*(4), 1-4.

Banning, J. H. (1993). A taxonomy for classroom understanding. *The Campus Ecologist, 11*(3), 3-4.

Banning, J. H. (1993). Learning and the physical environment. *The Campus Ecologist, 11*(4), 3.

Banning, J. H. (1995). Where do I sit? The landscape of informal learning. *The Campus Ecologist, 13*(4), 1-4.

Banning, J. H. (2001). Ecological campus. *NEA Higher Education Advocate, 18*(5), 4-8.

Banning, J. H. (2003). The institution's commitment to diversity: An aid or hindrance to teachers of diversity. In W. M. Timpson, S. Canetto, E. Borrayo, & R. Yang (Eds.), *Teaching Diversity: Challenges and complexities, identities and integrity* (pp. 187-196). Madison, WI: Atwood Publishers.

Blocher, D. H. (1978). Campus learning environments and the ecology of student development. In J. H. Banning (Ed.), *Campus Ecology: A Perspective for student affairs* (pp. 19-26). Cincinnati, OH: National Association of Student Personnel Administrators.

Brown Leonard, B. J. (2007). *Integrative learning as a developmental process: A grounded theory of college students' experiences in Integrative Studies* (Doctoral Dissertation). Retrieved from ProQuest Dissertation and Theses Global database. (UMI No. 3283405)

Chepchieng, M. C., Mbugua, S. N., & Kariuki, M. W. (2006). University students' perception of lecturer-student relationships: A comparative study of public and private universities in Kenya. *Educational Research and Reviews, 1*(3), 80-84.

Deffenbaugh, D. G. (2011). 'Big questions' in the introductory religion classroom: Expanding the integrative approach. *Teaching Theology & Religion, 14*(4), 307-322. doi:10.1111/j.1467-9647.2011.00735.x

Folkestad, J. E., & Banning, J. H. (2010). The ecology model of learning: Evaluating digital media applications (DMAS) using established ecological subsystems of learning. *i-Manager's Journal of Educational Technology, 7*(2), 41-51.

Forden, C. (2006). Conducting research on the campus community in a community psychology course. *The Community Psychologist, 39*(2), 35-36.

Griffin, T. D. (1990). The physical environment of the college classroom and its effects on students. *The Campus Ecologist, 8*(1-3).

Jaffee, D. (2003). Virtual transformation: Web-based technology and pedagogical change. *Teaching Sociology, 31*(2), 227-236.

Johnson, M. L. (2003). *Differential analysis of student and teacher instructional expectations* (Doctoral Dissertation). Retrieved from ProQuest Dissertation and Theses Global database. (UMI No. 3114682)

Jones, C. (2011). *Teaching entrepreneurship to undergraduates.* Cheltenham, UK: Edward Elgar.

Kleberg, J. (1987). Academics and campus architecture linked. *The Campus Ecologist, 5*(1), 3.

Magolda, M. B. B. (1997). Promoting Cocurricular Learning. In E. Whitt (Ed.), *College Student Affairs Administration* (pp. 349-360). Boston, MA: Pearson Custom Printing.

Peterson, M. W. (1986). *The organizational context for teaching and learning. A review of the research literature.* Ann Arbor, MI: University of Michigan.

Reed, T. A. (2001). *Student leaders in the classroom: A study of Virginia Tech student leaders and their accounts of curricular and co-curricular leadership* (Doctoral Dissertation). Retrieved from ProQuest Dissertation and Theses Global database. (UMI No. 3040286)

Ruland, J. P. (1999). *Relationship of classroom environment to growth in critical thinking ability of first year college students* (Doctoral Dissertation). Retrieved from ProQuest Dissertation and Theses Global database. (UMI No. 9940767)

Sommer, R. (1967). Classroom ecology. *The Journal of Applied Behavioral Science, 3*(4), 189-503.

Veltri, S., Banning, J. H., & Davies, T. G. (2006). The community college classroom: Student perceptions. *The College Student Journal, 40*(3), 517-527.

Watson, V. L. (1998). *Relationship between student perceptions of classroom climate and satisfaction in institutions of higher education* (Doctoral Dissertation). Retrieved from ProQuest Dissertation and Theses Global database. (UMI No. 9835921)

Zandvliet, D. B. (2013). Developing Smiles: Evaluating place-based learning. In D. B. Zandvliet (Ed.), *The Ecology of School* (pp. 105-119). Rotterdam, NL: Sense Publishers.

Chapter 5

Student Affairs and Campus Ecology

The campus ecology concepts and applications are most prevalent in the general student affairs literature. Three themes are used to organize this work. One, again similar to the presentation of the students' journey in academic affairs, a student affairs journey is also a way to look at the following topics: engagement/involvement, mattering, student satisfaction, student development, behavioral issues, and activism. A second theme centers on student affairs administration including theory and practice, professional training, and ethical behavior. The third theme address the administrative departments or units typically found in a student affairs division. These include counseling centers, housing, recreational/outdoor programs, campus unions, health programs, learning communities, first-year programs, leadership programs, faith programs, and student activities (honors, athletics, and Greeks).

The Student Affairs Journey
Applications: Engagement/Involvement and Campus Ecology

Alford, S. M. (1998). The impact of inner-city values on student social adjustment in commuter colleges. *NASPA Journal, 35*(3), 225-233.

Boyd, K. D., & Brackmann, S. (2012). Promoting civic engagement to educate institutionally for personal and social responsibility. *New Directions for Student Services 139*, 39-50.

Butcher, J. L. (1997). *Involvement and persistence: Nontraditional student perceptions of the student-college relationship* (Doctoral Dissertation). Retrieved from ProQuest Dissertation and Theses Global database. (UMI No. 9819077)

Froman, R. (2003). *An examination in expectations of student involvement, financial aid, and work at a private, liberal arts college* (Doctoral Dissertation). Retrieved from ProQuest Dissertation and Theses Global database. (UMI No. 3105607)

Hecker, M. J. (1994). *Assessing the effectiveness of a developmental educational program using GPA attainment, student retention, and student involvement as measurement variables* (Doctoral Dissertation). Retrieved from ProQuest Dissertation and Theses Global database. (UMI No. 9503712)

Heiss, J. K. (2006). *Moving into students' spaces: The impact of location of academic advising on student engagement among undecided students* (Doctoral Dissertation). Retrieved from ProQuest Dissertation and Theses Global database. (UMI No. 3222783)

Jamison, A. L. (1993). *Making it on campus: The interplay between student strategies and social structure* (Doctoral Dissertation). Retrieved from ProQuest Dissertation and Theses Global database. (UMI No. 9322688)

Jones-Malone, D. L. (2011). *The Black body as a counterspace: The experiences of African American students at a predominantly White institution* (Doctoral Dissertation). Retrieved from ProQuest Dissertation and Theses Global database. (UMI No. 3453909)

Kuk, L., Banning, J. H., & Thomas, D. (2009). Enhancing student organizations as agents for community development and civic engagement. *Journal of Student Affairs, 18,* 98-107.

Laker, J. A. (2005). *Beyond bad dogs: Toward a pedagogy of engagement of male students* (Doctoral Dissertation). Retrieved from ProQuest Dissertation and Theses Global database. (UMI No. 3162820)

Layman, R. W. (2005). *Exploring differences in level of involvement, educational outcomes, and satisfaction of resident students and commuter students at a rural community college* (Doctoral Dissertation). Retrieved from ProQuest Dissertation and Theses Global database. (UMI No. 3191233)

Long, J. C. (1993). *The relationship between psychosocial development and participation in collegiate activities for selected high-intensity-involvement groups* (Doctoral Dissertation). Retrieved from ProQuest Dissertation and Theses Global database. (UMI No. 9416272)

LoParco, L. B. (1991). *Collaboration between academic and student affairs at the multiversity level for the purpose of student involvement: A case study of Farmville University* (Doctoral

Dissertation). Retrieved from ProQuest Dissertation and Theses Global database. (UMI No. 9121190)

Marr, M. A. (2015). Welcoming environments: Student with disabilities and involvement in college. *Journal of Student Affairs, 25*, 45-51.

Okoli, D. T. (2013). *Sense of place and student engagement among undergraduate students at a major public research university* (Doctoral Dissertation). Retrieved from ProQuest Dissertation and Theses Global database. (UMI No. 3608379)

Price, J. M. (1992). *Community and campus culture: Out-of-class involvement at a midwest liberal arts college* (Doctoral Dissertation). Retrieved from ProQuest Dissertation and Theses Global database. (UMI No. 9335044)

Schuetz, P. (2008). Developing a theory-driven model of community college student engagement. *New Directions for Community Colleges, 144*, 17-28.

Schuetz, P. G. (2007). *Influences of campus environment on adult community college student engagement* (Doctoral Dissertation). Retrieved from ProQuest Dissertation and Theses Global database. (UMI No. 3288232)

Turner, D. J. (2012). *The impact of involvement in Mortar Board Senior Honor Society on lifelong views of civic engagement and leadership* (Doctoral Dissertation). Retrieved from ProQuest Dissertation and Theses Global database. (UMI No. 3526366)

Warmack, D. J. (2011). *Comparison of satisfaction levels of minority and non-minority students in higher education based on levels of student engagement* (Doctoral Dissertation). Retrieved from ProQuest Dissertation and Theses Global database. (UMI No. 3463493)

Whitaker, E. P. (1999). *The linkage of college and university seniors to their institution: A study of factors related to institutional loyalty* (Doctoral Dissertation). Retrieved from ProQuest Dissertation and Theses Global database. (UMI No. 9970087)

Winger, P. E. (1989). *Images of the student: The impact of three approaches to inquiry on the creation of knowledge about student involvement in higher education* (Doctoral Dissertation). Retrieved from ProQuest Dissertation and Theses Global database. (UMI No. 9014516)

Applications: Mattering and Campus Ecology

Decker, A. K. (2011). *Appalachian bridges to the baccalaureate: How community colleges affect transfer success* (Doctoral Dissertation). Retrieved from ProQuest Dissertation and Theses Global database. (UMI No. 3584050)

Fauber, T. L. (1996). *"Mattering" doesn't matter: An analysis of adult undergraduate persistence patterns* (Doctoral Dissertation). Retrieved from ProQuest Dissertation and Theses Global database. (UMI No. 9622278)

Gomez, D. M. (2009). *ACT 101 programs as learning communities: Using the construct of mattering to enhance higher education service delivery* (Doctoral Dissertation). Retrieved from ProQuest Dissertation and Theses Global database. (UMI No. 3338567)

Hillard, M. K. (1996). *An assessment of persistence and mattering among nontraditional, community college students* (Doctoral Dissertation). Retrieved from ProQuest Dissertation and Theses Global database. (UMI No. 9628684)

Kent, S. E. (2004). *Persistence of adult undergraduate students and their perceptions of how they matter to a public institution* (Doctoral Dissertation). Retrieved from ProQuest Dissertation and Theses Global database. (UMI No. 3130530)

Kettle, S. L. C. (2001). *A comparison of undergraduate traditional and nontraditional students' perceptions of mattering on a college campus* (Doctoral Dissertation). Retrieved from ProQuest Dissertation and Theses Global database. (UMI No. 3037959)

Kuhrik, N. S. (1996). *Mattering perceptions of students in midwestern rural and urban nursing programs* (Doctoral Dissertation). Retrieved from ProQuest Dissertation and Theses Global database. (UMI No. 9635020)

McGuire, S. (2012). *Mattering and marginality: Attitudes of Rowan University students* (Unpublished Master's Thesis). Rowan University, Glassboro, NJ.

Phillips, C. M. (2011). *Appalachian bridges to the baccalaureate: Institutional perceptions of community college transfer success* (Doctoral Dissertation). Retrieved from ProQuest Dissertation and Theses Global database. (UMI No. 3584185)

Preston, N. C. (2011). *Appalachian bridges to the baccalaureate: The influence of multiple roles and cultural norms on the baccalaureate persistence of location-bound Appalachian women* (Doctoral Dissertation). Retrieved from ProQuest Dissertation and Theses Global database. (UMI No. 3584189)

Schlossberg, N. K. (1990). *The Mattering Scales for Adult Students in Postsecondary Education*. Retrieved from http://eric.ed.gov/?id=ED341772

Applications: Student Satisfaction and Campus Ecology

Al-nusair, D. M. (2000). *An assessment of college experience and educational gains of Saudi students studying at U.S. colleges and universities* (Doctoral Dissertation). Retrieved from ProQuest Dissertation and Theses Global database. (UMI No. 9955796)

Bell, D. A. (2012). *An exploration of factors that impact the satisfaction and success of low socioeconomic status community college students* (Doctoral Dissertation). Retrieved from ProQuest Dissertation and Theses Global database. (UMI No. 3535408)

Bell, D. A., Hackett, C. D., & Hoffman, J. L. (2016). Student satisfaction and success in a low-income community college environment. *Journal of Applied Research in the Community College, 23*(1), 1-16.

Brown, J. T. (2004). *Student service satisfaction: Differences between traditional and distance learning students* (Master's Thesis). Retrieved from ProQuest Dissertation and Theses Global database. (UMI No. 1425242)

Cook, J. L. (2006). *The interrelationship among job satisfaction/dissatisfaction of student affairs professionals and selected demographic variables* (Doctoral Dissertation). Retrieved from ProQuest Dissertation and Theses Global database. (UMI No. 3218240)

Cox, D. H., & Strange, C. C. (2010). *Achieving student success: Effective student services in Canadian higher education.* Montreal, CA: McGill-Queen's Press-MQUP.

Davis, D. Z. (1979). *The effect of person-environment interaction on anxiety, depression, and subjective distress of optometry students*

(Doctoral Dissertation). Retrieved from ProQuest Dissertation and Theses Global database. (UMI No. 8112520)

Dunham, A. M. (2000). *Traditional-aged commuter student usage of and satisfaction with student services at four-year institutions* (Doctoral Dissertation). Retrieved from ProQuest Dissertation and Theses Global database. (UMI No. 9981500)

Edwards, M. T., & Zimet, C. N. (1976). Problems and concerns among medical students-1975. *Academic Medicine, 51*(8), 619-625.

Englesberg, P. M. (1992). *University student culture in China, 1978-1990: Formal and informal organization* (Doctoral Dissertation). Retrieved from ProQuest Dissertation and Theses Global database. (UMI No. 9305825)

Gilbreath, B., Kim, T., & Nichols, B. (2011). Person-environment fit and its effects on university students: A response surface methodology study. *Research in Higher Education, 52*(1), 47-62. doi:10.1007/s11162-010-9182-3

Gin, H. G. (1995). *The relationship between first-year college student satisfaction and place of residence* (Doctoral Dissertation). Retrieved from ProQuest Dissertation and Theses Global database. (UMI No. 9532667)

Greenlee, K. E. (1992). *An analysis of leadership styles and job satisfaction in student affairs* (Doctoral Dissertation). Retrieved from ProQuest Dissertation and Theses Global database. (UMI No. 9236741)

Hosokawa, E. P. (1990). Adapting employee assistance programs for academic settings. In J. H. Schuster & D. W. Wheeler (Eds.), *Enhancing Faculty Careers* (pp. 123-138). San Francisco, CA: Jossey-Bass.

Jamison, A. L. (1993). *Making it on campus: The interplay between student strategies and social structure* (Doctoral Dissertation). Retrieved from ProQuest Dissertation and Theses Global database. (UMI No. 9322688)

Levine, S. H. (1997). *Querying on quality: Assessing the assessment of student satisfaction* (Doctoral Dissertation). Retrieved from ProQuest Dissertation and Theses Global database. (UMI No. 9809512)

Lin, Y. (2011). University environment experience of the first two years of university graduates at a newly established small university located in suburban area in Taiwan. *College Student Journal, 45*(1), 65-83.

Maples, M. R. (2000). *Rural students' satisfaction with college environment: An ecological consideration* (Doctoral Dissertation). Retrieved from ProQuest Dissertation and Theses Global database. (UMI No. 9996133)

Powless, S. J. (2011). *College student satisfaction: The impact of Facebook and other factors* (Doctoral Dissertation). Retrieved from ProQuest Dissertation and Theses Global database. (UMI No. 3458021)

Watson, V. L. (1998). *Relationship between student perceptions of classroom climate and satisfaction in institutions of higher education* (Doctoral Dissertation). Retrieved from ProQuest Dissertation and Theses Global database. (UMI No. 9835921)

Applications: Student Development and Campus Ecology

Abiddin, N. Z., & Ismail, A. (2012). Exploring student development theory in enhancing learning through supervision.

International Journal of Academic Research in Progressive Education and Development, 1(1), 213-223.

Abrahamowicz, D. (1990). *The concept of balance: A futuristic perspective of student development.* Retrieved from http://files.eric.ed.gov/fulltext/ED317900.pdf

Banning, J. H. (1989). Creating a climate for successful student development: The Campus Ecology manager role. In U. Delworth & G. R. Hanson (Eds.), *Student services: A handbook for the profession* (pp. 304-322). San Francisco: Jossey-Bass.

Banning, J. H. (2002). Student development: In-between buildings. *Journal of Student Affairs, 11*, 21-25.

Banning, J. H., & Cunard, M. R. (1986). Environment supports student development. *ACU-I Bulletin, 54*(1), 8-10.

Banning, J. H., & Cunard, M. R. (1986). The physical environment supports student development. *The Campus Ecologist, 4*(1), 1-3.

Banning, J. H., & Cunard, M. R. (1996). Assessment and design of the physical environment in support of student development. In N. Metz (Ed.), *ACUI Classics: Student Development* (pp. 131-135). Bloomington, IN: Association of College Unions-International.

Blocher, D. H. (1974). Toward an ecology of student development. *Personnel and Guidance Journal, 32*(6), 360-365.

Blocher, D. H. (1978). Campus learning environments and the ecology of student development. In J. H. Banning (Ed.), *Campus Ecology: A Perspective for student affairs* (pp. 19-26). Cincinnati, OH: National Association of Student Personnel Administrators.

Boyle, K. M. (2009). Student development theory as a backdrop for employment. In B. Perrozzi (Ed.), *Enhancing student learning through college employment* (pp. 3-30). Indianapolis, IN: Dog Ear Publishing.

Brown, R. D., & Barr, M. J. (1990). Student development: yesterday, today, and tomorrow. *New Directions for Student Services, 51*, 83-95.

Coomes, M. D., & DeBard, R. (2004). A generational approach to understanding students. *New Directions for Student Services, 106*, 5-16.

Creamer, D. G. (Ed.). (1990). *College Student Development: Theory and Practice for the ACPA Media Publication No. 49.* Alexandria, VA: American College Personnel Association.

Cress, C. M. (1999). *The impact of campus climate on students' cognitive and affective development* (Doctoral Dissertation). Retrieved from ProQuest Dissertation and Theses Global database. (UMI No. 9939058)

Evans, N. J., Forney, D. S., Guido, F. M., Patton, L. D., & Renn, K. A. (2009). Ecological approaches to college student development. *Student development in college: Theory, research, and practice* (pp. 157-175). San Francisco, CA: Jossey-Bass.

Furr, S. R., & Elling, T. W. (2000). The influence of work on college student development. *NASPA Journal, 37*(2), 454-470.

Gertner, D. (1991). Men and student development: Emerging notions from the perspective of campus ecology. *The Campus Ecologist, 9*(1), 1-2.

Gillett-Karam, R. (2016). Moving from student development to student success. *New Directions for Community Colleges, 174*,

9-21. Howard-Hamilton, M., Hinton, K. G., & Hughes, R. L. (2010). Student development theoretical perspectives applied to cultural centers. In L. Patton, *Culture centers in higher education: Perspectives on identity, theory, and practice* (105-118). Sterling, VA: Stylus Publishing.

Jones, S. R., & Stewart, D-E. (2016). Evolution of student development theory. *New Directions for Student Services, 154*, 17-28.

Knefelkamp, L. L., & Stewart, S. (1983). Toward a new conceptualization of commuter students: The developmental perspective. In S. S. Stewart (Ed.), *New directions for student services, no. 24: Enhancing their educational experience* (61-70). San Francisco: Jossey-Bass.

Morrill, W. H., Ivey, A. E., & Oetting, E. R. (1968). The college counseling center: a center for student development. In J. C. Heston & W. B. Frick (Eds.), *Counseling for the Liberal Arts Campus* (pp. 141-157). Yellow Springs, OH: Antioch Press.

Hsieh, P. C. (1990). *The formulation of a student development model for the California community college* (Doctoral Dissertation). Retrieved from ProQuest Dissertation and Theses Global database. (UMI No. 9034046)

Hurst, J. C. (1987). Student development and campus ecology: A rapprochement. *NASPA Journal, 25*(1), 5-17.

Jacobs, B. S. (1985). *The effectiveness of two selected student development programs in four-year public institutions in Arkansas, Louisiana, Oklahoma, and Texas (Personal affairs)* (Doctoral Dissertation). Retrieved from ProQuest Dissertation and Theses Global database. (UMI No. 8528334)

Johnson, C. S. (1993.) Student development in higher education. In G. R. Walz & J. C. Bleuer (Eds.), *Counselor efficacy: Assessing and using counseling outcomes research* (pp. 51-62). Ann Arbor, MI: ERIC Clearinghouse on Counseling and Personnel Services.

Johnson, M. L. (1995). Stages and transitions in cognitive development. *Journal of Thought, 30*(3), 45-69.

Jordan, M. L. (2012). Heterosexual ally identity development: A conceptual model. *Journal of the Indiana University Student Personnel Association*, 67-78.

Kennedy, A. A. (2000). *A qualitative analysis of college student development as expressed through personal living environments: A comparison of freshmen and seniors* (Doctoral Dissertation). Retrieved from ProQuest Dissertation and Theses Global database. (UMI No. 9983077)

King, A. R. (2008). Student perspectives on multiracial identity. *New Directions for Student Services, 123*, 33-41.

Korschoreck, L., Cseri, C., & Miller, D. (1987). The establishment of a responsible living environment to promote student development. *The Campus Ecologist, 5*(3), 2-3.

Kuh, G. D. (1988). *Personal Development and the College Student Experience: A Review of the Literature.* Retrieved from http://files.eric.ed.gov/fulltext/ED304972.pdf

Kuh, G. D. (1991). *The influence of student effort, college environments, and campus culture on undergraduate student learning and personal development.* Paper presented at the Annual Meeting of the Association for the Study of Higher Education, Boston, MA. Retrieved from http://files.eric.ed.gov/fulltext/ED339315.pdf

Larson, V. C., Jr. (2003). *Student perceptions of moral development at three liberal arts institutions* (Doctoral Dissertation). Retrieved from ProQuest Dissertation and Theses Global database. (UMI No. 3090369)

Long, J. C. (1993). *The relationship between psychosocial development and participation in collegiate activities for selected high-intensity-involvement groups* (Doctoral Dissertation). Retrieved from ProQuest Dissertation and Theses Global database. (UMI No. 9416272)

Magolda, M. B. B. (1997). Promoting Cocurricular Learning. In E. J. Whitt (Ed.), *College student affairs administration* (pp. 349-360). Boston, MA: Pearson Publishing.

May, R. J. (1988). The developmental journey of the male college student. *New Directions for Student Services,* (42), 5-18.

McCoy, D. L., & Rodricks, D. J. (2015). Critical race theory in higher education: 20 years of theoretical and research innovations. *ASHE Higher Education Report, 41*(3), 1-117.

Mickle, A. R. (2001). *An analysis of the psychosocial development of college student-athletes* (Doctoral Dissertation). Retrieved from ProQuest Dissertation and Theses Global database. (UMI No. 3000323)

Rastall, P. W. (1998). *A phenomenological exploration of two high ropes course elements* (Doctoral Dissertation). Retrieved from ProQuest Dissertation and Theses Global database. (UMI No. 9835028)

Rideout, C. A., & Richardson, S. A. (1989). A teambuilding model: Appreciating differences using the Myers Briggs type indicator with developmental theory. *Journal of Counseling & Development, 67*(9), 529-533.

Rodgers, R. F. (1990). An integration of campus ecology and student development: The Olentangy project. In D. G. Creamer (Ed.), *College student development* (pp. 155-180). Alexandria, VA: American College Personnel Association.

Sanchez, F. D. (1993). Meeting the needs for at-risk black students: A developmental program. *Colorado State University Journal of Student Affairs, 2,* 67-73.

Schroeder, C. C. (1981). Student development through environmental management. *New Directions for Student Services, 13,* 35-49.

Spooner, S. E. (1988). Ecological development: The mirror and the lamp. *The Campus Ecologist, 6*(2), 2.

Stage, F., Watson, L., & Terrell, M. C. (Eds.). (1999). *Enhancing student learning.* Washington, DC: American College Personnel Association.

Strange, C. C. (1993). Developmental impacts of campus living environments. In R. B. Winston, Jr. & S. Anchors (Eds.), *Student housing and residential life: A handbook for professionals dedicated to student development goals* (pp. 134-166). San Francisco, CA: Jossey-Bass.

Strange, C. C., & King, P. M. (1990). The professional practice of student development. In D. G. Creamer (Ed.), *College student development* (pp. 9-24). Alexandria, VA: American College Personnel Association.

Tankersley, C. J. (2013). *Becoming an orientation leader: A catalyst for self-authorship development* (Doctoral Dissertation). Retrieved from ProQuest Dissertation and Theses Global database. (UMI No. 3671167)

Taylor, S. H. (1994). *Enhancing tolerance: The confluence of moral development with the college experience* (Doctoral Dissertation). Retrieved from ProQuest Dissertation and Theses Global database. (UMI No. 9513491)

Thomas, R. L. (1985). *An ecological implementation strategy for fostering college student development utilizing a synchrony of five psychosocial and cognitive development theories* (Doctoral Dissertation). Retrieved from ProQuest Dissertation and Theses Global database. (UMI No. 8522596)

Upcraft, M. L. (1999). Assessing student learning. In F. Stage, L. Watson, & M. C. Terrell (Eds.), *Enhancing student learning: setting the campus context* (pp. 123-138). Lanham, MD: University Press of America, Inc.

Winkle-Wagner, R. (2012). Self, college experiences, and society. *College Student Affairs Journal, 30*(2), 45-60.

Winslow, R. P. (2006). *Ethos and its influences on religious identity: An undergraduate articulation of campus ethos from denominational perspectives* (Doctoral Dissertation). Retrieved from ProQuest Dissertation and Theses Global database. (UMI No. 3218574)

Applications: Student Behavior and Campus Ecology

Banning, J. H. (1989). The ecology of vandalism. *The Campus Ecologist, 7*(2), 3.

Banning, J. H. (1991). Campus buildings and behavior. *The Campus Ecologist, 9*(1), 3.

Boyd, K. D. (2010). *The nature of the student-institution relationship and behavioral indicators of personal and social responsibility: an exploration of the association between relational quality outcomes, alcohol use, and academic honesty* (Unpublished Doctoral Dissertation). University of Georgia, Athens, GA. Retrieved from https://getd.libs.uga.edu/pdfs/boyd_karen_d_201005_phd.pdf

Dennis, D. M. (1988). *University misconduct cases: An analysis of characteristics of student offenders* (Doctoral Dissertation). Retrieved from ProQuest Dissertation and Theses Global database. (UMI No. 8820706)

Downey, J. P., & Jennings, P. (1993). *Insights and implications of campus hate speech codes.* Paper presented at the Annual Meeting of the National Association of Student Personnel Administrators, Boston, MA.

Griffin, T. D., & Salter, D. W. (1993). Psychological type and involvement in a university residence hall judicial system. *Journal of Psychological Type, 27,* 32-38.

Jacobson, K. A. (2013). *Transforming hierarchical relationships in student conduct administration* (Doctoral Dissertation). Retrieved from ProQuest Dissertation and Theses Global database. (UMI No. 3588562)

Jones, L. B. (2004). *Social norms, environmental management, campus culture and context: A case study of the dynamics shaping high-risk drinking behaviors of college students* (Doctoral Dissertation). Retrieved from ProQuest Dissertation and Theses Global database. (UMI No. 3136426)

Klinedinst, S. S. (2008). *Influences that affect dangerous drinking of alcohol as reported by intercollegiate athletes at a small college in southeastern Pennsylvania* (Doctoral Dissertation). Retrieved from ProQuest Dissertation and Theses Global database. (UMI No. 3312906)

Kuh, G. P. (1991). *Environmental influences on alcohol use by college students.* Retrieved from https://eric.ed.gov/?q=ED331336

Miller, L. A. (2009). *Understanding the epistemological development of substance abusing college students: A construct exploration study* (Doctoral Dissertation). Retrieved from ProQuest Dissertation and Theses Global database. (UMI No. 3385175)

Navas, M. M. (2010). *Do student values at honor code schools change from freshman to senior year?* (Master's Thesis). Retrieved from http://libres.uncg.edu/ir/asu/f/Navas,%20Michelle_2010_Thesis.pdf

Nelson, S., & McHugh Engstrom, C. (2013). Fraternity influences on binge drinking and grade point averages. *Journal of Student Affairs Research and Practice, 50*(4), 393-415.

Prince, P. E. (1998). *Binge drinking among college students* (Doctoral Dissertation). Retrieved from ProQuest Dissertation and Theses Global database. (UMI No. 9919188)

Ray-Tomasek, J. (2004). *Credibility perceptions and intention to conform to a campus media campaign designed to reduce alcohol misuse* (Doctoral Dissertation). Retrieved from ProQuest Dissertation and Theses Global database. (UMI No. 3158491)

Rickert, P. R. (2012). *Examining crime among college-aged Christians: Are Christian religious beliefs associated with low levels of criminal activity?* (Doctoral Dissertation). Retrieved from ProQuest Dissertation and Theses Global database. (UMI No. 3548569)

Stein, J. L. (2004). *Predictors of male college students willingness to prevent rape moderated by a rape prevention peer education program* (Doctoral Dissertation). Retrieved from ProQuest Dissertation and Theses Global database. (UMI No. 3134069)

Von Holle, T. R. (1986). Environmental study of alcohol use in fraternity houses. *The Campus Ecologist, 4*(3), 1-2.

Wonnett, R. (2010). *A place apart: The judicial interpretation of campus place as a public forum* (Doctoral Dissertation). Retrieved from ProQuest Dissertation and Theses Global database. (UMI No. 3441285)

Applications: Activism and Campus Ecology

Adesina, O. O. (2006). *Crisis in Nigerian higher education: 1980 through 2002* (Doctoral Dissertation). Retrieved from ProQuest Dissertation and Theses Global database. (UMI No. 3206574)

Aluede, O. O., & Imhanlahimi, J. E. (2004). Towards a psychological frame for explicating student unrest in Nigerian Universities. *College Student Journal, 38*(1), 135-142.

Atkinson, S. (2014). *Bridging the Divide: Perceptions of effective responses to student protests as perceived by administrators and student activists* (Doctoral Dissertation). Retrieved from ProQuest Dissertation and Theses Global database. (UMI No. 3685175)

Banning, J. H., & McKinley, D. (1988). Activism and the campus ecology. In K. M. Miser (Ed.), *Student affairs and the campus dissent: Reflection of the past and challenge for the future* (pp. 41-54). Cincinnati, OH: National Association of Student Personnel Administrators.

Biddix, J. P. (2006). *The power of "student protest": A study of electronically enhanced student activism* (Doctoral Dissertation). Retrieved from ProQuest Dissertation and Theses Global database. (UMI No. 3224938)

Broadhurst, C., & Martin, G. L. (2014). Part of the "establishment"? Fostering positive campus climates for student activists. *Journal of College & Character, 15*(2), 75-85.

Guan, L. H. (2013). Student Activism in Malaysia: Crucible, Mirror, Sideshow by Meredith L. Weiss (review). *SOJOURN Journal of Social Issues in Southeast Asia, 28*(2), 361-363.

Hobson-Panico, S. (1989). An application on the transactional view: A unique role for ombudsmen in campus protest. *The Campus Ecologist, 7*(2), 1-2.

Miser, K. M. (Ed.) (1988). *Student affairs and campus dissent: Reflection of the past and challenge for the future. NASPA Monograph Series, Volume 8.* Washington, DC: National Association of Student Personnel Administrators, Inc.

Page, J. D. (2010). *Activism and leadership development: Examining the relationship between college student activism involvement and socially responsible leadership capacity* (Doctoral Dissertation). Retrieved from ProQuest Dissertation and Theses Global database. (UMI No. 3426286)

Rezai, H. (2012). *State, dissidents, and contention: Iran, 1979-2010* (Doctoral Dissertation). Retrieved from ProQuest Dissertation and Theses Global database. (UMI No. 3494562)

Weiss, M. L. (2009). Intellectual containment. *Critical Asian Studies, 41*(4), 499-522. doi:10.1080/14672710903328005

Zhao, D. (1995). *Reform and discontent: The causes of the 1989 Chinese Student Movement* (Doctoral Dissertation). Retrieved from ProQuest Dissertation and Theses Global database. (UMI No. NN05819)

Zhao, D. (1998). Ecologies of social movements: Student mobilization during the 1989 Prodemocracy Movement in Beijing. *American Journal of Sociology, 103*(6), 1493-1529.

Student Affairs Administration

Applications: Student Affairs Theory and Practice and Campus Ecology

Aldridge, D. V. (1997). *Leadership and management behaviors of the Deans of Student Services within the Los Angeles Community College District* (Doctoral Dissertation). Retrieved from ProQuest Dissertation and Theses Global database. (UMI No. 9803457)

Ball, G. A. (2002). *Technology integration in student services, retention, and satisfaction of first time freshmen in the California State University System* (Doctoral Dissertation). Retrieved from ProQuest Dissertation and Theses Global database. (UMI No. 3071358)

Banning, J. H. (1980). The campus ecology manager role. In U. Delworth & G. R. Hanson (Eds.), *Student services: A handbook for the profession* (pp. 209-227). San Francisco, CA: Jossey-Bass.

Banning, J. H. (1987). Environmental change: A seven question process. *The Campus Ecologist, 5*(3), 1-3.

Banning, J. H. (1995). Ecological thinking and behavior in student affairs organizations: Importance of feminist leadership. *Journal of Student Affairs, 4*, 2-7.

Banning, J. H., & Sherman, R. (1988). The politics of change: A different view of working together. *ACUI Bulletin, 56*(6), 4-7, 29.

Chapin, T. J. (1987). An application of campus ecology: The development of a student affairs based paraprofessional program. *The Campus Ecologist, 5*(2), 2-3.

Chavez, A. F. (1998). *Coping with restructuring and fiscal constraint in student affairs: A critical review* (Doctoral Dissertation). Retrieved from ProQuest Dissertation and Theses Global database. (UMI No. (9912082)

Clower, J. S. (1987). *A comparative study of values of student personnel administrators and college students in the United States.* (Doctoral Dissertation). Retrieved from ProQuest Dissertation and Theses Global database. (UMI No. 8711714)

Coffman, J., & Paratore, J. (1987). Operationalizing the ecological perspective: The Southern Illinois University experience. *The Campus Ecologist, 5*(1), 1-2.

Cook, J. L. (2006). *The interrelationship among job satisfaction/ dissatisfaction of student affairs professionals and selected demographic variables* (Doctoral Dissertation). Retrieved from ProQuest Dissertation and Theses Global database. (UMI No. 3218240)

DeVillo, S. (1990). The ecology of campus information systems. *The Campus Ecologist, 8*(3), 1-2.

Harper, S. R. (2011). Strategy and intentionality in practice. In S. Komives & D. B. Woodward (Eds.), *Student services: A handbook for the profession* (pp. 287-302). San Francisco: Jossey-Bass.

Ellis, S. E. (2010). Introduction to strategic planning in student affairs: A model for process and elements of a plan. *New Directions for Student Services, 132*, 5-16.

Farrell, R. J., II. (1996). *Perceptions of student services held by staff at National Collegiate Athletic Association institutions participating in the life skills program* (Doctoral Dissertation). Retrieved from ProQuest Dissertation and Theses Global database. (UMI No. 9709129)

Fawcett, G., Huebner, L., & Banning, J. H. (1978). Campus ecology: Implementing the design process. In J. H. Banning (Ed.), *Campus ecology: A perspective for student affairs* (pp. 35-52). Cincinnati, OH: National Association of Student Personnel Administrators.

Fluker, R. C., Sr. (1995). *Leadership styles of chief student services administrators in Texas community colleges* (Doctoral Dissertation). Retrieved from ProQuest Dissertation and Theses Global database. (UMI No. 9534786)

Garland, P. H., & Grace, T. W. (1993). *New perspectives for student affairs professionals: Evolving realities, responsibilities and roles. ASHE-ERIC Higher Education Report No. 7.* Retrieved from https://eric.ed.gov/?q=New+Perspectives+for+Student+Affairs+Professionals%3a+Evolving+Realities%2c+Responsibilities+and+Roles.+ASHE-ERIC+Higher+Education+Report+No.+7%3a&id=ED370508

Greenlee, K. E. (1992). *An analysis of leadership styles and job satisfaction in student affairs* (Doctoral Dissertation). Retrieved from ProQuest Dissertation and Theses Global database. (UMI No. 9236741)

Halberg, L. J. (1987). *A comparison of sex-role stereotypes, achievement motivation and decision-making styles of college and university women chief student affairs officers and women middle managers* (Doctoral Dissertation). Retrieved from ProQuest Dissertation and Theses Global database. (UMI No. 8729466)

Harpel, R. I. (1978). Evaluating from a management perspective. *New Directions for Student Services, 1*, 19-34.

Hosokawa, E. P. (1990). Adapting employee assistance programs for academic settings. In J. H. Schuster & D. W. Wheeler (Eds.), *Enhancing faculty careers* (pp. 123-138). San Francisco, CA: Jossey-Bass.

Hubiak, W., & Banning, J. H. (1994). The implications of place attachment for campus workplaces. *The Campus Ecologist, 12*(3), 1-4.

Hurst, J. C., & Jacobson, J. K. (1985). Theories underlying students' needs for programs. In M. J. Barr & L. A. Keating (Eds.), *Developing effective student services programs: Systematic approaches for practitioners* (pp. 113-136). San Francisco, CA: Jossey-Bass.

Hurst, J. C., & Ragle, J. D. (1979). Application of the ecosystem perspective to a dean of students' office. *New Directions for Student Services, 8*, 69-84.

Johnson-Majedi, K. (2002). *Optimal integration of technology in student services* (Doctoral Dissertation). Retrieved from ProQuest Dissertation and Theses Global database. (UMI No. 3077735)

Kelly, J. L. (2012). *Factors affecting the promotion of women to senior level administrative positions in student affairs* (Unpublished Master's Thesis) Emporia State University, Emporia, KS. Retrieved from https://esirc.emporia.edu/bitstream/handle/123456789/1696/Kelly%201994.pdf?sequence=1

Kleemann, G. L. (1984*). Student perceptions of effectiveness at three state universities (organizational, strategic management, theory,* *non-traditional students)* (Doctoral Dissertation). Retrieved from ProQuest Dissertation and Theses Global database. (UMI No. 8504267)

Knock, G. W. (1985). Development of Student Services in Higher Education. In M. J. Barr & L. A. Keating (Eds.), *Developing effective student services programs* (pp. 15-42). San Francisco, CA: Jossey-Bass.

Knoll, D. A. (1987). *Formulating student affairs missions and priorities* (Doctoral Dissertation). Retrieved from ProQuest Dissertation and Theses Global database. (UMI No. 8715220)

Krager, L. L. (1987). *The effects of time, administrative level, and problem content on student affairs program evaluation decisions* (Doctoral Dissertation). Retrieved from ProQuest Dissertation and Theses Global database. (UMI No. 8722408)

Kuh, G. D. (1987). *A brief for incorporating Organizational Theory in student affairs preparation and research.* Paper presented at the ASHE Annual Meeting, Baltimore, MD. Retrieved from https://eric.ed.gov/?q=A+Brief+for+Incorporating+Organizational+Theory+in+Student+Affairs+Preparation+and+Research&id=ED292409

Kuk, L., & Banning, J. H. (2016). *Student affairs leadership: Defining the role through an ecological framework.* Sterling, VA: Stylus Publishing.

Kuk, L., Banning, J. H., & Amey, M. J. (2012). *Positioning student affairs for sustainable change: Achieving organizational effectiveness through multiple perspectives*: Sterling, VA: Stylus Publishing.

Kuk, L., Thomas, D., & Banning, J. (2008). Student organizations and their relationship to the institution: A dynamic framework. *Journal of Student Affairs, 17,* 9-20.

Lohsandt, M. C. (2005). *Online or in line: Perceptions of online learners in South Dakota regarding online student services* (Doctoral Dissertation). Retrieved from ProQuest Dissertation and Theses Global database. (UMI No. 3206234)

LoParco, L. B. (1991). *Collaboration between academic and student affairs at the multiversity level for the purpose of student involvement: A case study of Farmville University* (Doctoral Dissertation). Retrieved from ProQuest Dissertation and Theses Global database. (UMI No. 9121190)

Manning, K., Kinzie, J., & Schuh, J. H. (2013). *One size does not fit all: Traditional and innovative models of student affairs practice.* New York: Routledge.

Meyer, H. T. (1986). *A national effort to build standards for the student services/development functions: An historical analysis* (Doctoral Dissertation). Retrieved from ProQuest Dissertation and Theses Global database. (UMI No. 8709336)

Neukrug, E. (2011). *The world of the counselor: An introduction to the counseling profession,* Pacific Grove, CA: Brooks/Cole.

Sandeen, A. (2011). Does student affairs have an enduring mission? *Journal of College and Character, 12*(4), 1-8. Retrieved from http://journals.naspa.org/jcc

Skarlis, D. P. (1998). *Student affairs outcomes: An exploratory assessment* (Doctoral Dissertation). Retrieved from ProQuest Dissertation and Theses Global database. (UMI No. 9919337)

Sloan, D. (1990). The ecology of campus information systems. *The Campus Ecologist, 8*(3), 1-2.

Smith, B. L., & Hughey, A. W. (2006). Leadership in higher education–its evolution and potential: a unique role facing critical challenges. *Industry and Higher Education, 20*(3), 157-163.

Thomas, M. (2014). *Outsourcing technology and support in higher education* (Doctoral Dissertation). Retrieved from ProQuest Dissertation and Theses Global database. (UMI No. 3643190)

Tull, A., & Medrano, C. I. (2008). Character values congruence and person-organization fit in student affairs: Compatibility between administrators and institutions that employ them. *Journal of College & Character, 9*(3), 1-16. Retrieved from http://journals.naspa.org/jcc

Upcraft, M. L. (1993). Translating theory into practice. In M. J. Barr (Ed.), *The handbook of student affairs administration* (pp. 260-273). San Francisco, CA: Jossey-Bass.

Wallace, H. *Campus ecology theory and websites: One example of applying traditional student affairs to technology.* Retrieved from http://studentaffairs.com/ejournal/Fall_2000/wallace.htm

Webster, D. (2005). *Designing the ideal off-campus housing website* (Master's Thesis). Retrieved from ProQuest Dissertation and Theses Global database. (UMI No. 1429744)

Whitner, P. A. (1993). *Responsible student affairs practice: Merging student development and quality management.* Paper presented at the Annual Conference of the National Association of Student Personnel Administrators, Boston, MA. Retrieved from https://eric.ed.gov/?q=Responsible+Student+Affairs+Practice%3a+Me

rging+Student+Development+and+Quality+Management.+&id=ED357292

Whitner, P. A., & Abrahamowicz, D. J. (1995). Accountability in a university counseling center through Total Quality Management and qualitative research. *California Association for Counseling and Development Journal, 16,* 37-44. Retrieved from http://files.eric.ed.gov/fulltext/ED400499.pdf

Wilson, D. J. (1998). *Visionary leadership of chief student affairs officers and its impact on partnership initiatives with Academic Affairs and student retention* (Doctoral Dissertation). Retrieved from ProQuest Dissertation and Theses Global database. (UMI No. 9908700)

Applications: Student Affairs Training and Campus Ecology

Baker, D. E. (2004). *A national set of competencies for paraprofessionals in residential college or living/learning programs* (Doctoral Dissertation). Retrieved from ProQuest Dissertation and Theses Global database. (UMI No. 3136156)

Breeden-Lee, D., Kirsch, R., Malutich, K., Norris, D., & Wright, J. (1982). Aggregate perceptions of "Supportiveness" in a student Personnel Preparation Program. *Journal of the Indiana University Student Personnel Association*, (1982 Edition), 5-10.

Bresciani, M. L. (2008). Global competencies in student affairs/services professionals: A literature synthesis. *College Student Journal, 42*(3), 906-919. Retrieved from https://ezproxy2.library.colostate.edu/login?url=http://search.ebscohost.com/login.aspx?direct=true&AuthType=cookie,ip,url,cpid&custid=s4640792&db=aph&AN=34262681&site=ehost-live

Bryan, W. A., & Mullendore, R. H. (1991). Operationalizing CAS standards for program evaluation and planning. *New Directions for Student Services, 53,* 29-44.

Carpenter, D. S., Jr. (1979). *The professional development of student affairs workers: An analysis* (Doctoral Dissertation). Retrieved from ProQuest Dissertation and Theses Global database. (UMI No. 8000985)

Cuyjet, M. J., & Duncan, A. D. (2013). The impact of cultural competence of the moral development of student affairs professional. *Journal of College & Character, 14*(5), 301-309.

Franco, M. A. (2005). *The development of student affairs professionals: A proactive response to change in higher education*

(Master's Thesis). Retrieved from ProQuest Dissertation and Theses Global database. (UMI No. 1429278)

Garland, P. H., & Grace, T. W. (1993). *New perspectives for student affairs professionals: Evolving realities, responsibilities and roles. ASHE-ERIC Higher Education Report No. 7.* Retrieved from https://eric.ed.gov/?q=New+Perspectives+for+Student+Affairs+Professionals%3a+Evolving+Realities%2c+Responsibilities+and+Roles.+ASHE-ERIC+Higher+Education+Report+No.+7%3a&id=ED370508

Gelowitz, A. C. (1979). *A proposal for professional preparation in college student personnel work for western Canada.* Retrieved from http://ir.library.oregonstate.edu/xmlui/handle/1957/9059

Henry, J. (1985). *Professional competencies for entry-level student affairs professionals* (Unpublished Doctoral Dissertation). Texas Tech University, Lubbock, TX. Retrieved from https://repositories.tdl.org/ttu-ir/handle/2346/16566

Hunter, D. E., & Beeler, K. J. (1991). Peering through the "looking glass" at preparation needed for student affairs research. In D. E. Hunter & K. J. Beeler (Eds.), *Puzzles and pieces in Wonderland: The promise and practice of student affairs research* (pp. 106-123). Washington, DC: National Association for Student Affairs Professionals. Retrieved from http://files.eric.ed.gov/fulltext/ED360598.pdf

Jones, S. R., & Abes, E. S. (2011). The nature and uses of theory. In S. Komives & D. B. Woodward (Eds.), *Student services: A handbook for the profession* (pp. 149-167). San Francisco, CA: Jossey-Bass.

Kelso, D. K. (2006). *An empirical investigation of the intercultural sensitivity of student affairs practitioners at a midwest metropolitan university* (Doctoral Dissertation). Retrieved from ProQuest Dissertation and Theses Global database. (UMI No. 3220256)

Lasswell, S. J. (1976). *Student personnel administration: A preparation program for the future* (Master's Thesis). Retrieved from ProQuest Dissertation and Theses Global database. (UMI No. EP30349)

Mastrodicasa, J. M. (2004). *The impact of diversity courses in student affairs graduate programs on multicultural competence of student affairs professionals* (Doctoral Dissertation). Retrieved from ProQuest Dissertation and Theses Global database. (UMI No. 3135202)

Nwenyi, S. E. (2013). *Factors influencing New York doctoral graduate student satisfaction: A quantitative multiple regression analysis* (Doctoral Dissertation). Retrieved from ProQuest Dissertation and Theses Global database. (UMI No. 3571478)

O'Connell, E. C. (1991). *An investigation of the relationship of psychological type to completion of the Doctor of Philosophy degree* (Doctoral Dissertation). Retrieved from ProQuest Dissertation and Theses Global database. (UMI No. 9119834)

Pierre, D. E. (2013). *No place like home: The coming out experiences of gay men in student affairs and higher education administration preparation programs* (Unpublished Master's Thesis). University of Georgia, Athens, GA. Retrieved from https://getd.libs.uga.edu/pdfs/pierre_darren_e_201305_phd.pdf

Pruitt, A. S. (1979). Preparation of student development specialists during the 1980s. *Counselor Education and Supervision, 18*(3), 190-198.

Schneider, J. S. (2014). *Self-perceived competence of new student affairs professionals* (Doctoral Dissertation). Retrieved from ProQuest Dissertation and Theses Global database. (UMI No. 3665868)

Schoper, S. E. (2011). *A narrative analysis of the process of self-authorship for student affairs graduate students* (Doctoral Dissertation). Retrieved from ProQuest Dissertation and Theses Global database. (UMI No. 3479067)

Smith, P. R. (1993). *A meeting of cultures: Faculty and part-time doctoral students in an EdD program* (Doctoral Dissertation). Retrieved from ProQuest Dissertation and Theses Global database. (UMI No. 9420290)

Swanbrow, M. A., & Drum, D. J. (2015). Essential counseling knowledge and skills to prepare student affairs staff to promote emotional wellbeing and to intervene with students in distress. *Journal of College & Character, 16*(4), 201-208.

Timko, G. M. (1999). *Assessing student needs for educational programming in student affairs* (Doctoral Dissertation). Retrieved from ProQuest Dissertation and Theses Global database. (UMI No. 9941446)

Tsai, C., & Shih, Y. (2015). On-the-job professional development programs for middle school and elementary school principals in Taiwan. *International Journal of Science Commerce and Humanities, 3*(5), 55-78.

Young, D. G., & Dean, L. A. (2015). Overall alumni confidence and effect of culminating experiences on learning in student affairs preparation programs: CAS professional studies standards. *College Student Affairs Journal, 33*(1), 66-86.

Young, D. G., & Dean, L. A. (2015). Validation of subject areas of CAS professional studies standards for Masters' level student affairs professional preparation programs. *Journal of College Student Development, 56*(4), 386-391.

Applications: Student Affairs Ethics and Campus Ecology

Banning, J. H. (1986). A template for an issue/context model for doing research and evaluation ethically. *The Campus Ecologist, 4*(2), 3.

Banning, J. H. (1989). Participation: The road to an ethical community. *The Campus Ecologist, 7*(1), 1-2.

Banning, J. H. (2001). Designing campus housing facilities with past, present, and future students. *Reslife.net.* Retrieved from http://www/reslife.net/html/facilities_0101a.html.

Dunn, M. S., & Hart-Steffes, J. S. (2012). Sustainability as moral action. *New Directions for Student Services, 139,* 73-82.

Mouritsen, M. M., & Quick, T, M. (1987). A curricular approach to ethical issues in student leadership development. *NASPA Journal, 25*(1) 63-78.

Shea, D. B. (1984). Perceptions of ethical standards in the student affairs profession (Doctoral Dissertation). Retrieved from ProQuest Dissertation and Theses Global database. (UMI No. 8415616)

Sundberg, D. C., & Fried, J. (1997). Ethical dialogues on campus. In J. Fried (Ed.), *New Directions for Student Services 77* (pp. 67-79). San Francisco, CA: Jossey-Bass.

Student Affairs Departments and Programs
Applications: Student Affairs Counseling and Campus Ecology

Archer Jr., J., & Cooper, S. (1999). An Initiator-Catalyst Approach to College Counseling Outreach. *Journal of College Counseling, 2*(1), 76-88.

Banning, J. H. (1985). College counseling centers and mental health centers: Relationship by "myth". *The Campus Ecologist, 3*(3), 1-2.

Banning, J. H. (1985). Quotes on ecology. *The Campus Ecologist, 3*(4), 3.

Banning, J. H. (1986). Quotes: Counseling psychologist as travel agent. *The Campus Ecologist, 4*(3), 2.

Banning, J. H. (1989). Ecotherapy: A life space application of the ecological perspective. *The Campus Ecologist, 7*(3), 1-3.

Beidert, J. W. (1993). *Defining "intelligent" student behavior at the college level* (Master's Thesis). Retrieved from ProQuest Dissertation and Theses Global database. (UMI No. EP17911)

Brown, R. D. (1987). Evaluating counseling centers. *New Directions for Institutional Research,* (56), 59-70.

Cimini, M. D., & Rivero, E. M. (2013). Postsuicide intervention as a prevention tool: Campus response to suicide and related risk. *New Directions for Student Services, 141,* 83-96.

Conyne, R. K. (2009). *Prevention program development and evaluation: An incidence reduction, culturally relevant approach.* Thousand Oaks, CA: Sage.

Creamer, D. G. (1983). Preparing and nurturing professional counselors. *New Directions for Community Colleges, 1983*(43), 85-97.

Crego, C. A. (1990). Consulting careers in college counseling. In B. Collison & N. J. Garfield (Eds.), *Careers in counseling and human development* (pp. 49-59). Alexandria, VA: American Counseling Association.

Crego, C. A. (1996). Consultation and mediation. In S. Komives & D. B. Woodward (Eds.), *Student services: A handbook for the profession* (pp. 361-379). San Francisco, CA: Jossey-Bass.

Davis, B. A. (1988). *Personality characteristics and counseling effectiveness of Black and White community college probationary students* (Doctoral Dissertation). Retrieved from ProQuest Dissertation and Theses Global database. (UMI No. 8818613)

Davis, D. Z. (1979). The effect of person-environment interaction on anxiety, depression, and subjective distress of optometry students (Doctoral Dissertation). Retrieved from ProQuest Dissertation and Theses Global database. (UMI No. 8112520)

Dey, F., & Cruzvergara, C. Y. (2014). Evolution of career services in higher education. *New Directions for Student Services, 148*, 5-18.

Forden, C. (2006). Conducting research on the campus community in a community psychology course. *The Community Psychologist, 39*(2), 35-36.

Getting, E. R. (1968). *The college counseling center: A center for student development.* Paper presented at the Counseling for the liberal arts campus: The Albion symposium.

Harrison, T. C., Maples, M. F., Testa, A. M., & Jones, P. (1993). Academic self concept of university students: Implications for counseling. *The Journal of Humanistic Education and Development, 32*(2), 69-75.

Holahan, C. J. (1977). Consultation in environmental psychology: A case study of a new counseling role. *Journal of Counseling Psychology, 24*(3), 251-254.

Hotelling, K. (1989). A model for addressing the problem of bulimia on college campuses. *Journal of College Student Psychotherapy, 3*(2-4), 241-255.

Huebner, L. A. (1987). The impact of the ecological approach on therapy and diagnosis. *NASPA Journal, 25*(2), 103-109.

Hurst, J. C., & McKinley, D. L. (1988). An ecological diagnostic classification plan. *Journal of Counseling & Development, 66*(5), 228-232.

Ivey, A. E., & Collins, N. M. (2003). Social justice: A long-term challenge for counseling psychology. *The Counseling Psychologist, 31*(3), 290-298.

Klein, S. M. (1990). *A model for a comprehensive career development program for liberal arts seniors* (Doctoral Dissertation). Retrieved from ProQuest Dissertation and Theses Global database. (UMI No. 9102384)

LaPoint, L. A. (2011). Cornell University suicides: A crisis response critique. *Journal of Student Affairs, 21*, 34-39.

Leonard, M. Q. (2002). An outreach framework for retaining nontraditional students at open admissions institutions. *Journal of College Counseling, 5*(1), 60-73.

MacKean, G. (2011, June). *Mental health and well-being in post-secondary education settings.* Paper presented at the CACUSS preconference workshop on mental health, Toronto, OT. http://campusmentalhealth.ca/wp-content/uploads/2014/02/Post_Sec_Final_Report_June6.pdf

Mackie, K. L. (2006). *Keeping faith: The negotiated professionalism of counselors in higher education contexts* (Doctoral Dissertation). Retrieved from ProQuest Dissertation and Theses Global database. (UMI No. 3213203)

Mallinckrodt, B., Gelso, C. J., & Royalty, G. M. (1990). Impact of the research training environment and counseling psychology students' Holland personality type on interest in research. *Professional Psychology: Research and Practice, 21*(1), 26-32.

Massey, C. P. (1982). Student counseling and the supportive environment. In O. Johnson (Ed.), *Retaining students of diverse backgrounds in schools of Nursing* (pp. 128-141). Atlanta, GA: Southern Regional Education Board.

Matson, J. E. (1983). Primary roles for community college counselors. *New Directions for Community Colleges, 1983*(43), 19-28.

May, R. J. (1984). Achieving long-term gains in interpersonal skill training with medical students: Ideas for the second decade. *Professional Psychology: Research and Practice, 15*(1), 9-17

Morrill, W. H. (2000). James C. Hurst: Reflections of a leader in counseling psychology. *The Counseling Psychologist, 28*(3), 311-334.

Morrill, W. H., Ivey, A. E., & Oetting, E. R. (1968). The college counseling center: A center for student development. In J. C.

Heston & W. B. Frick (Eds.), *Counseling for the liberal arts campus* (pp. 141-157). Yellow Springs, OH: Antioch Press.

Neukrug, E. (2011). *The world of the counselor: An introduction to the counseling profession* (2nd ed.). Pacific Grove, CA: Brooks/Cole.

O'Halloran, S., & Spooner, S. (1992). Eating disorders and applied campus ecology. *The Campus Ecologist, 10*(3), 1-2.

Openlander, P. (1983). From the network: Counseling: An ecological vignette. *The Campus Ecologist, 1*(2), 3.

Pace, D., & Stamler, V. L. (1996). Rounding out the cube: Evolution to a global model for counseling centers. *Journal of Counseling & Development, 74*(4), 321-325.

Peglow-Hoch, M. A. (1997). *Counselor intervention with academically low achieving community college students: Does it make a difference?* (Doctoral Dissertation). Retrieved from ProQuest Dissertation and Theses Global database. (UMI No. 9805291)

Rion, C. (2007). *Major changes: Student shifts among liberal arts, S.T.E.M. and occupational majors* (Doctoral Dissertation). Retrieved from ProQuest Dissertation and Theses Global database. (UMI No. 3270276)

Sandusky, C. H. (1995). *Perceptions of career counseling and utilization of career counseling services by older women students at a four-year urban university* (Master's Thesis). Retrieved from ProQuest Dissertation and Theses Global database. (UMI No. 1377457)

Schwitzer, A. M. (2005). Self-development, social support, and student help-seeking: Research summary and implications for college psychotherapists. *Journal of College Student Psychotherapy, 20*(2), 29-52.

Solovitz, B. L. (1985). The effect of person-environment fit on the psychological well-being of psychiatric aids working in a state hospital (coping resources, social support, occupational stress, locus-of-control (Doctoral Dissertation). Retrieved from ProQuest Dissertation and Theses Global database. (UMI No. 8601802)

Spooner, S. (2000). The college counseling environment. In D. C. Davis & K. M. Humphrey (Eds.), *College counseling: Issues and strategies for a new millennium* (pp. 3-14). Alexandria, VA: American Counseling Association.

Stone, G. L., & Archer, J. (1990). College and university counseling centers in the 1990s: Challenges and limits. *The Counseling Psychologist, 18*(4), 539-607.

Taub, D. J., & Servaty Seib, H. L. (2008). Developmental and contextual perspectives on bereaved college students. *New Directions for Student Services,* (121), 15-26.

Thurston, A. S. (1983). The decade ahead for community college counseling. *New Directions for Community Colleges, 43*, 113-120.

Troy, W. G., & Magoon, T. M. (1979). Activity analysis in a university counseling center: Daily time recording or time estimates? *Journal of Counseling Psychology, 26*(1), 58-63.

Werner, K. M. (2001). *Transitioning and adapting to college: A case-study analysis of the experience of university students with psychiatric disabilities* (Doctoral Dissertation). Retrieved from ProQuest Dissertation and Theses Global database. (UMI No. 3007031)

Whitner, P. A., & Abrahamowicz, D. J. (1995). Accountability in a university counseling center through Total Quality Management and qualitative research. *California Association for Counseling and Development Journal, 16*, 37-44.

Yates, S. A. (1987). Organization, services, and staffing of selected university placement and cooperative education offices (Doctoral Dissertation). Retrieved from ProQuest Dissertation and Theses Global database. (UMI No. 8802158)

Zaddach, C. W. (2014). *Beyond retention: Exploring mental health benefits of living learning programs* (Doctoral Dissertation). Retrieved from ProQuest Dissertation and Theses Global database. (UMI No. 3641175)

Zucker, A. L. (1999). *Presenting problems, symptoms, abuse history, and demographic characteristics of students requesting services at a university counseling center* (Doctoral Dissertation). Retrieved from ProQuest Dissertation and Theses Global database. (UMI No. 9941596)

Applications: Student Affairs Housing and Campus Ecology

Bachman, W. C. (1989). *A comparative study of the effectiveness of residence hall student government and selected perceptions and characteristics of resident hall student staff members and student government officers* (Doctoral Dissertation). Retrieved from ProQuest Dissertation and Theses Global database. (UMI No. 9019155)

Banning, J. H. (1989). Three is a crowd, but four is not? *The Campus Ecologist, 7*(4), 3.

Banning, J. H. (1990). Campus ecology: Recent publications of interest. *The Campus Ecologist, 8*(3), 3.

Banning, J. H. (1995). Cocooning: A qualitative analysis of the ecology of college housing trends. *The Campus Ecologist, 13*(2), 1-4.

Banning, J. H. (1997). Point of view: Designing for community: Thinking "outside the box" with porches. *The Journal of College and University Student Housing, 26*(2), 3-6.

Banning, J. H. (2001, June). Designing campus housing facilities with past, present, and future students. *Reslife.net*. Retrieved from http://www/reslife.net/html/facilities_0101a.html.

Banning, J. H. (2001). Developing the environmental program. In Bartley-Taylor (Ed.), *Higher Education housing facilities: Options for construction, renovation, privatization, and financing* (pp. 38-43). Columbus, OH: The National Association of College Auxiliary Services.

Banning, J. H., & Kuk, L. (2011). College housing dissertations: A bounded qualitative meta-study. *Journal of College & University Student Housing, 37*(2), 90-105.

Blimling, G., S. (2015). *Student learning in college residence halls: What works, what doesn't and why.* San Francisco, CA: Jossey-Bass.

Grimes J. C. (1993). Residential alternatives. In R. B. Winston, Jr. & S. Anchors (Eds.), *Student housing and residential life: A handbook for professionals committed to student development* (pp. 248-268). San Francisco, CA: Jossey-Bass.

Campbell, M. H. (1998). *The impact of residential environment on psychological adjustment of college students* (Doctoral

Dissertation). Retrieved from ProQuest Dissertation and Theses Global database. (UMI No. 9837362)

Casey-Powell, D. (Ed.). (1999). *College and university apartment housing.* Columbia, OH: The Association of College and University Housing Officers – International.

Cinnamond, J. H. (1989). *The development of intersubjective trust: Rules and practices* (Doctoral Dissertation). Retrieved from ProQuest Dissertation and Theses Global database. (UMI No. 8913629)

Clemons, S. A., Banning, J. H., & McKelfresh, D. A. (2004). The importance of sense of place and sense of self in residence hall room design. *Journal of Student Affairs, 13*, 8-15.

Conlogue, J. A. (1993). *Resident assistant perceptions of their roles and responsibilities* (Doctoral Dissertation). Retrieved from ProQuest Dissertation and Theses Global database. (UMI No. 9406339)

Dishno, A. S. (2010). *Development and validation of the university student housing application and student matching and placement methodology* (Doctoral Dissertation). Retrieved from ProQuest Dissertation and Theses Global database. (UMI No. 3480320)

Farni, A. C. (1987). *Perceptions of residence hall living environment by resident assistants by Myers-Briggs type indicator* (Doctoral Dissertation). Retrieved from ProQuest Dissertation and Theses Global database. (UMI No. 8716765)

Fisher, J. S. (1981). *The development and use of an environmental assessment and redesign program for residence halls at Central Michigan University* (Doctoral Dissertation). Retrieved from ProQuest Dissertation and Theses Global database. (UMI No. 1316784)

Fleming, W. J. B. (2001). *The effects of campus ecology on incoming freshmen students: Toward a model for a residential learning community* (Doctoral Dissertation). Retrieved from ProQuest Dissertation and Theses Global database. (UMI No. 3023578)

Foubert, J. D., Boss, K., Ginther, A., & Komives, S. R. (2000). Students living in substance free housing: Attitudes toward their residential experience and predictors of their satisfaction. *The Journal of College and University Student Housing, 29*(1), 15-21.

Foubert, J. D., Tepper, R., & Morrison, D. (1998). Predictors of student satisfaction in university residence halls. *The Journal of College and University Student Housing, 27*(1), 41-46.

Grahmn, P. A., Hurtado, S. S., & Gonyea, R. M. (2015). Living on campus: Does it still make a difference? Report retrieved from http://nsse.indiana.edu/pdf/presentations/2016/ACPA_2016_Graham_et_al_paper.pdf

Griffin, T. D., & Salter, D. W. (1993). Psychological type and involvement in a university residence hall judicial system. *Journal of Psychological Type, 27,* 32-38.

Hallenbeck, D. A. (2002). *Relations of leadership and motivational factors and residential setting of college students* (Doctoral Dissertation). Retrieved from ProQuest Dissertation and Theses Global database. (UMI No. 3080524)

Harrison, J. T. (2003). *Residence life and programming as a contributing factor to student success and retention* (Master's Thesis). Retrieved from ProQuest Dissertation and Theses Global database. (UMI No. MQ82413)

Hirsch, S. L. (1999). *Sense of community, leadership development, and social support in college student housing: A comparison* of residence halls and cooperatives (Doctoral Dissertation). Retrieved from ProQuest Dissertation and Theses Global database. (UMI No. 9943325)

Isakson, R. (1988). *Implementing a wellness and ecosystem program in a university housing system: Heritage developmental community.* Paper presented at the American College Personnel Association, Miami, FL. Retrieved from http://files.eric.ed.gov/fulltext/ED296197.pdf

Kennedy, A. A. (2000). *A qualitative analysis of college student development as expressed through personal living environments: A comparison of freshmen and seniors* (Doctoral Dissertation). Retrieved from ProQuest Dissertation and Theses Global database. (UMI No. 9983077)

Korschoreck, L., Cseri, C., & Miller, D. (1987). The establishment of a responsible living environment to promote student development. *The Campus Ecologist, 5*(3), 2-3.

Krafft, L. R. (2014). *The impact of college students' perceptions of residence hall environment on retention risks, as moderated by attachment style* (Doctoral Dissertation). Retrieved from ProQuest Dissertation and Theses Global database. (UMI No. 3643411)

Maleski, S. S. (1988). *The relationship between the effectiveness of resident assistants and the variables of assertiveness, empathy, unconditional positive regard, and congruence* (Doctoral Dissertation). Retrieved from ProQuest Dissertation and Theses Global database. (UMI No. 8824061)

McClinton, L. (2006). *Exploring the difference in housing satisfaction between first-year black and white on-campus residential students* (Doctoral Dissertation). Retrieved from

ProQuest Dissertation and Theses Global database. (UMI No. 3239065)

O'Beirne, B. (1991). The role of residential programs in the recruitment and orientation of new students. In W. Zeller (Ed.), *Residence Life programs and the first-year experience* (pp. 21-28). Columbia, SC: National Resource Center for the Freshman Year Experience.

Owens, J. T. (2010). *The impact of university housing construction type on psychosocial development of first-year students* (Doctoral Dissertation). Retrieved from ProQuest Dissertation and Theses Global database. (UMI No 3439374)

Paape, T. (2012). *The impact of residence halls on the sense of community and belonging of gay and bisexual college men* (Unpublished Master's Thesis). University of Minnesota, Minneapolis, MN. Retrieved from http://s3.amazonaws.com/academia.edu.documents/31093733

Pustorino, A. M. (2014). *Differences in perceptions of student experiences between residential and commuter sub-populations in higher education* (Doctoral Dissertation). Retrieved from ProQuest Dissertation and Theses Global database. (UMI No. 3643668)

Rafuls, S. E., Howard-Hamilton, M., & Jennie, J. (1999). Multicultural models and campus ecology theory: Applications to diversity in apartment communities. In D. Casey-Powell (Ed.), *College and university apartment housing* (pp. 93-118). Columbus, OH: ACUHO-I Publisher

Roecks, A. L. (1973). *A comparative study of the non-cognitive, cognitive and demographic characteristics of undergraduates who resided in double rooms with undergraduates who resided in single* rooms at Gonzaga University (Unpublished Master's Thesis) Gonzaga University, Spokane, WA. Retrieved from http://files.eric.ed.gov/fulltext/ED119087.pdf

Rose, A., York, M. F., & Polley, L. D. (1997). GROUPS 1996: Goals, values, and perceptions in intentional residence life interventions. *Journal of the Indiana University Student Personnel Association*, (1997 Edition) 47-64.

Rowe, L. P. (1998). *"The least thing you hear about in the dorm": Cultural themes for academic activity in a women's residence hall at a public comprehensive university* (Doctoral Dissertation). Retrieved from ProQuest Dissertation and Theses Global database. (UMI No. 9902316)

Schroeder, C. C. (1981). Student development through environmental management. *New Directions for Student Services, 13*, 35-49.

Schroeder, C. C., & Jackson, G. S. (1987). Creating conditions for student development in campus living environments. *NASPA Journal, 25*(1), 45-53.

Schuh, J. H. (1990). Streamlining the ecosystem approach to residence hall environmental assessment. *NASPA Journal, 27*(3), 185-191.

Schuh, J. H., & Triponey, V. L. (1993). Fundamentals of program design. In R. B. Winston, Jr. (Ed.), *Student housing and residential life: A handbook for professionals dedicated to student development goals* (pp. 423-442). San Francisco, CA: Jossey-Bass.

Seplow, S. L. (2001). *Students' perceptions of the impacts of construction and environmental influences on their participation, experience and learning in their residence hall community*

(Doctoral Dissertation). Retrieved from ProQuest Dissertation and Theses Global database. (UMI No. 3024087)

Strange, C. C. (1993). Developmental impacts of campus living environments. In R. B. Winston, Jr. & S. Anchors (Eds.), *Student housing and residential life: A handbook for professionals dedicated to student development goals* (pp. 134-166). San Francisco, CA: Jossey-Bass.

Suhr, D. D., & Isaacson, M. *Using factor analysis to develop Health Enhancement Lifestyle Management (HELM) profiles for Residence Life students at the University of Northern Colorado.* Paper presented at the Wuss-95, Honolulu, HI.

Suitor, D. T. (2013). *Social support, sense of community, and psychological distress among college students: Examining the impact of university housing units* (Doctoral Dissertation). Retrieved from ProQuest Dissertation and Theses Global database. (UMI No. 557140)

Tennant, A. (2013). *Intrusive advising and its implementation in residence halls* (Unpublished Master's Thesis). Kansas State University, Manhattan, KS. Retrieved from http://krex.k-state.edu/dspace/bitstream/handle/2097/15291/AbigailTennant2013.pdf?sequence=1&isAllowed=y

Twale, D. J., & Damron, J. (1991, April). *The quality of residence life at Auburn University.* Paper presented at the Annual Meeting of the American Educational Research Association Chicago, IL. Retrieved from http://files.eric.ed.gov/fulltext/ED330260.pdf

Ware Jr., T. E., & Miller, M. T. (1997). *Literature related to college housing for adult undergraduate students.* Retrieved from http://files.eric.ed.gov/fulltext/ED414799.pdf

Ware Jr., T. E. (1997). *Adult undergraduates and residential life: Services, recruitment, and the chief housing officer* (Doctoral Dissertation). Retrieved from ProQuest Dissertation and Theses Global database. (UMI No. 9735763)

Webster, D. (2005). *Designing the ideal off-campus housing website* (Master's Thesis). Retrieved from ProQuest Dissertation and Theses Global database. (UMI No. 1429744)

Wilson, K., & Banning, J. H. (1993). From home to hall: An ecological transition. *The Campus Ecologist, 11*(2), 1-4.

Applications: Student Affairs Recreation and Campus Ecology

Banning, J. H., & Burfeind, H. S. (1993). Why rope courses work: An ecological perspective. *Journal of Student Affairs, 2*, 27-31.

Murphy, D. M. (1985). *The influence of participation in intramural sports on the development of Chickering's vector of identity* (Doctoral Dissertation). Retrieved from ProQuest Dissertation and Theses Global database. (UMI No. 8605818)

Rastall, P. W. (1998). *A phenomenological exploration of two high ropes course elements* (Doctoral Dissertation). Retrieved from ProQuest Dissertation and Theses Global database. (UMI No. 9835028)

Applications: Student Affairs Unions and Campus Ecology

Banks, W. L., Hammond, D. L., & Hernandez, E. (2014). Serving diverse student populations in college unions. *New Directions for Student Services, 145*, 13-23.

Banning, J. H. (2000). Bricks and mortarboards: How student union buildings learn and teach. *College Services, 23*(6), 16-19.

Banning, J. H., & Cunard, M. R. (1996). An ecological perspective of buildings and behavior. *College Services Administration, 19*(4), 38-41.

Barrett, L. A. (2014). *The college union and a sense of community for students in public higher education: Is there a relationship* (Unpublished Doctoral Dissertation.), St. John Fisher College, Rochester, NY. Retrieved from http://fisherpub.sjfc.edu/cgi/viewcontent.cgi?article=1177&context=education_etd.

Harrell, K. L. (2012). *Green student centers' influence on the campus environment* (Doctoral Dissertation). Retrieved from ProQuest Dissertation and Theses Global database. (UMI No. 3535753)

Janisz, M. A. (2014). *College student unions: A Delphi study regarding purposes, amenities, barriers and future influences* (Doctoral Dissertation). Retrieved from ProQuest Dissertation and Theses Global database. (UMI No. 3670575)

Johnson, A. D. (2000). *Campus ecology and the functions of physical settings: a review of Ball State University's current Student Center* (Unpublished Master's Thesis). Ball State University, Muncie, IN.

Tierno, S. A. (2013). *College union facilities and their perceived influence on institutional retention* (Doctoral Dissertation). Retrieved from ProQuest Dissertation and Theses Global database. (UMI No. 3567824)

Walch, D. (2010). *Physical environments and their influence on student utilization of public spaces in the Texas Tech University Student Union facility* (Unpublished Master's Thesis). Texas Tech University, Lubbock, TX. Retrieved from http://repositories.tdl.org/ttu-ir/handle/2346/ETD-TTU-2010-12-1103

Applications: Student Affairs Learning Communities and Campus Ecology

Akens, C. A. (2001). *Students' recollections of participating in a first year residential learning community experience* (Doctoral Dissertation). Retrieved from ProQuest Dissertation and Theses Global database. (UMI No. 3031602)

Baker, D. E. (2004). *A national set of competencies for paraprofessionals in residential college or living/learning programs* (Doctoral Dissertation). Retrieved from ProQuest Dissertation and Theses Global database. (UMI No. 3136156)

Burright, D. L. V. (2002). *Student voices: The residential business learning community experience* (Doctoral Dissertation). Retrieved from ProQuest Dissertation and Theses Global database. (UMI No. 3061817)

Cress, C. M. (2008). Creating inclusive learning communities: the role of student–faculty relationships in mitigating negative campus climate. *Learning Inquiry, 2*(2), 95-111.

Engstrom, Z. B. (2008). *The impact of learning community involvement and campus climate on student satisfaction and the retention of Latino students at a highly selective private institution* (Doctoral Dissertation). Retrieved from ProQuest Dissertation and Theses Global database. (UMI No. 3311110)

Fleming, W. J. B. (2001). *The effects of campus ecology on incoming freshmen students: Toward a model for a residential learning community* (Doctoral Dissertation). Retrieved from ProQuest Dissertation and Theses Global database. (UMI No. 3023578)

Gomez, D. M. (2009). *ACT 101 programs as learning communities: Using the construct of mattering to enhance higher education service delivery* (Doctoral Dissertation). Retrieved from ProQuest Dissertation and Theses Global database. (UMI No. 3338567)

Jessup-Anger, J. E. (2009). *Inspiring the life of the mind: An examination of the roles of residential college environments and motivational attributes in promoting undergraduate students' inclination to inquire and capacity for lifelong learning* (Doctoral Dissertation). Retrieved from ProQuest Dissertation and Theses Global database. (UMI No. 3381260)

Jones, J. B. (2000). *A study of the effects that multiple living learning programs have on residence hall students at a large research university* (Doctoral Dissertation). Retrieved from ProQuest Dissertation and Theses Global database. (UMI No. 9980621)

Martinson Zunkel, K. A. (2002). *Relationships among learning community participation, student self-efficacy, confidence, outcome expectations, and commitment* (Doctoral Dissertation). Retrieved from ProQuest Dissertation and Theses Global database. (UMI No. 3061881)

Powell, M. J. (2009). *From Ujima to emergence: An historical case study of a community college learning community* (Doctoral Dissertation). Retrieved from ProQuest Dissertation and Theses Global database. (UMI No. 3379603)

Steele, J. R. (2014). *Housing and residential life: Determining the connection between theme communities and student's retention rates* (Unpublished Master's Thesis). California State University-Sacramento, Sacramento, CA. Retrieved from http://scholarworks.calstate.edu/bitstream/

handle/10211.3/122158/Joan%20R%20Steele%20Thesis%20Edited%205-11-14%20FINAL.pdf?sequence=2.

Walker-Guyer, L. A. (1999). *Making connections for students and educators in higher education through a systemic learning community model* (Doctoral Dissertation). Retrieved from ProQuest Dissertation and Theses Global database. (UMI No. 9917989)

Williams, P. (2012). *Design and development of residential learning communities at the University of the Virgin Islands, St. Croix campus* (Doctoral Dissertation). Retrieved from ProQuest Dissertation and Theses Global database. (UMI No. 3523407)

Wood, V. M. (2012). *A case study of learning community curriculum models implemented in business programs in three public community colleges in ohio* (Doctoral Dissertation). Retrieved from ProQuest Dissertation and Theses Global database. (UMI No. 3563274)

Zaddach, C. W. (2014). *Beyond retention: Exploring mental health benefits of living learning programs* (Doctoral Dissertation). Retrieved from ProQuest Dissertation and Theses Global database. (UMI No. 3641175)

Applications: Student Affairs Health and Campus Ecology

Angle, S. P. (1999). *Perceptions of college students diagnosed with panic disorder with agoraphobia: Academic, psychosocial, and environmental views of their college experience* (Doctoral Dissertation). Retrieved from ProQuest Dissertation and Theses Global database. (UMI No. 3000292)

Babb, E. J. (1996). *A qualitative investigation of eating disorder programs on selected college campuses* (Doctoral Dissertation). Retrieved from ProQuest Dissertation and Theses Global database. (UMI No. 9701318)

Babers-Henry, M. M. (2105). *Psychological and physical health predictions of academic achievement for African American college students* (MS). California State University, Long Beach, CA.

Banning, J. H. (1985). College counseling centers and mental health centers: Relationship by "myth". *The Campus Ecologist, 3*(3), 1-2.

Banning, J. H., & Kuk, L. (2005). Campus ecology and college Health. *Spectrum, November,* 9-15.

Barr, S. L. (2000). *The role of the college environment in developing and maintaining eating and weight control attitudes and behaviors* (Doctoral Dissertation). Retrieved from ProQuest Dissertation and Theses Global database. (UMI No. 9971454)

Best, A., Stokols, D., Green, L., Leischow, S., Holmes, B., & Buchholz, K. (2003). An integrative framework for community partnering to translate theory into effective health promotion strategy. *American Journal of Health Promotion, 18*(2), 168-176.

Buchanan, J. K. (2015). *The role of Kentucky state-supported postsecondary education in creating a healthier citizenship* (Doctoral Dissertation). Retrieved from ProQuest Dissertation and Theses Global database. (UMI No. 3731256)

Cimini, M. D., & Rivero, E. M. (2013). Postsuicide intervention as a prevention tool: Campus response to suicide and related risk. *New Directions for Student Services, 141,* 83-96.

Drum, D. J., & Denmark, A. B. (2012). Campus suicide prevention: Bridging paradigms and forging partnerships. *Harvard Review of Psychiatry, 20*(4), 209-221. doi:10.3109/10673229.2012.712841

Garden, R. S. (2009). *Learning about serious illnesses: Implications for instructional communication* (Doctoral Dissertation). Retrieved from ProQuest Dissertation and Theses Global database. (UMI No. 3360084)

Hotelling, K. (1989). A model for addressing the problem of bulimia on college campuses. *Journal of College Student Psychotherapy, 3*(2-4), 241-255.

Isakson, R. (1988). *Implementing a wellness and ecosystem program in a university housing system: Heritage developmental community.* Paper presented at the American College Personnel Association Miami, FL.

Jodoin, E. C., & Robertson, J. (2013). The public health approach to campus suicide prevention. *New Directions for Student Services,* (141), 15-25. doi:10.1002/ss.20037

John, H., & Grizzell, J. (2014). *Low grades and student health: At the core of the university mission (Part II).* Retrieved from http://scholar.google.com/scholar?q=Low+Grades+and+Student+Health%3A+At+the+Core+of+the+University+Mission+%28Part+II%29&btnG=&hl=en&as_sdt=0%2C6

Klinedinst, S. S. (2008). *Influences that affect dangerous drinking of alcohol as reported by intercollegiate athletes at a small college in southeastern Pennsylvania* (Doctoral Dissertation). Retrieved from ProQuest Dissertation and Theses Global database. (UMI No. 3312906)

Kowa, S. R. (1994). *A comparative study of the personality characteristics of adult children of alcoholics compared with the personality characteristics of non-adult children of alcoholics among a college student population* (Doctoral Dissertation). Retrieved from ProQuest Dissertation and Theses Global database. (UMI No. 9507992)

LaPoint, L. A. (2011). Cornell University suicides: A crisis response critique. *Journal of Student Affairs, 21,* 34-39.

Miller, L. A. (2009). *Understanding the epistemological development of substance abusing college students: A construct exploration study* (Doctoral Dissertation). Retrieved from ProQuest Dissertation and Theses Global database. (UMI No. 3385175)

Moore, M., Pfeiffer, B., Ruggiero, K., & Savoca, M. (1995). Women's perceptions of body image, dieting, exercise, and self-concept in an undergraduate residence center. *Journal of the Indiana University Student Personnel Association,* (1995 Edition), 23-36.

Morrison, G. (2006). *Interaction between cultures: The recovery process amongst undergraduates participating in Alcoholics Anonymous and/or Narcotics Anonymous* (Doctoral Dissertation). Retrieved from ProQuest Dissertation and Theses Global database. (UMI No. 3205343)

Moses, K. S. (2012). *The effect of stress on self-reported academic performance measures among Hispanic undergraduate students at Arizona State University* (Doctoral Dissertation). Retrieved from ProQuest Dissertation and Theses Global database. (UMI No. 3505892)

O'Halloran, S., & Spooner, S. (1992). Eating disorders and applied campus ecology. *The Campus Ecologist, 10*(3), 1-2.

Palombi, B. J. (2006). An alcohol treatment program for college students: Community model of inclusion in the university setting. *Professional Psychology: Research and Practice, 37*(6), 622.

Porter, J. E., Camerlengo, R., DePuye, M., & Sommer, M. (1999). *Campus life and the development of postsecondary deaf and hard of hearing students: Principles and practices.* Retrieved from https://eric.ed.gov/?q=Campus+life+and+the+development+of+postsecondary+deaf+and+hard+of+hearing+students%3a+Principles+and+practices+(&id=ED509241)

Prince, P. E. (1998). *Binge drinking among college students* (Doctoral Dissertation). Retrieved from ProQuest Dissertation and Theses Global database. (UMI No. 9919188)

Quirolgico, R. P. R. (2010). *The employment of human dignity and social responsibility: College health promotion comes of age in the time of AIDS* (Doctoral Dissertation). Retrieved from ProQuest Dissertation and Theses Global database. (UMI No. 3416985)

Racher, F. E., Hyndman, K., Anonson, J., Arries, E., & Foster, C. (2014). Taking the right action in the right way: A comparison of frameworks for assessing the health and quality of life of postsecondary student campus community. *Research and Theory for Nursing Practice, 28*(3), 228-251.

Sallis, J. F., & Owen, N. (1996). Ecological models. In K. Clanz, F. M. Lewis, & B. K. Rimer (Eds.), *Health behaviors and health education: Theory, Research, and Practice* (pp. 403-424). San Francisco, CA: Jossey-Bass.

Schwitzer, A. M., Bergholz, K., Dore, T., & Salimi, L. (1998). Eating disorders among college women: Prevention, education, and treatment responses. *Journal of American College Health, 46*(5), 199-207.

Silverman, D. C., Underhile, R., & Keeling, R. (2008). Student health reconsidered: A radical proposal for thinking differently about health-related programs and services for students. *Spectrum, June,* 4-11.

Stein, J. L. (2004). *Predictors of male college students' willingness to prevent rape moderated by a rape prevention peer education program* (Doctoral Dissertation). Retrieved from ProQuest Dissertation and Theses Global database. (UMI No. 3134069)

Suhr, D. D., & Isaacson, M. *Using factor analysis to develop Health Enhancement Lifestyle Management (HELM) profiles for Residence Life students at the University of Northern Colorado.* Paper presented at the Wuss-95, Honolulu, HI.

Sullivan, C. E. (1987). Developmental, ecological theories and wellness approaches: A synthesis for student life programming. *NASPA Journal, 25*(1), 18-27.

Taub, D. J., & Servaty Seib, H. L. (2008). Developmental and contextual perspectives on bereaved college students. *New Directions for Student Services, 121,* 15-26.

Waxman, M. (1986). Ecology of educational institutions: The teaching hospital as a model. *The Campus Ecologist, 4*(1), 2-3.

Werner, K. M. (2001). *Transitioning and adapting to college: A case-study analysis of the experience of university students with psychiatric disabilities* (Doctoral Dissertation). Retrieved from ProQuest Dissertation and Theses Global database. (UMI No. 3007031)

Zimring, C., Joseph, A., Nicoll, G., & Tespas, S. (2005). Influences of building design and site design on physical activity. *American Journal of Preventive Medicine, 28*(2S2), 186-193.

Applications: Student Affairs First Year Programs and Campus Ecology

Akens, C. A. (2001). *Students' recollections of participating in a first year residential learning community experience* (Doctoral Dissertation). Retrieved from ProQuest Dissertation and Theses Global database. (UMI No. 3031602)

Alderman, L. V. (1997). *Student support services and their impact on persistence of first-year students at a rural community college* (Doctoral Dissertation). Retrieved from ProQuest Dissertation and Theses Global database. (UMI No. 9817088)

Attinasi Jr, L. C. (1989). Getting in: Mexican Americans' perceptions of university attendance and the implications for freshman year persistence. *The Journal of Higher Education, 60*(3), 247-277.

Ball, G. A. (2002). *Technology integration in student services, retention, and satisfaction of first time freshmen in the California State University System* (Doctoral Dissertation). Retrieved from ProQuest Dissertation and Theses Global database. (UMI No. 3071358)

Banning, J. H. (1989). Impact of college environments on freshman students. In M. L. Upcraft & J. N. Gardner (Eds.), *The Freshman year experience* (pp. 53-62). San Francisco, CA: Jossey-Bass.

Bennett, M. A., & Benton, S. L. (2001). What are the buildings saying? A study of first-year undergraduate students' attributions about college campus architecture. *NASPA Journal, 38*(2), 159-177.

Bergeron, D. M. (2013). *The relationship of perceived intellectual and social attainment to academic success of first-generation, first-year college students participating in a first generation access program* (Doctoral Dissertation). Retrieved from ProQuest Dissertation and Theses Global database. (UMI No. 3588545)

Boone, C. A. (2003). *Person-environment fit and college freshmen retention: Effects of congruence between the precollegiate and collegiate settings* (Doctoral Dissertation). Retrieved from ProQuest Dissertation and Theses Global database. (UMI No. 3101153)

Bradbury, B. L., & Mather, P. C. (2009). The integration of first-year, first generation college students from Ohio Appalachia. *NASPA Journal, 46*(2), 258-281.

Clark, S. B., & Crawford, S. L. (1992). An analysis of African-American first-year college student attitudes and attrition rates. *Urban education, 27*(1), 59-79.

Conway, M. S. D. (2008). *So this is college: An examination of the academic, social, and personal experiences that influence freshman adjustment* (Doctoral Dissertation). Retrieved from ProQuest Dissertation and Theses Global database. (UMI No. 3318138)

Cowart, C. V. (1990). *The contribution of freshman orientation programs to academic and social integration of sophomore students* (Doctoral Dissertation). Retrieved from ProQuest Dissertation and Theses Global database. (UMI No. 9116728)

DeBard, R., Lake, T., & Binder, R. S. (2006). Greeks and grades: The first-year experience. *NASPA Journal, 43*(1), 56-68.

Dextras, S. (1993). *Freshmen perceptions of academic and social changes during the first year of college* (Doctoral Dissertation). Retrieved from ProQuest Dissertation and Theses Global database. (UMI No. 9407239)

Douglas, K. B. (1997). *Pictures and perceptions: First-year, African American students' impression of a predominantly White university* (Doctoral Dissertation). Retrieved from ProQuest Dissertation and Theses Global database. (UMI No. 9810757)

Douglas, K. B. (1998). Impressions: African American first-year students' perceptions of a predominantly white university. *Journal of Negro Education, 67*(4), 416-431.

Dykes, M. (2011). *Appalachian bridges to the baccalaureate: Mattering perceptions and transfer persistence of low-income, first-generation community college students* (Doctoral Dissertation). Retrieved from ProQuest Dissertation and Theses Global database. (UMI No. 3584058)

Fleming, W. J. B. (2001). *The effects of campus ecology on incoming freshmen students: Toward a model for a residential learning community* (Doctoral Dissertation). Retrieved from ProQuest Dissertation and Theses Global database. (UMI No. 3023578)

Fuller, B. E. (1998). *Understanding the transition into college: An exploration of the psychosocial and environmental factors that predict successful academic outcome* (Doctoral Dissertation). Retrieved from ProQuest Dissertation and Theses Global database. (UMI No. 9924882)

Gansas, K. M. (2016). The college transition for first-year students from rural Oregon communities. *Journal of Student*

Affairs and Practice. Retrieved from: http://dx.doi.org/10.1080/19496591.2016.1157487

Gengler-Dunn, D. (2007). *A narrative inquiry of four female first-year, first-generation student perspectives of the university experience* (Doctoral Dissertation). Retrieved from ProQuest Dissertation and Theses Global database. (UMI No. 3299793)

Gillis, M. E. (1993). *The effects of a continuous orientation course on the academic and social integration of college freshmen* (Doctoral Dissertation). Retrieved from ProQuest Dissertation and Theses Global database. (UMI No. 9329777)

Gin, H. G. (1995). *The relationship between first-year college student satisfaction and place of residence* (Doctoral Dissertation). Retrieved from ProQuest Dissertation and Theses Global database. (UMI No. 9532667)

Harrington, C. E., & Schibik, T. J. (2003). Reflexive photography as an alternative method for the study of the freshman year experience. *NASPA Journal, 41*(1), 23-40.

Hernandez, Y. (2013). *Latino student's perceptions of the university campus climate: Exploratory study of first generation students* (Doctoral Dissertation). Retrieved from ProQuest Dissertation and Theses Global database. (UMI No. 3558345)

Musselman, R. A. (1986). *Value patterns of freshmen entering Temple University, fall 1985: A descriptive study (Pennsylvania)* (Doctoral Dissertation). Retrieved from ProQuest Dissertation and Theses Global database. (UMI No. 8627491)

O'Beirne, B. (1991). The role of residential programs in the recruitment and orientation of new students. In W. Zeller (Ed.), *Residence Life programs and the first-year experience* (pp.

21-28). Columbia, SC: National Resource Center for the Freshman Year Experience.

Ouimet, J. A. (1998). *The freshman experience: Benchmarking student perceptions of quality of life* (Doctoral Dissertation). Retrieved from ProQuest Dissertation and Theses Global database. (UMI No. 9838072)

Owens, J. T. (2010). *The impact of university housing construction type on psychosocial development of first-year students* (Doctoral Dissertation). Retrieved from ProQuest Dissertation and Theses Global database. (UMI No. 3439374)

Rapp, S. P. (1999). *Experiences of first-year students regarding the personal, social, and academic expectations of a private Midwestern university* (Doctoral Dissertation). Retrieved from ProQuest Dissertation and Theses Global database. (UMI No. 9960420)

Reed, R. J. (1993). *The effects of structured-group membership on the new freshmen college experience* (Doctoral Dissertation). Retrieved from ProQuest Dissertation and Theses Global database. (UMI No. 9410284)

Reynolds, A. L., & Weigard, M. J. (2010). The relationship among academic attitudes, psychological attitudes, and the first-semester academic achievement of first-year college students. *Journal of Student Affairs Research and Practice, 47*(2), 175-195.

Ruland, J. P. (1999). *Relationship of classroom environment to growth in critical thinking ability of first year college students* (Doctoral Dissertation). Retrieved from ProQuest Dissertation and Theses Global database. (UMI No. 9940767)

Salahu-Din, H. A. (1987). *An investigation of campus perceptions of first-year, undergraduate students in arts and sciences at a Midwestern, land-grant university: Considerations in strategic planning* (Doctoral Dissertation). Retrieved from ProQuest Dissertation and Theses Global database. (UMI No. 8724699)

Stanley. D. A. (1988). *The relationship between roommate rapport and social skills development of first semester female college freshmen* (Doctoral Dissertation). Retrieved from ProQuest Dissertation and Theses Global database. (UMI No. 8908531)

Upcraft, M. L. (1995). Insights from theory: Understanding first-year student development. In M. L. Upcraft & G. L. Kramer (Eds.), *First-year academic advising: Patterns in the present, pathways to the future.* (Monograph Series No. 18, pp. 15-24). Columbia, SC: National Center for the Freshman Year Experience and Students in Transition.

White, A. (2012). *A study abroad course for first-generation college students* (Unpublished Master's Thesis). Ball State University, Muncie, IN.

Yang, H. W. (2001). *A comparison of academic achievement, continuous full-time enrollment, and persistency rate between first-semester freshman students who participated in one of the two types of freshman orientation programs at Fresno City College* (Doctoral Dissertation). Retrieved from ProQuest Dissertation and Theses Global database. (UMI No. 3022946)

Applications: Student Affairs Student Leadership and Campus Ecology

Ban, A. O. (2001). *Reform of Romanian higher education from 1990: Perceptions, intentions and procedures affecting leadership development* (Doctoral Dissertation). Retrieved from ProQuest Dissertation and Theses Global database. (UMI No. 3003793)

Berman, L. A. (2013). *John Dewey's experiential theories and leadership preparation in higher education* (Doctoral Dissertation). Retrieved from ProQuest Dissertation and Theses Global database. (UMI No. 3611022)

Bradley, M. J. (1994). *The effectiveness of leadership training for traditional-aged college students* (Doctoral Dissertation). Retrieved from ProQuest Dissertation and Theses Global database. (UMI No. 9524815)

Cadenhead, J. K. (2004). *The tripartite self: Gender, identity, and power* (Doctoral Dissertation). Retrieved from ProQuest Dissertation and Theses Global database. (UMI No. 3126153)

Cole, M. L. (1999). *An analysis of teacher and student leadership and gender differentiation within academic divisions at three Virginia and Tennessee liberal arts colleges* (Doctoral Dissertation). Retrieved from ProQuest Dissertation and Theses Global database. (UMI No. 9955484)

Hallenbeck, D. A. (2002). *Relations of leadership and motivational factors and residential setting of college students* (Doctoral Dissertation). Retrieved from ProQuest Dissertation and Theses Global database. (UMI No. 3080524)

Hirsch, S. L. (1999). *Sense of community, leadership development, and social support in college student housing: A comparison of residence halls and cooperatives* (Doctoral Dissertation). Retrieved from ProQuest Dissertation and Theses Global database. (UMI No. 9943325)

Holloway, E. A. (1998). *Candidates' and non-candidates' perceptions of student leadership factors at the University of Southern*

Mississippi (Doctoral Dissertation). Retrieved from ProQuest Dissertation and Theses Global database. (UMI No. 9840826)

Komives, S., & Wagner, W. (2009). *Leadership for a better world: Understanding the social change model of leadership development.* San Francisco, CA: Jossey-Bass.

Komives, S. R. (2005). Spirituality and Leadership. *Journal of College & Character, 6*(5). Retrieved from http://journals.naspa.org/jcc

McComb, T. A. (2007). *"I won't, I might, I am." Undergraduate women and Stages of Change for participation in leadership development activities* (Doctoral Dissertation). Retrieved from ProQuest Dissertation and Theses Global database. (UMI No. NR41017)

Mouritsen, M. M., & Quick, T. M. (1987). A curricular approach to ethical issues in student leadership development. *NASPA Journal, 25*(1) 63-78.

Newman, E. B. L. (2013). *A theory on becoming an entrepreneurial leader: A student's developmental journey to a creation-driven mindset* (Doctoral Dissertation). Retrieved from ProQuest Dissertation and Theses Global database. (UMI No. 3592348)

Quick, T. M. (1988). *A descriptive study of developmental issues among a group of college leadership students in a specific academic environment* (Doctoral Dissertation). Retrieved from ProQuest Dissertation and Theses Global database. (UMI No. 8825186)

Reed, T. A. (2001). *Student leaders in the classroom: A study of Virginia Tech student leaders and their accounts of curricular and co-curricular leadership* (Doctoral Dissertation). Retrieved from ProQuest Dissertation and Theses Global database. (UMI No. 3040286)

Romano, C. R. (1994). *Going against the grain: Women student leaders at coeducational institutions* (Doctoral Dissertation). Retrieved from ProQuest Dissertation and Theses Global database. (UMI No. 9518437)

Salazar, E. (2009). *Leadership development: Perceptions of gay and lesbian student leaders in Jesuit universities* (Doctoral Dissertation). Retrieved from ProQuest Dissertation and Theses Global database. (UMI No. 3383807)

Tankersley, C. J. (2013). *Becoming an orientation leader: A catalyst for self-authorship development* (Doctoral Dissertation). Retrieved from ProQuest Dissertation and Theses Global database. (UMI No. 3671167)

Warren, L. D. (2009). *Ain't I a leader: Exploring the leadership narratives of Black female undergraduate student leaders at a predominantly White institution* (Doctoral Dissertation). Retrieved from ProQuest Dissertation and Theses Global database. (UMI No. 3409803)

Whitt, E. J. (1993). *"I can be anything!" Student leadership in three women's colleges.* Paper presented at the ASHE Annual Meeting, Pittsburg, PA. Retrieved from https://eric.ed.gov/?q=ED365192&id=ED365192

Workman, N. (Ed). (2009). *Change.* San Francisco, CA: Jossey-Bass.

Applications: Student Affairs Faith Programs and Campus Ecology

Apassa, C. O. (1996). *Perceptions of pastors, principals, and teachers of the Catholic identity of the Roman Catholic high schools in Owerri Archecclesiastical Province, Nigeria* (Doctoral

Dissertation). Retrieved from ProQuest Dissertation and Theses Global database. (UMI No. 9639159)

Deffenbaugh, D. G. (2011). 'Big questions' in the introductory religion classroom: Expanding the integrative approach. *Teaching Theology & Religion, 14*(4), 307-322. doi:10.1111/j.1467-9647.2011.00735.x

Forbes, G. D. (1998). *The concept of religious fit and student retention at Christian colleges* (Doctoral Dissertation). Retrieved from ProQuest Dissertation and Theses Global database. (UMI No. 9918363)

Haggray, D. A. (1993). *A description of the faith development of five students attending a church-related college* (Doctoral Dissertation). Retrieved from ProQuest Dissertation and Theses Global database. (UMI No. 9321155)

Haque, M. T., Miller, A., Miller, S., Tai, L. (2003). Sacred by design: Shifting to higher ground through the design of meditation and memorial gardens. *Garden History (Jan.-June), 56*, 68.

Krebs, S. R. (2014). *Voices of interfaith dialogue: A phenomenological analysis* (Doctoral Dissertation). Retrieved from ProQuest Dissertation and Theses Global database. (UMI No. 3635638)

Larson, V. C., Jr. (2003). *Student perceptions of moral development at three liberal arts institutions* (Doctoral Dissertation). Retrieved from ProQuest Dissertation and Theses Global database. (UMI No. 3090369)

Lemley, E. Y. (1990). *Effects of selected extracurricular involvement on persistence in a church-related university* (Doctoral

Dissertation). Retrieved from ProQuest Dissertation and Theses Global database. (UMI No. 9104815)

Lion, B. (2015). *Catholic student experiences and perceptions at a non-Catholic Christian institution* (Doctoral Dissertation). Retrieved from ProQuest Dissertation and Theses Global database. (UMI No. 3726095)

Maher, M. J., & Sever, L. M. (2007). What educators in Catholic schools might expect when addressing gay and lesbian issues: A study of needs and barriers. *Journal of Gay & Lesbian Issues in Education, 4*(3), 79-111.

Patel, E. (2014). What it means to build the bridge: Identity and diversity at ELCA colleges. *Intersections, (40)*6, 1-25. Retrieved from http://digitalcommons.augustana.edu/intersections/vol2014/iss40/6

Patel, E., Meyer, C. (2012). Interfaith leaders as social entrepreneurs. *Journal of College & Character, 13*(4). Retrieved from http://journals.naspa.org/jcc

Patel, E., & Meyer, C. (2011). Introduction to "interfaith cooperation on campus": Interfaith cooperation as an institutional-wide priority. *Journal of College & Character, 12*(2). Retrieved from http://search.proquest.com/docview/1037909638?accountid=10223

Rogers, K. L. (2000). *Student services in bible colleges and universities accredited by the Accrediting Association of Bible Colleges (AABC)* (Doctoral Dissertation). Retrieved from ProQuest Dissertation and Theses Global database. (UMI No. 3064417)

Riggers-Piehl, T. A., & Lehman, K. J. (2016). Modeling the relationship between campus spiritual climate and the sense of belonging for Christian, Muslim, and Jewish students. *Religion and Education*, DOI: 10.1080/15507394.2016.11175843

Talboys, W. M. (1995). *Using financial ratios in the analysis of four private universities in the southwest United States: A case study* (Doctoral Dissertation). Retrieved from ProQuest Dissertation and Theses Global database. (UMI No. 9615638)

Thompson, D. W. (2002). *The relationship between mentoring functions and personality temperaments of seminarians called into vocational ministry* (Doctoral Dissertation). Retrieved from ProQuest Dissertation and Theses Global database. (UMI No. 3050701)

Tuttle, J. K. (2006). *The effects of a commuter collegium on Christian college commuter students' sense of community* (Doctoral Dissertation). Retrieved from ProQuest Dissertation and Theses Global database. (UMI No. 3228566)

Winslow, R. P. (2006). *Ethos and its influences on religious identity: An undergraduate articulation of campus ethos from denominational perspectives* (Doctoral Dissertation). Retrieved from ProQuest Dissertation and Theses Global database. (UMI No. 3218574)

Zingales, J. A. (2001). *Mission statement values and behavioral outcomes at seven Benedictine colleges and universities* (Doctoral Dissertation). Retrieved from ProQuest Dissertation and Theses Global database. (UMI No. 3019330)

Applications: Student Affairs Honors Activities and Campus Ecology

Collins, B., Dolly, D., Leonard, M. B., & Whitaker, J. L. (2016). Bridging the gap: meaningful connections after the Group

Scholar Program. *Journal of the Indiana University student Personnel Association, 2015-16 Edition,* 71-83.

Pindar, L. M. (2014). *The implications of a university brand: Institutional brand alignment and the experience of honors students attending Clemson University* (Doctoral Dissertation). Retrieved from ProQuest Dissertation and Theses Global database. (UMI No. 3636845)

Shushok, F. X., Jr. (2002). *Educating the best and the brightest: Collegiate honors programs and the intellectual, social and psychological development of students* (Doctoral Dissertation). Retrieved from ProQuest Dissertation and Theses Global database. (UMI No. 3070562)

Turner, D. J. (2012). *The impact of involvement in Mortar Board Senior Honor Society on lifelong views of civic engagement and leadership* (Doctoral Dissertation). Retrieved from ProQuest Dissertation and Theses Global database. (UMI No. 3526366)

Applications: Student Affairs Athletics and Campus Ecology

Dowhower, A. L. (2000). *The experiences of female athletes at a women's college and a coed college* (Doctoral Dissertation). Retrieved from ProQuest Dissertation and Theses Global database. (UMI No. 9971539)

Farrell, R. J., II. (1996). *Perceptions of student services held by staff at National Collegiate Athletic Association institutions participating in the life skills program* (Doctoral Dissertation). Retrieved from ProQuest Dissertation and Theses Global database. (UMI No. 9709129)

Fremont, R. H., II. (2002). *College graduation rates and the elite student-athlete* (Doctoral Dissertation). Retrieved from ProQuest Dissertation and Theses Global database. (UMI No. 3045678)

Gabay, D. N. (2013). *Race, gender and interuniversity athletics: Black female student athletes in Canadian higher education* (Doctoral Dissertation). Retrieved from ProQuest Dissertation and Theses Global database. (UMI No. 3665976)

Klinedinst, S. S. (2008). *Influences that affect dangerous drinking of alcohol as reported by intercollegiate athletes at a small college in southeastern Pennsylvania* (Doctoral Dissertation). Retrieved from ProQuest Dissertation and Theses Global database. (UMI No. 3312906)

Leibold, M. B. (2001). *An exploratory study of the influence of culture on the stress and coping processes of collegiate student-athletes: Application of the multicultural stress model* (Doctoral Dissertation). Retrieved from ProQuest Dissertation and Theses Global database. (UMI No. 3006643)

Mickle, A. R. (2001). *An analysis of the psychosocial development of college student-athletes* (Doctoral Dissertation). Retrieved from ProQuest Dissertation and Theses Global database. (UMI No. 3000323)

Thelin, J. R. (2015). From sports page to front page: Intercollegiate athletics and American higher education. In E. Comeaux (Ed.), *Introduction to intercollegiate athletics* (pp. 2-33). Baltimore, MD: Johns Hopkins University Press.

Tontz, P. A. (2008). *A chameleon on the court: Understanding factors that contribute to invisibility/visibility for Division I intercollegiate gay athletes* (Doctoral Dissertation). Retrieved

from ProQuest Dissertation and Theses Global database. (UMI No. 3320587)

Applications: Student Affairs Greeks and Campus Ecology

Allison, D. J. (2016). *We matter, we're relevant and we are Black women in sororities: An exploration of the experience of black sorority members at a predominately White institution* (Master's Thesis). Retrieved from http://digitalcommons.unl/cehseddiss/367

Boyle, J. P. (1992). *Fraternities and sororities: The development and initial assessment of a model for institutional self-study* (Doctoral Dissertation). Retrieved from ProQuest Dissertation and Theses Global database. (UMI No. 9319143)

DeBard, R., Lake, T., & Binder, R. S. (2006). Greeks and grades: The first-year experience. *NASPA Journal, 43*(1), 56-68.

McGuire, J. J. (1993). *The effect of deferring fraternity and sorority rush upon scholastic achievement, satisfaction, and quality and quantity of involvement among students at a small, private liberal arts university* (Doctoral Dissertation). Retrieved from ProQuest Dissertation and Theses Global database. (UMI No. 9318033)

Nelson, S., & McHugh Engstrom, C. (2013). Fraternity influences on binge drinking and grade point averages. *Journal of Student Affairs Research and Practice, 50*(4), 393-415.

Von Holle, T. R. (1986). An analysis of the relationship between the social ecology of university fraternity residences and the use of alcohol (drug, drinking) (Doctoral Dissertation). Retrieved

from ProQuest Dissertation and Theses Global database. (UMI No. 8622267)

Von Holle, T. R. (1986). Environmental study of alcohol use in fraternity houses. *The Campus Ecologist, 4*(3), 1-2.

Zacker, T. Y. (2001). *An exploratory study of the institutional factors relating to the quality of social Greek letter societies* (Doctoral Dissertation). Retrieved from ProQuest Dissertation and Theses Global database. (UMI No. 3037163)

Chapter 6

Diversity Affairs and Campus Ecology

The campus ecology model is built on the premise that campus environments can change to better meet the educational and developmental needs of students. Nowhere is this change more necessary than in addressing the important educational and personal needs of students who represent diversity. Given that the history of higher education has not always been open to all students or designed to meet the needs of all students, the campus ecology model has been a significant contributor to the diversity movement in higher education. Two major themes are addressed. One addresses how campus ecology is noteworthy in the development and implementation of campus diversity policies and programs. The second addresses a number of diversity categories including race/ethnicity/culture, disability, gender/sexual identity, and diversity of particular circumstances (commuter, low-income, non-traditional, first generation, and geography).

Campus Diversity Policies and Programs

Applications: Diversity Policies/Programs and Campus Ecology

Banks, W. L., Hammond, D. L., & Hernandez, E. (2014). Serving diverse student populations in college unions. *New Directions for Student Services, 145*, 13-23.

Banning, J. H. (1985). A pending collision in our college environments "Diversity or decline: Different is not dumb". *The Campus Ecologist, 3*(2), 1-2.

Banning, J. H. (1985). Quotes on ecology. *The Campus Ecologist, 3*(1), 3.

Banning, J. H. (1986). An outline: The ecology of racism and sexism. *The Campus Ecologist, 4*(3), 3.

Banning, J. H. (1987). Racism and sexism: White male perspective. *The Campus Ecologist, 5*(4), 3.

Banning, J. H. (2003). The institution's commitment to diversity: An aid or hindrance to teachers of diversity. In W. M. Timpson, S. Canetto, E. Borrayo, & R. Yang (Eds.), *Teaching Diversity: Challenges and complexities, identities and integrity* (pp. 187-196). Madison, WI: Atwood Publishers.

Banning, J. H., & Bartels, S. (1997). A taxonomy: Campus physical artifacts as communicators of campus multiculturalism. *NASPA Journal, 35*(1), 29-37.

Banning, J. H., & Bass de Martinez, B. M. (1983). Diversity: An ecological perspective. *The Campus Ecologist, 1*(1), 2.

Banning, J. H., Middleton, V., & Deniston, T. L. (2008). Using photographs to assess equity climate: A taxonomy. *Multicultural Perspectives, 10*(1), 41-46. doi:10.1080/15210960701869611

Banning, J. H., & Minter, J. (1983). Are campus environments ready for diversity? *The Campus Ecologist, 1*(1), 3.

Blezien, P. (2004). *The impact of summer international short-term missions experiences on the cross-cultural sensitivity of undergraduate college student participants* (Doctoral Dissertation). Retrieved from ProQuest Dissertation and Theses Global database. (UMI No. 3119089)

Borman, K. M., Halperin, R. H., & Tyson, W. (2010). Introduction: The scarcity of scientists and engineers, a hidden crisis in the United States. In K. M. Borman, R. H. Halperin, & W. Tyson (Eds.), *Becoming an engineer in public universities: Pathways for women and minorities* (pp. 1-20). New York: Palgrave Macmillan.

Chun, E., & Evans, E. (Eds.). (2016). *Rethinking cultural competence in higher education: An ecological framework for student development: ASHE higher education report, volume 42, number 4*. San Francisco, CA: Jossey-Bass.

Collins, B., Dolly, D., Leonard, M. B., & Whitaker, J. L. (2016). Bridging the gap: Meaningful connections after the Group Scholar Program. *Journal of the Indiana University Student Personnel Association, 2015-16 Edition*, 71-83.

Crittenden, M. A. (1992). *The consequences of campus ecology and multicultural personal development* (Unpublished Master's Thesis.). Radford University, Radford, VA.

Fried, J. (1997). Editor's notes. *New Directions for Student Services, 77*, 1-4.

Harper, S. R., Berhanu, J., Davis III, C. H. F., & McGuire, K. M. (2015). Engaging college men of color. In S. J. Quaye & S. R.

Harper (Eds.), *Student engagement in higher education* (pp. 55-74). New York: Routledge.

Hathaway, R. S., III. (1999). *College student definitions of key concepts and thinking in a multicultural education course* (Doctoral Dissertation). Retrieved from ProQuest Dissertation and Theses Global database. (UMI No. 9938385)

Howard-Hamilton, M., Hinton, K. G., & Hughes, R. L. (2010). Student development theoretical perspectives applied to cultural centers. In L. Patton, *Culture centers in higher education: Perspectives on identity, theory, and practice* (105-118). Sterling, VA: Stylus Publishing.

Hoyt, K. L. (1998). *The diversity challenge: Institutional factors that affect minority student retention at Ohio independent colleges* (Doctoral Dissertation). Retrieved from ProQuest Dissertation and Theses Global database. (UMI No. 9829171)

Huesca, R. (1996). Diversity in communication for social change. *Peace Review, 8*(1), 69-73.

Kelso, D. K. (2006). *An empirical investigation of the intercultural sensitivity of student affairs practitioners at a midwest metropolitan university* (Doctoral Dissertation). Retrieved from ProQuest Dissertation and Theses Global database. (UMI No. 3220256)

Kuh, G. (2015). Foreword. In S. J. Quaye & S. R. Harper (Eds.), *Student Engagement in Higher education* (pp. ix-xii). New York: Routledge.

Mastrodicasa, J. M. (2004). *The impact of diversity courses in student affairs graduate programs on multicultural competence of student affairs professionals* (Doctoral Dissertation). Retrieved

from ProQuest Dissertation and Theses Global database. (UMI No. 3135202)

Matejczyk, E., Rubin, E., & Travers, S. (1996). The Diversity Advocate Program: Through the perceptual lens. *Journal of the Indiana University Student Personnel Association* (1996 Edition), 36-48.

McCoy, D. L., & Rodricks, D. J. (2015). Critical race theory in higher education: 20 years of theoretical and research innovations. *ASHE Higher Education Report, 41*(3), 1-117.

McDowell, A. M., & Higbee, J. L. (2014). Responding to the concerns of student cultural groups: Redesigning spaces for cultural centers. *Contemporary Issues in Education Research, 7*(3), 227-236.

Miville, M. L., & Ferguson, A. D. (Eds.). (2014). *Handbook of race-ethnicity and gender in psychology.* New York: Springer.

Morrison, N. J. (2007). *The meaning of place in an urban context for the under-represented minority student experience at NYU* (Doctoral Dissertation). Retrieved from ProQuest Dissertation and Theses Global database. (UMI No. 3255856)

Museus, S. D., & Jayakumar, U. M. (2011). Mapping the intersections of campus culture and equitable outcomes among racially diverse student populations. In S. D. Museus & U. M. Jayakumar (Eds.), *Creating campus cultures: Fostering success among racially diverse student populations* (pp. 1-27). London, UK: Routledge.

Museus, S. D., Ravello, J. N., & Vega, B. E. (2011). The campus racial culture: A critical case counterstory. In S. D. Museus & U. M. Jayakumar (Eds.), *Creating campus cultures: Fostering* success among racially diverse student populations (pp. 28-45). London, UK: Routledge.

Odell, M., & Mock, J. J. (1989). *A crucial agenda: Making colleges and universities work better for minority students.* Boulder, CO: Western Interstate Commission for Higher Education.

Ozaki, C. C., & Renn, K. (2015). Engaging multiracial students. In S. J. Quaye & S. R. Harper (Eds.), *Student engagement in higher education* (pp. 91-104). New York: Routledge.

Paguyo, C. H. (2014). *Enacting diversity and racial projects on college campuses: Tensions and possibilities for transforming pedagogical practices* (Doctoral Dissertation). Retrieved from ProQuest Dissertation and Theses Global database. (UMI No. 3635893)

Patel, E. (2015). What it means to build the bridge: Identity and diversity at ELCA colleges. *Intersections, 40,* 1-25.

Powers, S. M. (1996). *An implementation study of hypermedia-based multicultural training* (Doctoral Dissertation). Retrieved from ProQuest Dissertation and Theses Global database. (UMI No. 9701389)

Rafuls, S. E., Howard-Hamilton, M., & Jennie, J. (1999). Multicultural models and campus ecology theory: Applications to diversity in apartment communities. In D. Casey-Powell (Ed.), *College and university apartment housing* (pp. 93-118). Columbus, OH: ACUHO-I Publisher.

Roque, M. (2013). *Multiracial identity development and the impact of race-oriented student services* (Unpublished Master's Thesis). Kansas State University, Manhattan, KS.

Sanford, M. R. (1990). *The effectiveness of summer orientation programs on retention and subsequent academic performance of minority students: A follow-up study* (Doctoral Dissertation). Retrieved from ProQuest Dissertation and Theses Global database. (UMI 9100501).

Strayhorn, T. L. (2015). *A return on investment analysis for Black graduates of historically Black colleges and universities: Insights from three studies.* Retrieved from https://www2.gse.upenn.edu/cmsi/sites/gse.upenn.edu.cmsi/files/HBCU%20final%20paper.pdf

Tajuba, D. L. (1996). *An appraisal of the multicultural educational environment at an urban community college setting as perceived by students* (Doctoral Dissertation). Retrieved from ProQuest Dissertation and Theses Global database. (UMI No. 9903074)

Taylor, S. H. (1994). *Enhancing tolerance: The confluence of moral development with the college experience* (Doctoral Dissertation). Retrieved from ProQuest Dissertation and Theses Global database. (UMI No. 9513491)

Warmack, D. J. (2011). *Comparison of satisfaction levels of minority and non-minority students in higher education based on levels of student engagement* (Doctoral Dissertation). Retrieved from ProQuest Dissertation and Theses Global database. (UMI No. 3463493)

Diversity Groups

Applications: African Americans and Campus Ecology

Allison, D. J. (2016). *We matter, we're relevant and we are Black women in sororities: An exploration of the experience of Black sorority members at a predominately White institution*

(Master's Thesis). Retrieved from http://digitalcommons.unl/cehseddiss/367

Birk, N. A. (2009). *A day in the life of African American and European American college students: Daily affective experience and perceptions of climate at a predominantly White institution* (Doctoral Dissertation). Retrieved from ProQuest Dissertation and Theses Global database. (UMI No. 3382022)

Blue, L. A. (2004). *"This culture is nurturing and caring": An ethnographic account of a campus climate from the perspective of African-American students* (Doctoral Dissertation). Retrieved from ProQuest Dissertation and Theses Global database. (UMI No. 3107719)

Burnes, T. R. (2006). *Opening the door of a bigger closet: Sexual orientation identity development for lesbian, bisexual, and queer college women of color* (Doctoral Dissertation). Retrieved from ProQuest Dissertation and Theses Global database. (UMI No. 3226253)

Cooper, R., & Davis, J. C. W. (2015). Problematizing the discourse: A quantitative analysis of African American high school students' academic aspirations and motivations to excel. *The Journal of Negro Education, 84*(3) 311-332.

Cox, J. C. (2012). *Building the bridges to opportunity: Understanding the persistence and departure of African Americans who integrated a southern urban university* (Doctoral Dissertation). Retrieved from ProQuest Dissertation and Theses Global database. (UMI No. 3520361)

Danley, L. L. (2003). *Truths about sojourner: African-American women and the professorship. Their struggles and their successes on negotiating promotion and tenure at a predominantly White institution* (Doctoral Dissertation). Retrieved from ProQuest Dissertation and Theses Global database. (UMI No. 3085899)

Davis, B. A. (1988). *Personality characteristics and counseling effectiveness of Black and White community college probationary students* (Doctoral Dissertation). Retrieved from ProQuest Dissertation and Theses Global database. (UMI No. 8818613)

De St. Aubin, T. M. (1982). *Black student mental health: A model for campus needs assessment* (Doctoral Dissertation). Retrieved from ProQuest Dissertation and Theses Global database. (UMI No. 8221927)

Dogan, S. L. (2002). *The relationship between African American student retention at predominantly White institutions and institutional proximity to African American communities* (Doctoral Dissertation). Retrieved from ProQuest Dissertation and Theses Global database. (UMI No. 3076760)

Elfe, L. B. (2011). *African American students' and African American professors' perceptions of campus climate at a predominantly White university in the New England region of the United States* (Doctoral Dissertation). Retrieved from ProQuest Dissertation and Theses Global database. (UMI No. 3492565)

Franklin, J. D. (2008). *Making the subtle the obvious: Underrepresented students on a historically White campus and implications for institutional fit and stress* (Unpublished Master's Thesis). The University of Utah, Salt Lake City. Retrieved from http://content.lib.utah.edu/utils/getfile/collection/etd2/id/1010/filename/373.pdf

Gabay, D. N. (2013). *Race, gender and interuniversity athletics: Black female student athletes in canadian higher education*

(Doctoral Dissertation). Retrieved from ProQuest Dissertation and Theses Global database. (UMI No. 3665976)

Gaines, N. D. (2012). *Exploring the perceptions of study abroad among Black undergraduates at historically Black colleges and universities* (Doctoral Dissertation). Retrieved from ProQuest Dissertation and Theses Global database. (UMI No. 3510805)

Guyton, C. (2011). *Exploring the lived experiences of rural African American millennials at predominantly White institutions* (Doctoral Dissertation). Retrieved from ProQuest Dissertation and Theses Global database. (UMI No. 3491227)

Harper, S. R. (2011). An anti-deficit achievement framework for research on students of color in STEM. In S. R. Harper & C. B. Newman (Eds.), *Students of Color in STEM: New Directions for Institutional Research, Number 148* (pp. 63-74). San Francisco, CA: John Wiley & Sons.

Hayes, R. E. (2013). *Understanding him in STEM: Sharing the stories of African American male scholars in engineering academic programs at a predominantly White university* (Doctoral Dissertation). Retrieved from ProQuest Dissertation and Theses Global database. (UMI No. 3562421)

Hellyer, S. J. (2005). *Diverse perceptions of a midwest university* (Doctoral Dissertation). Retrieved from ProQuest Dissertation and Theses Global database. (UMI No. 3178424)

Hotchkins, B. K. (2013). *The soul of leadership: African American students' experiences in historically Black and predominantly White organizations* (Doctoral Dissertation). Retrieved from ProQuest Dissertation and Theses Global database. (UMI No. 3600312)

Johnson, J. B. (1999). *A comparison of cognitive development between Whites and African Americans based on William Perry's scheme of intellectual and ethical development* (Doctoral Dissertation). Retrieved from ProQuest Dissertation and Theses Global database. (UMI No. 9961423)

Louis, D. A., Rawls, G. J., Jackson-Smith, D., Chambers, G. A., Phillips, L. L., & Louis, S. L. (2016). Listening to our voices: Experiences of Black faculty at predominantly White universities with microgression. *Journal of Black Studies*, DOI 10.1177/0021934716632983

Manthei, Jr., L. P. (2016). Cutting the deficit: An examination of factors contributing to the success of Black males seeking doctoral degrees at a predominately White institution (Doctoral Dissertation). Retrieved from http://etd.lsu.edu/docs/available/etd-05252016-161418/unrestricted/manthei_diss.pdf

Sanchez, F. D. (1993). Meeting the needs for at-risk Black students: A developmental program. *Journal of Student Affairs, 2,* 67-73.

Singer, J. (2002). *"Let us make man": The development of Black male (student)-athletes in a big-time college sport program* (Doctoral Dissertation). Retrieved from ProQuest Dissertation and Theses Global database. (UMI No. 3049116) Retrieved from https://etd.ohiolink.edu/

Thompson, J.-N. (1999). *Exploring diversity among African American students at a predominantly White university* (Doctoral Dissertation). Retrieved from ProQuest Dissertation and Theses Global database. (UMI No. 9932712)

Warren, L. D. (2009). *Ain't I a leader: Exploring the leadership narratives of Black female undergraduate student leaders at a predominantly White institution* (Doctoral Dissertation). Retrieved from ProQuest Dissertation and Theses Global database. (UMI No. 3409803)

Washington, C. M. (1996). *A study of early academic performance, attrition, and retention as related to selected cognitive, noncognitive, and adjustment variables for African-American college students attending a private, open admission, historically Black institution* (Doctoral Dissertation). Retrieved from ProQuest Dissertation and Theses Global database. (UMI No. 9711730)

Williams, P. (2012). *Design and development of residential learning communities at the University of the Virgin Islands, St. Croix campus* (Doctoral Dissertation). Retrieved from ProQuest Dissertation and Theses Global database. (UMI No. 3523407)

Zamani, E. M. (2003). African American student affairs professionals in community college settings: A commentary for the future. *Association of Student Affairs Professionals Journal, 6*(1), 91-104.

Zamani, E. M. (2003) African American women in higher education. *New Directions in Student Services, 104*, 5-18.

Applications: Latinas/os and Campus Ecology

Archibeque-Engle, S. L. (2015). The intersection of agriculture, Latinas/os, and higher education in the land grant system: A mixed methods study (Doctoral Dissertation). Retrieved from ProQuest Dissertation and Theses Global database. (UMI No. 3746139)

Attinasi Jr, L. C. (1989). Getting in: Mexican Americans' perceptions of university attendance and the implications for freshman year persistence. *The Journal of Higher Education, 60*(3), 247-277.

Banning, J. H., & Luna, F. C. (1992). Viewing the campus ecology for messages about Hispanic/Latino culture. *The Campus Ecologist, 10*(4), 1-4.

Castellanos, J. (1998). *Student effort and educational gains: A comparison of Hispanic/Latino/a and white students* (Doctoral Dissertation). Retrieved from ProQuest Dissertation and Theses Global database. (UMI No. 9917415)

Engstrom, Z. B. (2008). *The impact of learning community involvement and campus climate on student satisfaction and the retention of Latino students at a highly selective private institution* (Doctoral Dissertation). Retrieved from ProQuest Dissertation and Theses Global database. (UMI No. 3311110)

Estrada, L. J. (1990). *A comparative assessment of persistence factors impacting Anglo and Hispanic students at a predominantly Anglo institution of higher education* (Doctoral Dissertation). Retrieved from ProQuest Dissertation and Theses Global database. (UMI No. 9115273)

Faulkner, B. M. (2014). *An analysis of Hispanic students' recollections of perceived financial barriers to the completion of a baccalaureate degree* (Doctoral Dissertation). Retrieved from ProQuest Dissertation and Theses Global database. (UMI No. 3623833)

Gallegos, L. E. (2006). *Latinas: Life histories and the factors that influence success* (Doctoral Dissertation). Retrieved from

ProQuest Dissertation and Theses Global database. (UMI No. 3226126)

Hernandez, J. C. (1999). *En sus voces (in their voices): Understanding the retention of Latino/a college students* (Doctoral Dissertation). Retrieved from ProQuest Dissertation and Theses Global database. (UMI No. 9957158)

Hernandez, Y. (2013). *Latino student's perceptions of the university campus climate: Exploratory study of first generation students* (Doctoral Dissertation). Retrieved from ProQuest Dissertation and Theses Global database. (UMI No. 3558345)

James, M. C. (2005). *Promoting a sense of belonging among Latino college students* (Master's Thesis). Retrieved from ProQuest Dissertation and Theses Global database. (UMI No. EP69724)

Lozano, A. (2010). Latina/o culture centers: Providing a sense of belonging and promoting student success. In L. Patton (Ed.), *Culture centers in higher education: Perspectives on identity, theory, and practice* (pp. 3-25). Sterling, VA: Stylus Publishing.

Moses, K. S. (2012). *The effect of stress on self-reported academic performance measures among Hispanic undergraduate students at Arizona State University* (Doctoral Dissertation). Retrieved from ProQuest Dissertation and Theses Global database. (UMI No. 3505892)

Navarrette, K. (2014). *Validation: Latino voices in higher education* (Unpublished Master's Thesis). University of Nebraska, Lincoln, NE. Retrieved from http://digitalcommons.unl.edu/cehsedaddiss/188

Ortiz, D. A. (2006). *"Wrestling with the bear": A qualitative study of Mexican American male student success at a Christian *university* (Doctoral Dissertation). Retrieved from ProQuest Dissertation and Theses Global database. (UMI No. 3232580)

Rogers, N. E. M. (1995). *Mexican-American women in academe: Analysis of career progress and job satisfaction* (Doctoral Dissertation). Retrieved from ProQuest Dissertation and Theses Global database. (UMI No. 9617332)

Shelton, L. J. (2014). *The experiences of undocumented Latin students who demonstrate resilience in navigating higher education* (Doctoral Dissertation). Retrieved from ProQuest Dissertation and Theses Global database. (UMI No. 3634629)

Villanueva, V. A. (2015). *A study of Latino student persistence in emerging adulthood: A Grounded Theory study* (Doctoral Dissertation). Retrieved from ProQuest Dissertation and Theses Global database. (UMI No. 3689250)

Wilburn, B. S. (1999). *An examination of college persistence and Hispanic students' perceptions of academic and social integration at a two-year campus of a doctoral degree-granting university* (Doctoral Dissertation). Retrieved from ProQuest Dissertation and Theses Global database. (UMI No. 9963702)

Applications: Asian Americans and Campus Ecology

Bottrell, C. A. (2007). *Vietnamese-American students at Midwestern Community College: A narrative inquiry study* (Doctoral Dissertation). Retrieved from ProQuest Dissertation and Theses Global database. (UMI No. 3279495)

Do, T. H. (2005). *East meets west: The adaptation of Vietnamese international students to California community colleges* (Doctoral Dissertation). Retrieved from ProQuest Dissertation and Theses Global database. (UMI No. 3192327)

Hur, R. (1992). *Study of an East-West philosophical belief system among college students* (Doctoral Dissertation). Retrieved from ProQuest Dissertation and Theses Global database. (UMI No. 9233654)

Restar, A. C. (2005). *Personal, social and academic factors that impact educational outcomes for Asian-Americans in higher education* (Doctoral Dissertation). Retrieved from ProQuest Dissertation and Theses Global database. (UMI No. 3190610)

Applications: Native Americans and Campus Ecology

Engs, M. S. (1996). *Factors affecting the retention of Native American students at a southwestern community college* (Doctoral Dissertation). Retrieved from ProQuest Dissertation and Theses Global database. (UMI No. 9710193)

May, D. J. (1997). *Improving retention among Native Americans through enhanced understanding of critical academic pathways: Exploring the relationships among GPA, acculturation status, campus climate, age, gender and urbanicity* (Doctoral Dissertation). Retrieved from ProQuest Dissertation and Theses Global database. (UMI No. 9827966)

St. Clair, D. (1994). The Drum: Improving the campus ecology for native students. *The Campus Ecologist, 12*(1), 1-4.

Applications: International Students/Programs and Campus Ecology

Al-nusair, D. M. (2000). *An assessment of college experience and educational gains of Saudi students studying at U.S. colleges and universities* (Doctoral Dissertation). Retrieved from ProQuest Dissertation and Theses Global database. (UMI No. 9955796)

Arturo, O. L. (2015). The educational pathway through social and economic integration of highly educated immigrants: The case of Columbians in the United States of America (Doctoral Dissertation). Retrieved from http://stars.library.ucf.edu/cgi/viewcontent.cgi?article=2352&context=etd

Ban, A. O. (2001). *Reform of Romanian higher education from 1990: Perceptions, intentions and procedures affecting leadership development* (Doctoral Dissertation). Retrieved from ProQuest Dissertation and Theses Global database. (UMI No. 3003793)

Barratt, W. (1988). Ecology: An international experience. *The Campus Ecologist, 6*(2), 3.

Ben-Meir, Y. (2009). *Participatory development and its emergence in the fields of community and international development* (Doctoral Dissertation). Retrieved from ProQuest Dissertation and Theses Global database. (UMI No. 3359812}

Braskamp, L. A. (2009). Internationalization in higher education: Four issues to consider. *Journal of College and Character, 10*(6). Retrieved from http://dx.doi.org/10.2202/1940-1639.1688

Braskamp, L. A. (2010). Internationalizing a campus is world wide. *Journal of College and Character, 11*(2). Retrieved from http://dx.doi.org/10.2202/1940-1639.1258

Bresciani, M. L. (2008). Global competencies in student affairs/services professionals: A literature synthesis. *College Student Journal, 42*(3), 906-919. Retrieved from https://ezproxy2.library.colostate.edu/login?url=http://search.ebscohost.com/login.aspx?direct=true&AuthType=cookie,ip,url,cpid&custid=s4640792&db=aph&AN=34262681&site=ehost-live

Callalhan, K. M. (2015). *The internationalization in student affairs in the United States from 1951 to 1996* (Doctoral Dissertation).

Retrieved from ProQuest Dissertation and Theses Global database. (UMI No. 3724197)

Cuellar, M. M. (1999). *An assessment of student support services and needs at the University College of Belize* (Doctoral Dissertation). Retrieved from ProQuest Dissertation and Theses Global database. (UMI No. 9947949)

Englesberg, P. M. (1992). *University student culture in China, 1978-1990: Formal and informal organization* (Doctoral Dissertation). Retrieved from ProQuest Dissertation and Theses Global database. (UMI No. 9305825)

Fung, M. C. (1984). Ecosystem perspective, related definitions, origin, and theoretical background. *Bulletin of National Taiwan Normal University, 29*, 322-336.

Gaines, N. D. (2012). *Exploring the perceptions of study abroad among Black undergraduates at historically Black colleges and universities* (Doctoral Dissertation). Retrieved from ProQuest Dissertation and Theses Global database. (UMI No. 3510805)

Guan, L. H. (2013). Student Activism in Malaysia: Crucible, Mirror, Sideshow by Meredith L. Weiss (review). *SOJOURN: Journal of Social Issues in Southeast Asia, 28*(2), 361-363.

Jordan, K. A. F. (1981). The adaptation process of third culture dependent youth as they re-enter the United States and enter college: An exploratory study (Doctoral Dissertation). Retrieved from ProQuest Dissertation and Theses Global database. (UMI No. 8202458)

Lin, Y. (2011). University environment experience of the first two years of university graduates at a newly established small university located in suburban area in Taiwan. *College Student Journal, 45*(1), 65-83. Retrieved from https://ezproxy2.library.

colostate.edu/login?url=http://search.ebscohost.com/login.aspx?direct=true&AuthType=cookie,ip,url,cpid&custid=s4640792&db=aph&AN=59618807&site=ehost-live

Liu, J. (1992). *Investigation of the status of international education in colleges of education at land-grant and state universities* (Doctoral Dissertation). Retrieved from ProQuest Dissertation and Theses Global database. (UMI No. 9311509)

Neider, X. N. (2011). "When you come here, it is still like it is their space: Exploring the experiences of students of Middle Eastern heritages in post-9/11 US higher education. *Journal of International Education and Leadership, 1*(1), 1-19.

Owen, L. (2009). Serving international students. In K. J. Osfield (Ed.), *Internationalization of student affairs and services* (pp. 49-56). Washington, DC: National Association of Student Personnel Administrators.

Pickrell, A. (2008). *An evaluation of the effectiveness of a postsecondary transition program for Aboriginal students* (Master's Thesis). Retrieved from ProQuest Dissertation and Theses Global database. (UMI No. MR55263)

Pidgeon, M. E. (2001). *Looking forward...: A national perspective on Aboriginal student services in Canadian universities* (Master's Thesis). Retrieved from ProQuest Dissertation and Theses Global database. (UMI No. MQ62416)

Powell, M. J. (2009). *From Ujima to emergence: An historical case study of a community college learning community* (Doctoral Dissertation). Retrieved from ProQuest Dissertation and Theses Global database. (UMI No. 3379603)

Rampersad, C. M. (2007). *Diversity in question: Inclusionary and exclusionary social interactions among international graduate students* (Doctoral Dissertation). Retrieved from ProQuest Dissertation and Theses Global database. (UMI No. 3299041)

Rezai, H. (2012). *State, dissidents, and contention: Iran, 1979--2010* (Doctoral Dissertation). Retrieved from ProQuest Dissertation and Theses Global database. (UMI No. 3494562)

Rybalkina, O. (2009). Competence in student affairs administration. In K. J. Osfield (Ed.), *Internationalization of student affairs and services* (pp. 37-48). Washington, DC: National Association of Student Personnel Association.

Shupp, M. R. (2016). Creating healthy climates through intentionality of practice. In S. T. Gregory & J. Edwards, *Invitational education and practice in higher education: An international perspective* (pp. 179-192). Lexington, KY: Lexington Books.

Weiss, M. L. (2009). Intellectual containment. *Critical Asian Studies, 41*(4), 499-522.

White, A. (2012). *A study abroad course for first-generation college students* (Unpublished Master's Thesis). Ball State University, Muncie, IN.

Wu, X. (1993). *Patterns of adjustment concerns and needs perceived by international students in a community college environment in Iowa* (Doctoral Dissertation). Retrieved from ProQuest Dissertation and Theses Global database. (UMI No. 9334678)

Zhao, D. (1995). *Reform and discontent: The causes of the 1989 Chinese Student Movement* (Doctoral Dissertation). Retrieved from ProQuest Dissertation and Theses Global database. (UMI No. NN05819)

Diversity Affairs and Campus Ecology

Applications: White and Campus Ecology

Castellanos, J. (1998). *Student effort and educational gains: A comparison of Hispanic/Latino/a and white students* (Doctoral Dissertation). Retrieved from ProQuest Dissertation and Theses Global database. (UMI No. 9917415)

Davis, B. A. (1988). *Personality characteristics and counseling effectiveness of Black and White community college probationary students* (Doctoral Dissertation). Retrieved from ProQuest Dissertation and Theses Global database. (UMI No. 8818613)

Johnson, J. B. (1999). *A comparison of cognitive development between Whites and African Americans based on William Perry's scheme of intellectual and ethical development* (Doctoral Dissertation). Retrieved from ProQuest Dissertation and Theses Global database. (UMI No. 9961423)

Nixon, H. L., & Henry, W. J. (1991). White students at the Black university: Their experiences regarding acts of racial intolerance. *Equity & Excellence in Education, 25*(2-4), 121-123.

Webb, L. J. (2012). *Making meaning of whiteness: Life experiences that inform culturally conscious student affairs leaders* (Doctoral Dissertation). Retrieved from ProQuest Dissertation and Theses Global database. (UMI No. 3551665)

Applications: Multiracial Groups and Campus Ecology

Banning, J. H. (1987). Racism and Sexism: White male perspective. *The Campus Ecologist, 5*(4), 3.

Banning, J. H., & Bartels, S. (1997). A Taxonomy: Campus physical artifacts as communicators of campus multiculturalism. *NASPA Journal, 35*(1), 29-37.

Banning, J. H., Middleton, V., & Deniston, T. L. (2008). Using photographs to assess equity climate: A taxonomy. *Multicultural Perspectives, 10*(1), 41-46. doi:10.1080/15210960701869611

Capeheart-Meningall, J. D. (1998). *Quality of students of color effort on a predominantly White college campus and the internal environmental elements that influence involvement* (Doctoral Dissertation). Retrieved from ProQuest Dissertation and Theses Global database. (UMI No. 9822209)

Coleman, B. R. (2012). *Being mixed and Black: The socialization of mixed-race identity.* University of Illinois.

Crittenden, M. A. (1992). *The consequences of campus ecology and multicultural personal development* (M.S.). Radford University, Radford, VA.

Destinon, M. v., Ganz, B., & Engs, M. (1993). Outcomes assessment and minority students in community colleges. *Community College Journal of Research and Practice, 17*(6), 497-508.

Fortune, E. P. (1984). A model for recruiting and retaining minority students in criminal justice majors. *Journal of Crime and Justice, 7*(1), 43-62.

Fried, J. (1997). Editor's notes. *New Directions for Student Services, 77,* 1-4.

Guillaume, R. O. (2012). *Racial identity in biracial and multiracial students in postsecondary education, a mixed method study* (Doctoral Dissertation). Retrieved from ProQuest Dissertation and Theses Global database. (UMI No. 3537766)

Johnson, L. (2004). *"Other": Biracial students in the college environment* (Doctoral Dissertation). Retrieved from ProQuest Dissertation and Theses Global database. (UMI No. 3173531)

King, A. R. (2008). Student perspectives on multiracial identity. *New Directions for Student Services, 123*, 33-41.

Morrison, N. J. (2007). *The meaning of place in an urban context for the under-represented minority student experience at NYU* (Doctoral Dissertation). Retrieved from ProQuest Dissertation and Theses Global database. (UMI No. 3255856)

Museus, S. D., & Jayakumar, U. M. (2011). Mapping the intersections of campus culture and equitable outcomes among racially diverse student populations. In S. D. Museus & U. M. Jayakumar (Eds.), *Creating campus cultures: Fostering success among racially diverse student populations* (pp. 1-27). London, UK: Routledge.

Powell, M. H. (1998). Campus climate and students of color. In L. A. Valverde & L. A. Castenell Jr. (Eds.), *The multicultural campus: Strategies for transforming higher education* (pp. 95-118). Walnut Creek, CA: AltaMira Press.

Renn, K. A. (2003). Understanding the identities of mixed-race college students through a developmental ecology lens. *Journal of College Student Development, 44*(3), 383-403.

Roque, M. (2013). *Multiracial identity development and the impact of race-oriented student services* (Unpublished Master's Thesis). Kansas State University, Manhattan, KS.

Sanford, M. R. (1990). *The effectiveness of summer orientation programs on retention and subsequent academic performance of minority students: A follow-up study* (Doctoral Dissertation). Retrieved from ProQuest Dissertation and Theses Global database. (UMI No. 9100501)

Shang, P., & Moore, L. V. (1990). Applying cultural theory: The environmental variable. *New Directions for Student Services, 51,* 73-82.

Smith, T. D. (2010). *Asian American/European American and Latino/a/European American multiracial psychology students in higher education: Academic barriers, academic supports, perceptions of cultural diversity, and experiences* (Doctoral Dissertation). Retrieved from ProQuest Dissertation and Theses Global database. (UMI No. 3422861)

Stebleton, M. J., Soria, K. M., Huesman Jr, R. L., & Torres, V. (2014). Recent immigrant students at research universities: The relationship between campus climate and sense of belonging. *Journal of College Student Development, 55*(2), 196-202.

Tanaka, G. K. (2002). Higher education's self-reflexive turn: Toward an intercultural theory of student development. *The Journal of Higher Education, 73*(2), 263-296.

Tilson, L. M. (1989). *Campus ecology and minority students' perceptions of the Ball State University environment* (Unpublished Master's Thesis). Ball State University, Muncie, IN.

Wimms, H. E. (2008). *An exploratory study of the experiences and perspectives of African-American, Latina/o, Asian-American and European-American students: "Is one of these things still not like the others?"* (Doctoral Dissertation). Retrieved from ProQuest Dissertation and Theses Global database. (UMI No. 3324648)

Applications: Appalachian Students and Campus Ecology

Bradbury, B. L., & Mather, P. C. (2009). The integration of first-year, first generation college students from Ohio Appalachia. *NASPA Journal, 46*(2), 258-281.

Decker, A. K. (2011). *Appalachian bridges to the baccalaureate: How community colleges affect transfer success* (Doctoral Dissertation). Retrieved from ProQuest Dissertation and Theses Global database. (UMI No. 3584050)

Phillips, C. M. (2011). *Appalachian bridges to the baccalaureate: Institutional perceptions of community college transfer success* (Doctoral Dissertation). Retrieved from ProQuest Dissertation and Theses Global database. (UMI No. 3584185)

Preston, N. C. (2011). *Appalachian bridges to the baccalaureate: The influence of multiple roles and cultural norms on the baccalaureate persistence of location-bound Appalachian women* (Doctoral Dissertation). Retrieved from ProQuest Dissertation and Theses Global database. (UMI No. 3584189)

Applications: Disability and Campus Ecology

Abreu-Ellis, C., Ellis, J., & Hayes, R. (2009). College preparedness and time of learning disability identification. *Journal of Developmental Education, 32*(3), 28-38. Retrieved from https://ezproxy2.library.colostate.edu/login?url=http://search.ebscohost.com/login.aspx?direct=true&AuthType=cookie,ip,url,cpid&custid=s4640792&db=aph&AN=43157989&site=ehost-live

Casey, D. A. (2003). An administrative approach to universal design in allied health sciences. In J. L. Higbee & E.

Goff (Eds.), *Pedagogy and student services for institutional transformation. Implementing Universal Design in Higher Education* (pp. 321-336). Minneapolis, MN: University of Minnesota.

Marr, M. A. (2015). Welcoming environments: Student with disabilities and involvement in college. *Journal of Student Affairs, 25*, 45-51.

Milne, N. V. (1989). *The experiences of college students with learning disabilities* (Doctoral Dissertation). Retrieved from ProQuest Dissertation and Theses Global database. (UMI No. 9035642)

Myers, K. A., Lindburg, J. J., & Nied, D. M. (2014). *Allies for inclusion: Disability and equity in higher education: ASHE Volume 39, Number 5.* San Francisco: Jossey-Bass.

Nuttel, K. J., & Ringgenberg, L. J. (1993). Creating positive outcomes for students with disabilities. *New Directions for Student Services, 64*, 45-58.

Porter, J. E., Camerlengo, R., DePuye, M., & Sommer, M. (1999). *Campus life and the development of postsecondary deaf and hard of hearing students: Principles and practices.* Retrieved from http://eric.ed.gov/?id=ED440499.

Walsh North, R. (2003). *Fostering inclusive online learning environments for students with disabilities in higher education* (Master's Thesis). Retrieved from ProQuest Dissertation and Theses Global database. (UMI No. MQ89680)

Applications: Women and Campus Ecology

Allison, D. J. (2016). *We matter, we're relevant and we are Black women in sororities: An exploration of the experience of*

Black sorority members at a predominately White institution (Master's Thesis). Retrieved from http://digitalcommons.unl/cehseddiss/367

Banning, J. H. (1985). Ecology and domination. *The Campus Ecologist, 3*(2), 3.

Banning, J. H. (1992). Campus photographs of posters and cartoons: Images of women. *The Campus Ecologist, 10*(3), 2-3.

Banning, J. H. (1992). Visual anthropology: Viewing the campus ecology for messages of sexism. *The Campus Ecologist, 10*(1), 1-4.

Banning, J. H. (1995). Ecological thinking and behavior in student affairs organizations: Importance of feminist leadership. *Journal of Student Affairs, 4*, 2-7.

Borman, K. M., Halperin, R. H., & Tyson, W. (2010). Introduction: The scarcity of scientists and engineers, a hidden crisis in the United States. In K. M. Borman, R. H. Halperin, & W. Tyson (Eds.), *Becoming an engineer in public universities: Pathways for women and minorities* (pp. 1-20). New York: Palgrave Macmillan.

Bunderson, E. D., & Franz, K. B. (1995). *Fostering a woman-friendly campus through an innovative academic and non-academic living environment.* Paper presented at the Achieving Gender Equity in the Classroom and on the Campus: the Next Steps: AAUW pre-convention symposium, Disney's Contemporary Resort, Orlando, Florida, June 22-24, 1995.

Clark, V. F. (2000). *Reactions of nontraditional women students in an introductory class: Quilting conversations* (Doctoral Dissertation). Retrieved from ProQuest Dissertation and Theses Global database. (UMI No. 9978927)

Cotner, B. A., Whaler, C. W., & Tyson, W. (2010). Producing STEM graduates in Florida: Understanding the Florida context. In K. M. Borman, R. H. Halperin, & W. Tyson (Eds.), *Becoming an engineer in public universities. Pathways for women and minorities* (pp. 21-52). New York: Palgrave Macmillan.

Danley, L. L. (2003). *Truths about sojourner: African-American women and the professorship. Their struggles and their successes on negotiating promotion and tenure at a predominantly White institution* (Doctoral Dissertation). Retrieved from ProQuest Dissertation and Theses Global database. (UMI No. 3085899)

D'Lisa, A. S. (1988). *The relationship between roommate rapport and social skills development of first semester female college freshmen* (Master's Thesis). Retrieved from ProQuest Dissertation and Theses Global database. (UMI No. 8908531)

Dowhower, A. L. (2000). *The experiences of female athletes at a women's college and a coed college* (Doctoral Dissertation). Retrieved from ProQuest Dissertation and Theses Global database. (UMI No. 9971539)

Dziech, B. W., & Vaughan, G. B. (1983). Changing status of women. In G. B. Vaughan (Ed.), *Issues for community college leaders in a new era* (pp. 55-75). San Francisco, CA: Jossey-Bass.

Forrest, L., Hotelling, K., & Kuk, L. (1984, June). *The elimination of sexism in university environments.* Paper presented at the second annual Campus Ecology Symposium, Pemgree Park, CO.

Gallegos, L. E. (2006). *Latinas: Life histories and the factors that influence success* (Doctoral Dissertation). Retrieved from

ProQuest Dissertation and Theses Global database. (UMI No. 3226126)

Gengler-Dunn, D. (2007). *A narrative inquiry of four female first-year, first-generation student perspectives of the university experience* (Doctoral Dissertation). Retrieved from ProQuest Dissertation and Theses Global database. (UMI No. 3299793)

Halberg, L. J. (1987). *A comparison of sex-role stereotypes, achievement motivation and decision-making of college and university women chief student affairs officers and women middle managers* (Doctoral Dissertation). Retrieved from ProQuest Dissertation and Theses Global database. (UMI No. 8729466)

Hart, J. L., & Cress, C. M. (2008). Are women faculty just "worrywarts?" Accounting for gender. *Journal of Human Behavior in the Social Environment, 17*(1/2), 175-193. Retrieved from http://jhbase.haworthpress.com

Hoffmann, F. L. (1986). Sexual harassment in academia: Feminist theory and institutional practice. *Harvard Educational Review, 56*(2), 105-122.

Kelly, J. L. (1994). *Factors affecting the promotion of women to senior level administrative positions in student affairs* (Unpublished Master's Thesis). Emporia State University, Emporia, KS.

Kuk, L. (1990). Perspectives on gender differences. *New Directions for Student Services, 51*, 25-36.

McBride, R. A., & Lott, J. L. (2015). The ecology of volunteerism among college women: Identifying campus environments that inform volunteering behaviors. *NASPA Journal about Women in Higher Education, 8*(1), 47-65.

McComb, T. A. (2007). *"I won't, I might, I am." Undergraduate women and stages of change for participation in leadership development activities* (Doctoral Dissertation). Retrieved from ProQuest Dissertation and Theses Global database. (UMI No. NR41017)

Mimms, J. M. (1996). *African-American women in higher education administration* (Doctoral Dissertation). Retrieved from ProQuest Dissertation and Theses Global database. (UMI No. 9621756)

Rogers, N. E. M. (1995). *Mexican-American women in academe: Analysis of career progress and job satisfaction* (Doctoral Dissertation). Retrieved from ProQuest Dissertation and Theses Global database. (UMI No. 9617332)

Rowe, L. P. (1998). *"The least thing you hear about in the dorm": Cultural themes for academic activity in a women's residence hall at a public comprehensive university* (Doctoral Dissertation). Retrieved from ProQuest Dissertation and Theses Global database. (UMI No. 9902316)

Ryan, M. A. (2008). *Women who build buildings: The experiences of student affairs professionals in constructing student-focused space on university campuses* (Doctoral Dissertation). Retrieved from ProQuest Dissertation and Theses Global database. (UMI No. 3303431)

Sandusky, C. H. (1995). *Perceptions of career counseling and utilization of career counseling services by older women students at a four-year urban university* (Master's Thesis). Retrieved from ProQuest Dissertation and Theses Global database. (UMI No. 377457)

Schwitzer, A. M., Bergholz, K., Dore, T., & Salimi, L. (1998). Eating disorders among college women: Prevention, education, and treatment responses. *Journal of American College Health, 46*(5), 199. Retrieved from https://ezproxy2.library.colostate.edu/login?url=http://search.ebscohost.com/login.aspx?direct=true&AuthType=cookie,ip,url,cpid&custid=s4640792&db=aph&AN=470208&site=ehost-live

Whitt, E. J. (1993, November). *"I can be anything!" Student leadership in three women's colleges.* Paper presented at the ASHE Annual Meeting, Pittsburg, PA.

Zamani, E. M. (2003). African American student affairs professionals in community college settings. *Association of Student Affairs Professionals Journal, (6)*1, 91-104.

Zamani, E. M. (2003). African American women in higher education. *New Directions for Student Services, 104*, 5-18.

Applications: LGBT and Campus Ecology

Banning, J. H. (1995). Campus images: homopredjudice. *The Campus Ecologist, 13*(3), 3.

Brooks, S. E. (2002). *A critical pedagogy of residential education: Toward empowering representations of lesbian, gay and bisexual identity* (Doctoral Dissertation). Retrieved from ProQuest Dissertation and Theses Global database. (UMI No. 3045594)

Brown, R. D., & Gortmaker, V. J. (2009). Assessing campus climates for lesbian, gay, bisexual and transgender (LGBT) students: Methodological and political issues. *Journal of LGBT Youth, 6*(4), 416-435.

Burnes, T. R. (2006). *Opening the door of a bigger closet: Sexual orientation identity development for lesbian, bisexual, and queer college women of color* (Doctoral Dissertation). Retrieved from ProQuest Dissertation and Theses Global database. (UMI No. 3226253)

Evans, N. J., & Rankin, S. (1998). Heterosexism and campus violence: Assessment and intervention strategies. In R. Fenske, A. Hoffman, & J. H. Schuh (Eds.), *Violence on campus: Defining the problems, strategies for action* (pp. 169-186). Gaithersburg, MD: Aspen.

Fonken, L. E. (1995). Homoprejudice within the campus ecology. *The Campus Ecologist, 13*(3), 1-3.

Fonken, L. E. (1996). *A phenomenological study of lesbian faculty experience in institutions of higher education* (Doctoral Dissertation). Retrieved from ProQuest Dissertation and Theses Global database. (UMI No. 9719574)

Gutierrez, F. J. (1987, March). Managing the campus ecology of gay/lesbian students on Catholic college campuses. Paper presented at the Annual Meeting of the American College Personnel Association, Chicago, IL. Retrieved from http://search.proquest.com.ezproxy2.library.colostate.edu:2048/docview/62960952?accountid=10223

Hall, A. L. (2014). *Incredi-bull-ly inclusive?: Assessing the climate on a college campus* (Master's Thesis). Retrieved from ProQuest Dissertation and Theses Global database. (UMI No. 1563192)

Maher, M. J., & Sever, L. M. (2007). What educators in Catholic schools might expect when addressing gay and lesbian issues: A study of needs and barriers. *Journal of Gay & Lesbian Issues in Education, 4*(3), 79-111.

Maher, M. J. S., Jr. (1997). *The dis-integration of a child: Gay and lesbian youth in Catholic education* (Doctoral Dissertation).

Retrieved from ProQuest Dissertation and Theses Global database. (UMI No. 9803792)

McKinney, J. S. (2004). *"The most significant years of my life": The lived experiences of gay undergraduate men* (Doctoral Dissertation). Retrieved from ProQuest Dissertation and Theses Global database. (UMI No. 3162249)

Nichols, A. C. (1998). *An assessment of University of Wisconsin-La Crosse undergraduate student's attitudes toward gay men and lesbians* (Unpublished Master's Thesis) University of Wisconsin, Madison, WI.

Paape, T. (2012). *The impact of residence halls on the sense of community and belonging of gay and bisexual college men* (Unpublished Master's Thesis). University of Minnesota, Minneapolis, MN.

Perlis, S. M. (2001). *Sexual orientation and multiperspective identity on a small, Catholic campus: An analysis of the cultural climate and multicultural organizational change* (Doctoral Dissertation). Retrieved from ProQuest Dissertation and Theses Global database. (UMI No. 3014468)

Pierre, D. E. (2013). *No place like home: The coming out experiences of gay men in student affairs and higher education administration preparation programs* (Unpublished Doctoral Dissertation). University of Georgia, Athens, GA. Retrieved from: http://scholar.google.com/scholar?q=No+Place+Like+Home%3A+The+Coming+Out+Experience+of+Gay+Men&btnG=&hl=en&as_sdt=0%2C6

Rivera, D. P., Nadal, K. L., & Leroy, M. (2014). Understanding HIV and STI prevention for LGBT college students. In L. Wilson, R. T. Palmer, and D. C. Maramba, *Understanding*

HIV and STI prevention for college students (pp. 98-117). New York: Taylor and Francis.

Ritchie, C. A., & Banning, J. H. (2001). Gay, lesbian, bisexual, and transgender campus support office: A qualitative study of establishment experiences. *NASPA Journal, 38*(4), 482-494.

Rochenbach, A. N., Lo, M.A., & Mayhew, M. J. (2016). How LGBT college students perceive and engage the campus religious and spiritual climate. *Journal of Homosexuality*, DOI: 10.1080/00918369.2016.11911239

Salazar, E. (2009). *Leadership development: Perceptions of gay and lesbian student leaders in Jesuit universities* (Doctoral Dissertation). Retrieved from ProQuest Dissertation and Theses Global database. (UMI No. 3383807)

Salmi, R. P. (1994). *Changing attitudes toward lesbian women and gay men among college freshmen: The effects of a campus intervention program* (Doctoral Dissertation). Retrieved from ProQuest Dissertation and Theses Global database. (UMI No. 9428803)

Smith, A. R. (2014). *Making their own way: The experiences of gay male students in STEM fields* (Unpublished Master's Thesis). University of Nebraska, Lincoln, NE. Retrieved from http://scholar.google.com/scholar?q=No+Place+Like+Home%3A+The+Coming+Out+Experience+of+Gay+Men&btnG=&hl=en&as_sdt=0%2C6

Stevens, A. (1997). *Critical incidents contributing to the development of lesbian identities in college* (Doctoral Dissertation). Retrieved from ProQuest Dissertation and Theses Global database. (UMI No. 9808669)

Tontz, P. A. (2008). *A chameleon on the court: Understanding factors that contribute to invisibility/visibility for Division I intercollegiate gay athletes* (Doctoral Dissertation). Retrieved from ProQuest Dissertation and Theses Global database. (UMI No. 3320587)

Applications: Men and Campus Ecology

Gertner, D. (1991). Men and student development: Emerging notions from the perspective of campus ecology. *The Campus Ecologist, 9*(1), 1-2.

Harper, S. R., Berhanu, J., Davis III, C. H. F., & McGuire, K. M. (2015). Engaging college men of color. In S. J. Quaye & S. R. Harper (Eds.), *Student engagement in higher education* (2nd ed., pp. 55-74). New York: Routledge.

Harper, S. R., & Gasman, M. (2008). Consequences of conservatism: Black male students and the politics of historically Black colleges and universities. *Journal of Negro Education. 77*(4), 336-351. Retrieved from: http://www.jstor.org/journals/00222984.html

Laker, J. A. (2005). *Beyond bad dogs: Toward a pedagogy of engagement of male students* (Doctoral Dissertation). Retrieved from ProQuest Dissertation and Theses Global database. (UMI No. 3162820)

Manthei, Jr., L. P. (2016). Cutting the deficit: An examination of factors contributing to the success of Black males seeking doctoral degrees at a predominately White institution (Doctoral Dissertation). Retrieved from http://etd.lsu.edu/docs/available/etd-05252016-161418/unrestricted/manthei_diss.pdf

Stein, J. L. (2004). *Predictors of male college students willingness to prevent rape moderated by a rape prevention peer education program* (Doctoral Dissertation). Retrieved from ProQuest Dissertation and Theses Global database. (UMI No. 3134069)

Strayhorn, T. L. (2013). What role does grit play in the academic success of Black male collegians at predominantly White institutions? *Journal of African American Studies*, 18, 1-10. doi: 10.1007/s12111-012-9243-0

Warren, L. D. (2009). *Ain't I a leader: Exploring the leadership narratives of Black female undergraduate student leaders at a predominantly White institution* (Doctoral Dissertation). Retrieved from ProQuest Dissertation and Theses Global database. (UMI No. 3409803)

Williams, V. M., Jr. (1996). *Motivational orientations of reentry adult male graduate students to participate in higher education* (Doctoral Dissertation). Retrieved from ProQuest Dissertation and Theses Global database. (UMI No. 9622874)

Applications: Gender and Campus Ecology

Banning, J. H. (1985). Ecology and domination. *The Campus Ecologist*, 3(2), 3.

Banning, J. H. (1987). Racism and sexism: White male perspective. *The Campus Ecologist*, 5(4), 3.

Banning, J. H. (1992). Campus photographs of posters and cartoons: Images of women. *The Campus Ecologist*, 10(3), 2-3.

Banning, J. H. (1992). Visual anthropology: Viewing the campus ecology for messages of sexism. *The Campus Ecologist*, 10(1), 1-4.

Bunderson, E. D., & Franz, K. B. (1995). *Fostering a woman-friendly campus through an innovative academic and non-academic living environment.* Paper presented at the Achieving Gender Equity in the Classroom and on the Campus: the Next Steps: AAUW pre-convention symposium, Disney's Contemporary Resort, Orlando, Florida, June 22-24, 1995.

Cadenhead, J. K. (2004). *The tripartite self: Gender, identity, and power* (Doctoral Dissertation). Retrieved from ProQuest Dissertation and Theses Global database. (UMI No. 3126153)

Cole, M. L. (1999). *An analysis of teacher and student leadership and gender differentiation within academic divisions at three Virginia and Tennessee liberal arts colleges* (Doctoral Dissertation). Retrieved from ProQuest Dissertation and Theses Global database. (UMI No. 9955484)

Forrest, L., Hotelling, K., & Kuk, L. (1984, June). *The elimination of sexism in university environments.* Paper presented at the second annual Campus Ecology Symposium, Pingree Park, CO.

Gertner, D. (1991). Men and student development: Emerging notions from the perspective of campus ecology. *The Campus Ecologist, 9*(1), 1-2.

Harper, S. R., & Gasman, M. (2008). Consequences of conservatism: Black male students and the politics of historically Black colleges and universities. *Journal of Negro Education. Vol 77*(4), 336-351. Retrieved from: http://www.jstor.org/journals/00222984.html

Hart, J. L., & Cress, C. M. (2008). Are women faculty just "worrywarts?" Accounting for gender. *Journal of Human*

Behavior in the Social Environment, 17(1/2), 175-193. Retrieved from http://jhbase.haworthpress.com

Hoffmann, F. L. (1986). Sexual harassment in academia: Feminist theory and institutional practice. *Harvard Educational Review, 56*(2), 105-122.

Jordan, M. L. (2012). Heterosexual ally identity development: A conceptual model. *Journal of the Indiana University Student Personnel Association*, (2012 Edition), 67-78. Retrieved from http://scholarworks.iu.edu/journals/index.php/jiuspa/article/viewFile/1342/1947

Kuk, L. (1990). Perspectives on gender differences. *New Directions for Student Services, 51*, 25-36.

May, R. J. (1988). The developmental journey of the male college student. *New Directions for Student Services, 42*, 5-18.

Robbins, G. M. (1998). *The effect of higher education on attitudes and values: Gender and the academic environment* (Doctoral Dissertation). Retrieved from ProQuest Dissertation and Theses Global database. (UMI No. 9833562)

Rohrbacker, J. M., & Weber, K. (2014). Race-ethnicity and gender in higher education. In M. L. Miville & A.D. Ferguson (Eds.), *Handbook of race-ethnicity and gender in psychology* (pp. 189-218). New York: Springer.

Romano, C. R. (1994). *Going against the grain: Women student leaders at coeducational institutions* (Doctoral Dissertation). Retrieved from ProQuest Dissertation and Theses Global database. (UMI No. 9518437)

Waxman, M. (1987). Gender and ecological balance: Can the university function as a closed system. *The Campus Ecologist, 5*(4), 1-3.

Applications: Commuters and Campus Ecology

Alford, S. M. (1998). The impact of inner-city values on student social adjustment in commuter colleges. *NASPA Journal, 35*(3), 225-233.

Andreas, R., & Kubik, J. (1985). Redesigning our campuses to meet the needs of our commuting students: Study lounges. *The Campus Ecologist, 3*(1), 2.

Banning, J. H., & Hughes, B. M. (1986). Designing the environment with commuter students. *NASPA Journal, 24*(1), 17-24.

Dunham, A. M. (2000). *Traditional-aged commuter student usage of and satisfaction with student services at four-year institutions* (Doctoral Dissertation). Retrieved from ProQuest Dissertation and Theses Global database. (UMI No. 9981500)

Hail, R. M. G. (1997). *Why age 25? Should age be the determining factor in identifying non-traditional students' needs? A study of commuter students at a midwestern university* (Doctoral Dissertation). Retrieved from ProQuest Dissertation and Theses Global database. (UMI No. 98113610

Jacoby, B. (1983). Parents of dependent commuters: A neglected resource. *New Directions for Student Services, 24*, 49-59.

Jacoby, B. (1989). *The student as commuter: Developing a comprehensive institutional response.* ASHE-ERIC Report No. 7. Retrieved from http://eric.ed.gov/?q=ED319298.

Knefelkamp, L. L., & Stewart, S. (1983). Toward a new conceptualization of commuter students: The developmental perspective. In S. S. Stewart (Ed.), *New Directions for Student Services, 24,* 61-70. San Francisco: Jossey-Bass.

Masse, J. C. (2009). *An ecological perspective on commuter student success* (Master's Thesis). Retrieved from ProQuest Dissertation and Theses Global database. (UMI No. 1472234)

Ortman, J. (1995). *Commuter Students in Colleges and Universities.* Retrieved from http://eric.ed.gov/?q=ed398779

Pustorino, A. M. (2014). *Differences in perceptions of student experiences between residential and commuter sub-populations in higher education* (Doctoral Dissertation). Retrieved from ProQuest Dissertation and Theses Global database. (UMI No. 3643668)

Sloan, D. (1988). Ecological transitions and commuters: An interview with James H. Banning. *The Commuter, 14*(1), 2-5.

Sloan, D. (1988). Using campus ecology to serve commuter students. *The Commuter, 14*(1), 1.

Sloan, D. (1989). Advising adults from the commuter perspective. *NACADA Journal, 9*(2), 67-75.

Tuttle, J. K. (2006). *The effects of a commuter collegium on Christian college commuter students' sense of community* (Doctoral Dissertation). Retrieved from ProQuest Dissertation and Theses Global database. (UMI No. 3228566)

Weiss, M. (2014). *The college experience of commuter students and the concepts of place and space* (Doctoral Dissertation). Retrieved from ProQuest Dissertation and Theses Global database. (UMI No. 3619489)

Wiese, M. D. (1994). College choice cognitive dissonance: Managing student/institution fit. *Journal of Marketing for Higher Education, 5*(1), 35-48.

Applications: Low Income Students and Campus Ecology

Barratt, W. (2011). *Social class on campus: Theories and manifestations.* Sterling, VA: Stylus Publishing, LLC.

Bell, D. A. (2012). *An exploration of factors that impact the satisfaction and success of low socioeconomic status community college students* (Doctoral Dissertation). Retrieved from ProQuest Dissertation and Theses Global database. (UMI No. 3535408)

Bell, D. A., Hackett, C. D., & Hoffman, J. L. (2016). Student satisfaction and success in a low-income community college environment. *Journal of Applied Research in the Community College, 23*(1), 1-16.

Dykes, M. (2011). *Appalachian bridges to the baccalaureate: Mattering perceptions and transfer persistence of low-income, first-generation community college students* (Doctoral Dissertation). Retrieved from ProQuest Dissertation and Theses Global database. (UMI No. 3584058)

Wilson, B. D. (2006). *Contextual student differences and scoring patterns of the Motivated Strategies for Learning Questionnaire (MSQL)* (Doctoral Dissertation). Retrieved from ProQuest Dissertation and Theses Global database. (UMI No. 3221791)

Applications: Adults, Non-Traditionals, Veterans and Campus Ecology

Austin, L. (1992). *Factors influencing the academic success of adult college students after initial academic suspension* (Doctoral

Dissertation). Retrieved from ProQuest Dissertation and Theses Global database. (UMI No. 9303216)

Butcher, J. L. (1997). *Involvement and persistence: Nontraditional student perceptions of the student-college relationship* (Doctoral Dissertation). Retrieved from ProQuest Dissertation and Theses Global database. (UMI No. 9819077)

Fauber, T. L. (1996). *"Mattering" doesn't matter: An analysis of adult undergraduate persistence patterns* (Doctoral Dissertation). Retrieved from ProQuest Dissertation and Theses Global database. (UMI No. 9622278)

Hillard, M. K. (1996). *An assessment of persistence and mattering among nontraditional, community college students* (Doctoral Dissertation). Retrieved from ProQuest Dissertation and Theses Global database. (UMI No. 9628684)

Kleemann, G. L. (1984). Student perceptions of effectiveness at three state universities (Organizational, strategic management, theory, non-traditional students (Doctoral Dissertation). Retrieved from ProQuest Dissertation and Theses Global database. (UMI No. 8504267)

Nayman, R. L., & Patten, W. G. (1980). Offering effective student development programs for the adult learner. *New Directions for Student Services,* (11), 39-56.

Post, D. M. (1990). *A descriptive comparison of adult and traditional students in an undergraduate teacher education program* (Doctoral Dissertation). Retrieved from ProQuest Dissertation and Theses Global database. (UMI No. 9104956)

Schuetz, P. G. (2007). *Influences of campus environment on adult community college student engagement.* (Doctoral Dissertation).

Retrieved from ProQuest Dissertation and Theses Global database. (UMI No. 3288232)

Smith, P. R. (1993). *A meeting of cultures: Faculty and part-time doctoral students in an Ed.D. program* (Doctoral Dissertation). Retrieved from ProQuest Dissertation and Theses Global database. (UMI No. 9420290)

Ware, Jr., T. E., & Miller, M. T. (1997). *Literature related to college housing for adult undergraduate students.* Retrieved from http://files.eric.ed.gov/fulltext/ED414799.pdf

Ware, T. E., Jr. (1997). *Adult undergraduates and residential life: Services, recruitment, and the chief housing officer* (Doctoral Dissertation). Retrieved from ProQuest Dissertation and Theses Global database. (UMI No. 9735763)

White, A. H. (1999). *The focus on adult students: Institutional response to adult students at a small, private university* (Doctoral Dissertation). Retrieved from ProQuest Dissertation and Theses Global database. (UMI No. 9944341)

Williams, V. M., Jr. (1996). *Motivational orientations of reentry adult male graduate students to participate in higher education* (Doctoral Dissertation). Retrieved from ProQuest Dissertation and Theses Global database. (UMI No. 9622874)

Applications: First Generation Students and Campus Ecology

Bergeron, D. M. (2013). *The relationship of perceived intellectual and social attainment to academic success of first-generation, first-year college students participating in a first generation access program* (Doctoral Dissertation). Retrieved from ProQuest Dissertation and Theses Global database. (UMI No. 3588545)

Bradbury, B. L., & Mather, P. C. (2009). The integration of first-year, first generation college students from Ohio Appalachia. *NASPA Journal, 46*(2), 258-281.

Dykes, M. (2011). *Appalachian bridges to the baccalaureate: Mattering perceptions and transfer persistence of low-income, first-generation community college students* (Doctoral Dissertation). Retrieved from ProQuest Dissertation and Theses Global database. (UMI No. 3584058)

Gengler-Dunn, D. (2007). *A narrative inquiry of four female first-year, first-generation student perspectives of the university experience* (Doctoral Dissertation). Retrieved from ProQuest Dissertation and Theses Global database. (UMI No. 3299793)

Hernandez, Y. (2013). *Latino student's perceptions of the university campus climate: Exploratory study of first generation students* (Doctoral Dissertation). Retrieved from ProQuest Dissertation and Theses Global database. (UMI No. 3558345)

White, A. (2012). *A study abroad course for first-generation college students* (Unpublished Master's Thesis). Ball State University, Muncie, IN.

Applications: Geography and Campus Ecology

Gansas, K. M. (2016). The college transition for first-year students from rural Oregon communities. *Journal of Student Affairs and Practice*. Retrieved from: http://dx.doi.org/10.1080/19496591.2016.1157487

Maples, M. R. (2000). *Rural students' satisfaction with college environment: An ecological consideration* (Doctoral Dissertation). Retrieved from ProQuest Dissertation and Theses Global database. (UMI No. 9996133)

Richardson Jr., R. C., & Bender, L. W. (1985). *Students in urban settings: Achieving the baccalaureate degree. ASHE-ERIC Higher Education Report No. 6.* Washington D.C. Retrieved from http://eric.ed.gov/?q=Ed265798

Sharp, D. L. (1999). *The relationship between organizational cultures and organizational climates in three large urban higher education institutions in the United States* (Doctoral Dissertation). Retrieved from ProQuest Dissertation and Theses Global database. (UMI No. 9937344)

Shipes, J. F. (2002). *They did not teach: Veterans' experiences in a mid-career transition program at an urban university* (Doctoral Dissertation). Retrieved from ProQuest Dissertation and Theses Global database. (UMI No. 3068665)

Chapter 7

The Community College

An important campus environment in higher education is the community college. The curriculum mission, the student body, the array of student opportunities and programs, and the nature of the physical environment are often unique. Because of the ecological uniqueness of many of the community colleges in relation to the traditional four year plus graduate campuses, the use of the campus ecology model is highlighted in this chapter. The chapter is organized on a composite of the foregoing chapters: Institutional Affairs, Academic Affairs, Student Affairs, and Diversity Affairs.

Institutional Affairs and Campus Ecology

Applications: Planning and Campus Ecology

Demonica, D., & Ogurek, D. (2002). A new approach to community college master planning. *College Planning & Management, 5*(6), 42-44.

Applications: Campus Community/Culture and Campus Ecology

Knezevich, P. (2000). *A comparison of campus cultures between Ball State University and Lincoln Land Community College as seen through the ecological perspective* (Unpublished Master's Thesis). Ball State University, Muncie, IN.

Ousley, M. D. (2003). *Coffee pots and clocks: Cultural challenges to organizational change in higher education* (Doctoral Dissertation). Retrieved from ProQuest Dissertation and Theses Global database. (UMI No. 3107027)

Academic Affairs and Campus Ecology Applications: Retention and Campus Ecology

Alderman, L. V. (1997). *Student support services and their impact on persistence of first-year students at a rural community college* (Doctoral Dissertation). Retrieved from ProQuest Dissertation and Theses Global database. (UMI No. 9817088)

Brown-Weinstock, P. (2009). *Adjustment and persistence of students from an urban environment to a rural community college* (Doctoral Dissertation). Retrieved from ProQuest Dissertation and Theses Global database. (UMI No. 3410791)

Engs, M. S. (1996). *Factors affecting the retention of Native American students at a southwestern community college* (Doctoral Dissertation). Retrieved from ProQuest Dissertation and Theses Global database. (UMI No. 9710193)

McMillion, S. S. (1999). *Campus environment factors of two small, rural community colleges and their influences on persistence behaviors of African-American students in the college transfer program* (Doctoral Dissertation). Retrieved from ProQuest Dissertation and Theses Global database. (UMI No. 9922697)

Hillard, M. K. (1996). *An assessment of persistence and mattering among nontraditional, community college students* (Doctoral

Dissertation). Retrieved from ProQuest Dissertation and Theses Global database. (UMI No. 9628684)

Schuetz, P. (2005). UCLA community college review: Campus environment: A missing link in studies of community college attrition. *Community College Review, 32*(4), 60-80.

Williamson-Ashe, S. R. (2008). *The influence of academic and social integration, educational objectives, and intent on community college student persistence* (Doctoral Dissertation). Retrieved from ProQuest Dissertation and Theses Global database. (UMI No. 3325445)

Applications: Academic Advising and Campus Ecology

Hartsell, J. L. (1999). *The relationship between academic advising preferences, career decidedness and certain demographic characteristics of community college students* (Doctoral Dissertation). Retrieved from ProQuest Dissertation and Theses Global database. (UMI No. 9960178)

Johnson-Dedeaux, V. M. (2011). *An investigation of students' satisfaction with academic advising and students' impressions of academic advisors at a rural community college* (Doctoral Dissertation). Retrieved from ProQuest Dissertation and Theses Global database. (UMI No. 3487153)

Raushi, T. M. (1993). Developmental academic advising. *New Directions for Community Colleges, 82*, 5-19.

Applications: Academic Programs/Departments

Hodgkinson, H. L. (1983). Establishing alliances with business and industry. In G. B. Vaughan (Ed.), *Issues for community college leaders in a new era* (pp. 222-231). San Francisco, CA: Jossey-Bass.

Hubbard, B. (2010). *Manifestations of hidden curriculum in a community college online opticianry program: An ecological approach* (Doctoral Dissertation). Retrieved from ProQuest Dissertation and Theses Global database. (UMI No. 3425631)

Applications: Academic Outcomes

Aldridge, H. M., Jr. (2005). *Analysis of the perceptions of learning-centered changes in community college student affairs* (Doctoral Dissertation). Retrieved from ProQuest Dissertation and Theses Global database. (UMI No. 3174967)

Bell, D. A. (2012). *An exploration of factors that impact the satisfaction and success of low socioeconomic status community college students* (Doctoral Dissertation). Retrieved from ProQuest Dissertation and Theses Global database. (UMI No. 3535408)

Bell, D. A., Hackett, C. D., & Hoffman, J. L. (2016). Student satisfaction and success in a low-income community college environment. *Journal of Applied Research in the Community College, 23*(1), 1-16.

Choice, T. L. (1998). *An analysis of the assessment of general education outcomes in Illinois community colleges* (Doctoral Dissertation). Retrieved from ProQuest Dissertation and Theses Global database. (UMI No. 9918701)

Destinon, M. v., Ganz, B., & Engs, M. (1993). Outcomes assessment and minority students in community colleges. *Community College Journal of Research and Practice, 17*(6), 497-508.

Johnson, B. D. (2002). *Preparing students for the university: What is the effect of community college accommodation on students who transfer to state universities?* (Doctoral Dissertation). Retrieved from ProQuest Dissertation and Theses Global database. (UMI No. 3056242)

Layman, R. W. (2005). *Exploring differences in level of involvement, educational outcomes, and satisfaction of resident students and commuter students at a rural community college* (Doctoral Dissertation). Retrieved from ProQuest Dissertation and Theses Global database. (UMI No. 3191233)

Phillips, C. M. (2011). *Appalachian bridges to the baccalaureate: Institutional perceptions of community college transfer success* (Doctoral Dissertation). Retrieved from ProQuest Dissertation and Theses Global database. (UMI No. 3584185)

Applications: Academic Classrooms and Campus Ecology

Veltri, S., Banning, J. H., & Davies, T. G. (2006). The community college classroom: Student perceptions. *The College Student Journal, 40*(3), 517-527.

Student Affairs and Campus Ecology
Applications: Mattering and Campus Ecology

Decker, A. K. (2011). *Appalachian bridges to the baccalaureate: How community colleges affect transfer success* (Doctoral Dissertation). Retrieved from ProQuest Dissertation and Theses Global database. (UMI No. 3584050)

Dykes, M. (2011). *Appalachian bridges to the baccalaureate: Mattering perceptions and transfer persistence of low-income, first-generation community college students* (Doctoral Dissertation).

Retrieved from ProQuest Dissertation and Theses Global database. (UMI No. 3584058)

Hillard, M. K. (1996). *An assessment of persistence and mattering among nontraditional, community college students* (Doctoral Dissertation). Retrieved from ProQuest Dissertation and Theses Global database. (UMI No. 9628684)

Applications: Engagement/Involvement and Campus Ecology

Layman, R. W. (2005). *Exploring differences in level of involvement, educational outcomes, and satisfaction of resident students and commuter students at a rural community college* (Doctoral Dissertation). Retrieved from ProQuest Dissertation and Theses Global database. (UMI No. 3191233)

Schuetz, P. (2008). Developing a theory-driven model of community college student engagement. *New Directions for Community Colleges,* (144), 17-28.

Schuetz, P. G. (2007). *Influences of campus environment on adult community college student engagement* (Doctoral Dissertation). Retrieved from ProQuest Dissertation and Theses Global database. (UMI No. 3288232)

Applications: Student Satisfaction and Campus Ecology

Bilsky, J. H. (2000). *Student satisfaction among select demographic groups at a Florida community college* (Doctoral Dissertation). Retrieved from ProQuest Dissertation and Theses Global database. (UMI No. 9984391)

Applications: Student Development and Campus Ecology

Gillett-Karam, R. (2016). Moving from student development to student success. *New Directions for Community Colleges, 174*, 9-21.

Hsieh, P. C. (1990). *The formulation of a student development model for the California community college* (Doctoral Dissertation). Retrieved from ProQuest Dissertation and Theses Global database. (UMI No. 9034046)

Applications: Student Affairs Theory and Practice and Campus Ecology

Aldridge, D. V. (1997). *Leadership and management behaviors of the deans of student services within the Los Angeles Community College District* (Doctoral Dissertation). Retrieved from ProQuest Dissertation and Theses Global database. (UMI No. 9803457)

Dale, P., & Shoenhair, C. (2000). *Learning-centered practices in student services.* A Paradise Valley Community College Report. Retrieved from ERIC Database (ED445732).

Elsner, P. A., & Ames, W. C. (1983). Redirecting student services. In G. B. Vaughan (Ed.), *Issues for community college leaders in a new era* (pp. 139-158). San Francisco, CA: Jossey-Bass.

Fluker, R. C., Sr. (1995). *Leadership styles of chief student services administrators in Texas community colleges* (Doctoral Dissertation). Retrieved from ProQuest Dissertation and Theses Global database. (UMI No. 9534786)

Applications: Counseling and Campus Ecology

Creamer, D. G. (1983). Preparing and nurturing professional counselors. *New Directions for Community Colleges, 3,* 85-97.

Davis, B. A. (1988). *Personality characteristics and counseling effectiveness of Black and White community college probationary students* (Doctoral Dissertation). Retrieved from ProQuest Dissertation and Theses Global database. (UMI No. 8818613)

Hartsell, J. L. (1999). *The relationship between academic advising preferences, career decidedness and certain demographic characteristics of community college students* (Doctoral Dissertation). Retrieved from ProQuest Dissertation and Theses Global database. (UMI No. 9960178)

Matson, J. E. (1983). Primary roles for community college counselors. *New Directions for Community Colleges, 43,* 19-28.

Peglow-Hoch, M. A. (1997). *Counselor intervention with academically low achieving community college students: Does it make a difference?* (Doctoral Dissertation). Retrieved from ProQuest Dissertation and Theses Global database. (UMI No. 9805291)

Thurston, A. S. (1983). The decade ahead for community college counseling. *New Directions for Community Colleges, 1983*(43), 113-120.

Applications: Learning Communities and Campus Ecology

Powell, M. J. (2009). *From Ujima to emergence: An historical case study of a community college learning community* (Doctoral Dissertation). Retrieved from ProQuest Dissertation and Theses Global database. (UMI No. 3379603)

Wood, V. M. (2012). *A case study of learning community curriculum models implemented in business programs in three public community colleges in Ohio* (Doctoral Dissertation). Retrieved from ProQuest Dissertation and Theses Global database. (UMI No. 3563274)

Applications: First Year Programs and Campus Ecology

Alderman, L. V. (1997). *Student support services and their impact on persistence of first-year students at a rural community college* (Doctoral Dissertation). Retrieved from ProQuest Dissertation and Theses Global database. (UMI No. 9817088)

Diversity Affairs and Campus Ecology
Applications: Diversity Policies and Programs

Destinon, M. v., Ganz, B., & Engs, M. (1993). Outcomes assessment and minority students in community colleges. *Community College Journal of Research and Practice, 17*(6), 497-508.

Applications: African Americans and Campus Ecology

McMillion, S. S. (1999). *Campus environment factors of two small, rural community colleges and their influences on persistence behaviors of African-American students in the college transfer program* (Doctoral Dissertation). Retrieved from ProQuest Dissertation and Theses Global database. (UMI No. 9922697)

Thompkins, A. E. (1989). *Black students' environmental perceptions of their community college* (Doctoral Dissertation). Retrieved from ProQuest Dissertation and Theses Global database. (UMI No. 9012936)

Zamani, E. M. (2003). African American student affairs professionals in community college settings: A commentary for the future. *Association of Student Affairs Professionals Journal, 6*(1), 91-104.

Applications: Native Americans and Campus Ecology

Engs, M. S. (1996). *Factors affecting the retention of Native American students at a southwestern community college* (Doctoral Dissertation). Retrieved from ProQuest Dissertation and Theses Global database. (UMI No. 9710193)

Applications: Asian Americans and Campus Ecology

Bottrell, C. A. (2007). *Vietnamese-American students at Midwestern Community College: A narrative inquiry study* (Doctoral Dissertation). Retrieved from ProQuest Dissertation and Theses Global database. (UMI No. 3279495)

Do, T. H. (2005). *East meets west: The adaptation of Vietnamese international students to California community colleges* (Doctoral Dissertation). Retrieved from ProQuest Dissertation and Theses Global database. (UMI No. 3192327)

Applications: Multiracial Students and Campus Ecology

Tajuba, D. L. (1996). *An appraisal of the multicultural educational environment at an urban community college setting as perceived by students* (Doctoral Dissertation). Retrieved from ProQuest Dissertation and Theses Global database. (UMI No. 9903074)

Applications: International Students/Programs and Campus Ecology

Wu, X. (1993). *Patterns of adjustment concerns and needs perceived by international students in a community college environment in Iowa* (Doctoral Dissertation). Retrieved from ProQuest Dissertation and Theses Global database. (UMI No. 9334678)

Applications: Gender and Campus Ecology

Cadenhead, J. K. (2004). *The tripartite self: Gender, identity, and power* (Doctoral Dissertation). Retrieved from ProQuest Dissertation and Theses Global database. (UMI No. 3126153)

Applications: Women and Campus Ecology

Dziech, B. W., & Vaughan, G. B. (1983). Changing status of women. In G. B. Vaughan (ed.), *Issues for community college leaders in a new era* (pp. 55-75). San Francisco, CA: Jossey-Bass.

Applications: Adults, Non-Traditionals, Veterans and Campus Ecology

Hillard, M. K. (1996). *An assessment of persistence and mattering among nontraditional, community college students* (Doctoral Dissertation). Retrieved from ProQuest Dissertation and Theses Global database. (UMI No. 9628684)

Applications: Low Income Students and Campus Ecology

Bell, D. A. (2012). *An exploration of factors that impact the satisfaction and success of low socioeconomic status community college students* (Doctoral Dissertation). Retrieved from

ProQuest Dissertation and Theses Global database. (UMI No. 3535408)

Dykes, M. (2011). *Appalachian bridges to the baccalaureate: Mattering perceptions and transfer persistence of low-income, first-generation community college students* (Doctoral Dissertation). Retrieved from ProQuest Dissertation and Theses Global database. (UMI No. 3584058)

Applications: First Generation Students and Campus Ecology

Dykes, M. (2011). *Appalachian bridges to the baccalaureate: Mattering perceptions and transfer persistence of low-income, first-generation community college students* (Doctoral Dissertation). Retrieved from ProQuest Dissertation and Theses Global database. (UMI No. 3584058)

Applications: Geography and Campus Ecology

Alderman, L. V. (1997). *Student support services and their impact on persistence of first-year students at a rural community college* (Doctoral Dissertation). Retrieved from ProQuest Dissertation and Theses Global database. (UMI No. 9817088)

Brown-Weinstock, P. (2009). *Adjustment and persistence of students from an urban environment to a rural community college* (Doctoral Dissertation). Retrieved from ProQuest Dissertation and Theses Global database. (UMI No. 3410791)

Decker, A. K. (2011). *Appalachian bridges to the baccalaureate: How community colleges affect transfer success* (Doctoral Dissertation). Retrieved from ProQuest Dissertation and Theses Global database. (UMI No. 3584050)

Johnson-Dedeaux, V. M. (2011). *An investigation of students' satisfaction with academic advising and students' impressions of academic advisors at a rural community college* (Doctoral Dissertation). Retrieved from ProQuest Dissertation and Theses Global database. (UMI No. 3487153)

Layman, R. W. (2005). *Exploring differences in level of involvement, educational outcomes, and satisfaction of resident students and commuter students at a rural community college* (Doctoral Dissertation). Retrieved from ProQuest Dissertation and Theses Global database. (UMI No. 3191233)

McMillion, S. S. (1999). *Campus environment factors of two small, rural community colleges and their influences on persistence behaviors of African-American students in the college transfer program* (Doctoral Dissertation). Retrieved from ProQuest Dissertation and Theses Global database. (UMI No. 9922697)

Phillips, C. M. (2011). *Appalachian bridges to the baccalaureate: Institutional perceptions of community college transfer success* (Doctoral Dissertation). Retrieved from ProQuest Dissertation and Theses Global database. (UMI No. 3584185)

Part 3
The Future

In the final chapter, I speculate on the future of campus ecology. Important to this future is an in depth exploration of the principles of traditional/biological ecological concepts and their potential usefulness for campus ecology. Linking campus ecology to other "like minded" concepts and systems will also open up new directions in the future. Finally, an opportunity is presented to allow this book to becoming a "living" manuscript and to expand in the future.

Chapter 8

The Future:
An Epilogue

An epilogue is defined as a closing section providing further comment or interpretation (Guralnik, 1970). The history of the campus ecology concept illustrates that the ecological perspective that behavior is a transactional function between persons and environments is foundational to the model. The ecological concept of human behavior continues to be a basic tenet of modern social science. Campus ecology has a firm foundation. Also, the campus ecology model, as documented in this manuscript, has a long forty-plus year history signaling the endurance of the concept. The over 900 documents noted in the indexes of applications related to campus ecology attest to its utility and heuristic value. With this established foundation and ongoing use of the concept, the purpose of this brief epilogue is structured around the question: What is next for the campus ecology model? I think two paths lie ahead: (a) further development of concepts within the basic concepts of ecology, and (b) the development of linkages to other social science concepts and models.

Developments within the Concept of Ecology

In 1984, I began to think about concepts within the traditional biological use of the concept of ecology that could be used to help understand the social ecology of the campus environment (Banning, 1984). This was a metaphoric search, but several concepts emerged that had promise besides the already adopted "ecosystem." These included the notions of ecosystem resilience and stability, carrying capacity, niche, niche width, and territoriality. The connection of these concepts to the campus environment is noted in "On a Personal Note" 8-1: Cross-Fertilization. Since this early attempt to further the usefulness of the campus ecology concept by connecting to other more traditional concepts, a very useful step forward was made by Renn and Patton, 2011. They used the concept of ecological niche to illustrate the importance of campus cultural centers. They indicate that the cultural centers can serve as niches that contribute to the promotion of retention, engagement, and student success. Their discussion of the cultural center as an ecological niche supports further exploration of the concept. What are other niches on campus for what kinds of students? Can these be identified and highlighted for student use?

An additional biological concept, the edge effect or ecotone, also has promise for deepening the understanding of campus ecology (Dajoz, 1976). Ecotone is used to denote the transition zone between biological communities: "The fauna of an ecotone is more numerous and diverse than that of either adjacent community, since it includes species from both communities. This effect is also known as the edge effect" (Dajoz, 1976, p. 236). Where are the ecotones on campus? Certainly one ecotone is the zone produced by the campus edges as they bump up against the retail establishments of the community. These zones have often taken on a uniqueness as a behavioral setting encouraging partying and drinking behaviors

The Future: An Epilogue

not typically found on campus or in other parts of the community. Another application can be found in the academic arena. Are the interdisciplinary students in an ecotone? Are there important differences for students who are in biochemistry rather than biology or chemistry? Do student-athletes find themselves in a unique campus ecotone? Ecotone is just one example of the "metaphoric search" within biology for increasing the understanding of campus ecology. The concepts of density dependence, resource partitioning, structural inertia, and others may also be valuable in increasing the usefulness of the campus ecology model.

Gonzalez (1989) provides an excellent illustration of this notion of exploring biology to enhance the campus ecology perspective. He presents the four ecological/biological principles: "resource cycling, interdependence, adaptation, and succession" (p. 18) and how these concepts can increase the understanding of the campus environment.

"On a Personal Note" #8-1: Cross-Fertilization

My early attempt at cross-fertilization included the following:

Ecosystem

An ecosystem is a functioning interacting system composed of one or more living organisms—"biome"—and their effective environment, both physical and biological (Fosberg, 1963). Is the campus an ecosystem? What are the boundaries of the campus ecosystem? Some ecologists speculate that specific ecosystems may have distinctive emergent properties and undergo evolutionary change after the fashion of individual species (Margalef, 1968). What about developing universities?

What are the unique emergent properties? Can these be supportive of student development?

Ecosystem resilience

Ecosystem resilience determines the persistence of relationships within a system and is the measure of the ability of these systems to absorb changes of state variables and parameters, and still persist (Holling, 1973). How resilient is the campus to changes in student enrollment and/or student types?

Ecosystem stability

Ecosystem stability is the ability of the system to return to an equilibrium state after a temporary disturbance (Holling, 1973). Are some residence halls more stable than others? What are the conditions that relate to ecosystem stability?

Carrying capacity

Carrying capacity is the maximum population that a particular environment can support indefinitely without leading to degradation (Ellen, 1982). What are the carrying capacities of the sub-environment on campus, e.g., class size, residence hall capacity, and leadership opportunities? What is the relationship of carrying capacity to outcomes in student development? What are the support limits for a campus environment?

Ecological niche

Ecological niche represents the adaptive match between circumstances of the environment and the species schema (Hunt, 1961). Within a campus environment, can ecological niches be found and identified? Are there different niches for different students? Can campus ecological niches be designed?

What are the characteristics of an ecological niche that foster student growth and development?

Niche width

Niche width refers to the amount of different resources used and the extent to which each is relied upon by the organism within the ecological niche (Hardesty, 1975). Do different student populations consume resources at different rates? Do campus "widths" differ? Can we measure campus niche widths?

Territoriality

The concept of territoriality entails the acquisition, demarcation, and defense of a spatial area with related dimension of implied ownerships, personalization, and maximum control (Schroeder, 1977). How does the concept of territoriality impact our residence halls? Are behavior problems related to issues of territoriality?

Behavioral Sink

Calhoun (1962) coined the term "behavioral sink" to designate the gross distortions of behavior that appear to be the outcome when an unusually large number of animals are collected together. Are behaviors often observed in dorms related to a behavior sink phenomenon? Are the gross behaviors often associated with campus "Greek towns" related to this phenomena?

References:

Calhoun, J. B. (1962). Population density and social pathology. *Scientific American, 206,* 139-148.

Ellen, R. (1982). *Environment, subsistence, and system.* Cambridge: Cambridge University Press.

Fosberg, F. R. (Ed.). (1963). *Man's place in the island ecosystem.* Honolulu: Bernice P. Bishop Museum.

Hall, E. T. (1969). *The hidden dimension.* New York: Anchor Books.

Hardesty, D. L. (1975). The niche concept: suggestions for its use in studies of human ecology. *Human Ecology, 3,* 71-85.

Holling, C. S. (1973). Resilience and stability of ecological systems. *Annual Review of Ecology and Systematics, 4,* 1-23.

Hunt, J. M. (1961). *Intelligence and experience.* New York: Ronald Press.

Margalef, R. (1968). *Perspectives in ecological theory.* Chicago: University of Chicago Press.

Schroeder, C. C. (June, 1977). *Student development through environment management.* Paper presented at the Conference of the Association of College and University Housing Officers, Lexington, KY.

There is a second use of the concept of campus ecology in higher education whose development is associated with the National Wildlife Federation. In the early 1990s (Smith, 1993), their website defined campus ecology as a program to promote climate leadership and sustainability among colleges and universities by providing resources, technical support, networking opportunities, and by organizing events. Interaction between the two uses of *campus ecology* could also fall within an ecotone for further development of both uses of the concept. The continued cross-fertilization between biology and campus ecology is a directional path for the future.

> ### "On a Personal Note" #8-2: Lemmings to the Sea
>
> Lemmings to the sea is a personal example that I developed to illustrate the importance of the interface between campus ecology and biology. There may be other explanations for the lemming's behavior, but the "carry capacity" metaphor is instructive.

LEMMINGS TO THE SEA: STUDENT ATTRITION

From James Thurber

"'... It may interest you to know that I have made a lifelong study of lemmings, just as you have made a lifelong study of people. Like you, I have found but one thing about my subject which I do not understand.' 'And what is that?' asked the lemming. 'I don't understand', said the scientist, 'Why you lemmings all rush down to the sea and drown yourselves.' 'How curious,' said the lemming. 'The one thing I don't understand is why you human beings don't'" (Thurber, 1937).

Lemmings?

Lemmings are small, mouse like rodents and are well known for "suicidal" trips to the sea (Odum, 1975). Dubos (1965) gives the following account: "According to an ancient Norwegian belief, the lemmings periodically experience an irresistible 'collective urge' either to commit suicide or to search for their ancestral home on the lost Atlantic sea." "The migration of Norwegian lemmings was so massive in 1960-61 that a steamer entering the Trondheim Fjord took one hour to pass through a two-mile-long pack of swimming and sinking rodents!" (p. 103). While the exact mechanism for this population crash is not known, one factor that is suspected is crowding.

The "carrying capacity," or the maximum population that a particular environment can support indefinitely without leading to degradation, is a concept that is suggested by Ellen (1982). The concept may be useful in our attempt to understand student attrition.

Students as Lemmings

"I don't understand," said the campus administrator, "why you students all rush down to the registrar's office to a stop out or drop out?" "How curious," said the student. "The one thing I don't understand is why you administrators don't." (Apologies to Thurber!)

Student Attrition

While student attrition may not be "suicidal," it does represent the failure to reach an educational objective. It has been well documented that "between 40 and 45 of every 100 first-time entrants will leave without earning a degree of any sort" (Tinto, 1985). What is the "carrying capacity" of a campus environment? Do the students know something that we don't?

We do know that if all the enrolled students suddenly, for some reason, decided not to be an attrition statistic and continued their enrollment that the college or university would self-destruct. There would not be enough faculty, classrooms, staff, etc. We plan and design our educational environment based on the prediction of a status-quo attrition rate. Our ability to "carry" is based on a large number of our students rushing to the Sea of Attrition!

Improving Carrying Capacity

ACT (1985) lists the following as "common retention strategies" to improve what could be termed the "carrying capacity":

-Improved academic advising services

-Improved academic support service

-Mandatory assessment and course placement

-Increased career/life planning services

-Increased faculty/student contact

-Improved instruction

-New curricular developments

-Early warning systems

-Faculty/staff development programs

-Increased emphasis on co-curricular activities

-Enhancement of resident living

-Increased communication with parents

-Improvement in physical plant

Perhaps a "carrying environment" in higher education could be summarized as a "caring environment"!

References:

ACT (1985). *Midstate worksheets and activities.* Iowa City: The American College Testing Program.

Dubos, R. (1965). *Man adapting.* New Haven: Yale University Press.

Ellen, R. (1982*). Environment, subsistence and system.* Cambridge: Cambridge University Press.

Odum, E. P. (1975). *Ecology.* New York: Holt, Rinehart and Winston.

Thurber, J. (1937). *Interview with a lemming.* In *My world And welcome to it.* New York: Harcourt, Brace and Company.

Tinto, V. (1985). Dropping out and other forms of withdrawal from colleges. In L. Noel, R. Levitz, D. Saluri, and Associates (Eds.), *Increasing Student Retention.* San Francisco: Jossey-Bass.

The development of linkages to other social science concepts and models

Strange and Banning (2015) connected the concept of place to ecological thinking in their reference to Morrill, Snow, and White's (2005, p. 232) statement: "The meaning of place is not inherent in its 'objective' or physical attributes, but rather rises from the interpretive processes that occur in the interplay between people-to-place and person-to-person interactions." With the linkage between campus ecology and the concept of place, many useful connections are available for increasing the understanding of the campus environment. For example, Bott, Banning, Wells, Haas, and Lakey (2006) linked the "sense of place" to campus ecology. Okoli (2013) connected sense of place to the concept of involvement. Other linkages have also been made between important aspects of the student's campus journey and the concept of place: academic progress (Scott-Webber, Strickland, & Kapitual, 2013), alumni involvement (Reeve & Kassabaum, 1997), student organizations' relationship to the institution (Kuk, Thomas, & Banning, 2008), and residence hall room design (Clemons, Banning, & McKelfresh,

2004). The work of Cresswell (1996, 2014, & 2015) provides a linkage between ecology/place and the study of campus diversity by introducing the concept of "in place" or "out of place." Linkages and connections to the concept of place will enhance the future usefulness of the campus ecology model.

The concept of time, like place, is a complex one, but one worth exploration to fully understand the concept of campus ecology. Renn and Arnold (2003) noted the importance of time in the ecological perspective in their discussion of Bronfenbrenner's (1995) concept of chronosystem. On a practical level, even the simple notion that time denotes a particular point in a year or in the day has value for understanding the campus environment. The campus is a different place at night versus the day. Morning behavior that involves the arriving and starting of the campus activities is different than evening behavior that captures the exiting and closing of activities. Exploration of the concept of time and associated research will be an important addition to the campus ecology model in the future.

The Phenomenological Variant of Ecological Systems Theory (PVEST; Spencer, 1995; Spencer, Dupree, & Hartmann, 1997) is another potential enhancing linkage to the campus ecology model. PVEST is a research strategy described as a combination of the phenomenological approach with ecological systems. This combination allows the person to fully engage in the meaning making process in terms of the salient features of the environment. One study used the PVEST model to explore at-risk youths' experiences (Hayling, 2010), and many of the issues of these experiences can translate to the behavior associated with academic outcomes. In addition, the PVEST approach has been used to explore the developmental experiences of African Americans, which can have a direct link to the experience of diversity on the college campus (Lee, Spencer, & Harpalani, 2003; and Spencer, 1995).

The foregoing linkages are in concert with Renn and Patton's (2011) view of the future direction of campus ecology. They emphasize the role campus ecology can play in accountability and institutional productivity. Focusing on greater cross-fertilization between the use of traditional ecological concepts and the campus ecology model, exploring the role of place and time in ecological thinking, and seeking research models like PVEST should contribute to obtaining what Renn and Patton (2011) see as the future ecological perspective: "strong potential to contribute to demonstrating institutional efficacy in retaining and graduating diverse students …" (p. 253).

Final Note: A Living Book

The future use of the ecological perspective and the campus ecology model has yet to be written. This book found over 900 manuscripts that mentioned, referenced, and/or significantly used the concept of campus ecology. Nearly all of these manuscripts were located by the use of the *Google Scholar* search and notification program. To employ *Google Scholar* in a similar manner in the future by adding new studies to the established or new topical categories will make this document a *living* one. It is my hope that this book will grow as the concept of campus ecology becomes a more central component of professional training for higher education and a key focus of university affairs scholarship. To support the efforts of maintaining this book as current and "living," my website (http://www.campusecologist.com) will post manuscripts that mention, reference, or use the concept of campus ecology published after July 1, 2016. If you know of manuscripts that have been missed in the search effort for this book and/or become aware of new publications, please feel free to post them at the campusecologist.com website or contact Campusecologist@gmail.com.

References:

Banning, J. H. (1984). General ecology: An opportunity for cross-fertilization. *The Campus Ecologist, 2(*1), 1, 3.

Bott, S., Banning, J., Wells, M., Haas, G., & Lakey, J. (2006). A sense of place: A framework and its application to campus ecology. *College Services, 6,* 42-47.

Bronfenbrenner, U. (1995). Developmental ecology through space and time. A future perspective. In P. Moen & G. H. Elder, Jr. (Eds.), *Examining lives in context: Perspectives on the ecology of human development* (pp. 619-674). Washington, D.C.: American Psychological Association.

Clemons, S. A., Banning, J. H., & McKelfresh, D. A. (2004). The importance of sense of place and sense of self in residence hall room design. *Journal of Student Affairs, 13,* 8-15.

Cresswell , T. (1996). *In place/out of place: Geography, ideology, and transgression.* Minneapolis, MN: University of Minnesota Press.

Cresswell, T. (2004). *Place: A short introduction.* Malden, MA: Blackwell Publishing.

Cresswell, T. (2015). *Place: An introduction.* Malden, MA: Wiley Blackwell.

Dajoz, R. (1976). *Introduction to ecology.* New York: Crane, Russak, & Company, Inc.

Gonzalez, G. M. Understanding the campus community: An ecological paradigm. *New Directions in Student Services, 48,* 17-26.

Guralnik, D. B. (Ed.). (1970). *Webster's new world dictionary.* New York: The World Publishing Company.

Hayling, C. C. (2010). *The salience of context: A culturally-centered examination of the role of ecology in the behavioral outcomes of at-risk youth* (Doctoral Dissertation). Retrieved from ProQuest Dissertation and Thesis Database. (UMI No. 3419357).

Kuk, L., Thomas, D., & Banning, J. (2008). Student organizations and their relationship to the institution: A dynamic framework. *Journal of Student Affairs, 17*, 9-20.

Lee, C. D., Spencer, M. B., & Harpalani, V. (2003). "Every shut eye ain't sleep": Studying how people live culturally. *Educational Review, 32*(5), 6-13.

Morrill, C., Snow, D. A., & White, C. H. (Eds.). (2005). *Together alone: Personal relationships in public places.* Berkeley, CA: University of California Press.

Okoli, D. T. (2013). *Sense of place and student engagement among undergraduate students at a major public research university* (Doctoral Dissertation). Retrieved from ProQuest Dissertation and Theses database. (UMI No. 3608379)

Renn, K. A., & Arnold, K. D. (2003). Reconceptualizing research on college student peer culture. *The Journal of Higher Education, 74*(3), 261-291.

Renn, K. A., & Patton, L. D. (2011). Campus ecology and environments. In S. Komives & D. B. Woodward (Eds.), *Student services: A handbook for the profession* (pp. 242-256). San Francisco, CA: Jossey-Bass.

Reeve, J. R., & Kassabaum, D. G. (1997). A sense of place master plan: Linking mission and place. *1997 APPA Proceedings*, 209-228.

Scott-Webber, L., Strickland, A., & Kapitula, L. R. (2013). Built environments impact on behavior: Results of an active learning post-occupancy evaluation. *Planning for Higher Education Journal, 42*(1), 1-12.

Smith, A. A. (1993). *Campus ecology: A guide to assessing environmental quality and creating strategies for change.* Los Angeles: Living Planet Press.

Spencer, M. B. (1995). Old issues and new theorizing about African American youth: A phenomenological variant of ecological systems theory. In R. L. Taylor (Ed.), *Black Youth: Perspectives on their status in the United States* (pp. 37-70). Westport, CT: Praeger.

Spencer, M. B., Dupree, D., & Hartmann, T. (1997). A phenomenological variant of ecological systems theory (PVEST): A self-organization perspective in context. *Developmental and Psychopathology, 9,* 817-833.

Strange, C. C., & Banning, J. H. (2015). *Designing for learning: Creating campus environments for student success.* San Francisco, CA: Jossey-Bass.

About the Author

Jim Banning is professor emeritus in the School of Education at Colorado State University. After receiving his PhD in clinical psychology from the University of Colorado-Boulder, his career has focused on student services administration, ecological/environmental psychology, and the application of environmental psychology to educational settings. He has particularly focused on the application of the ecological perspective and the development of the campus ecology model and has taught a course in campus ecology in the Student Affairs in Higher Education Program at Colorado State University for more than 30 years and continues to teach an online version. In addition to teaching, Jim's administrative leadership experience has included Director of Counseling and Testing, University of Colorado, Vice Chancellor for Student Affairs, University of Missouri-Columbia, and Vice President for Student Affairs, Colorado State University. During his career, Jim has authored and co-authored several books, book chapters, and journal articles on the ecological perspective of student services, including the recent publications of *Designing for Learning: Creating Campus Environments for Student Success* and *Student Affairs Leadership: Defining the Role Through an Ecological Framework*. Jim maintains a website at http://www.campusecologist.com and welcomes participation.

Appendix A

First Paper on Campus Ecology by Dr. Leland Kaiser (Used with permission of the author)

CAMPUS ECOLOGY: IMPLICATIONS FOR ENVIRONMENTAL DESIGN

Leland R. Kaiser, M.A., M. P.H.
Division of Health Administration
University of Colorado Medical School

Task Force II -Epidemiology, Campus Ecology and Program Evaluation

For use in WICHE project -Improving Mental Health Services on Western Campuses

THE CONTEXT OF MENTAL HEALTH SERVICES

Mental health services are always provided in a given institutional context or setting. This context is a composite of (1) the attitudes and orientation of college administration towards the mental health center, (2) the philosophy of mental health and mental illness espoused by the staff of the center, (3) student definitions of the mental health center and its services, (4) financial resources of the center, and (5) policy constraints imposed on the center by administration, the Board of Trustees, state law, etc.

- Mental health services on the majority of college campuses are patterned after a traditional model and include:

- reliance upon the medical model to explain student distress (illness)

- an orientation towards treatment rather than prevention

- a focus upon pathology in the individual (intrapsychic) rather than pathology in the environment (contextual)

- limited participation in the formation of administrative policies and procedures

- limited review and comment upon the curriculum or faculty practices

An alternative model is available for the organization of mental health services on college campuses. It is an ecological model which stresses:

- reliance upon socio-environmental explanations of student distress

- an orientation toward prevention rather than treatment

- a focus upon disordered environments rather than disordered students

- the need for a close liaison between mental health center personnel and those persons responsible for formulation of administrative policies and procedures

- the need for a close liaison between mental health center personnel and the faculty, particularly in the area of curriculum development

Appendix A

The ecological approach to mental health is concerned with the creation of campus environments which potentiate students as physical, mental, social and spiritual beings. Through preventive environmental design, an attempt is made to "design out" pathology and enhance normal functioning. However, because of the transactional nature of students and their campus environments, some distress will always be present and must be treated. The ecological model does not replace the traditional treatment model. Rather, both models complement one another. The ecological model has only recently come into being and is still in the process of development.

THE DEVELOPMENT OF AN ECOLOGICAL MODEL

A number of investigators have expressed increasing dissatisfaction with the medical model as an explanatory scheme for student emotional disturbance. Typical of these sentiments are Cowen and Zax (1968a) who state: "The implicit assumption of analogy between psychological and physical disorder has doubtless been a stultifying one. Whereas physical disorder implicates invasion by some type of pathogenic agent, psychological dysfunction more likely reflects complex, long-standing determinants and processes and varied sources of influence, including important 'others' in the person's life space and key social institutions" (p. 48).

Cowen and Zax (1968b) feel that primary institutions exert an impact on emotional and personality development that deserves closer examination. They state: "We must learn more and do more about building for psychological resources and for health, rather than simply counter-punching against pathology. Such an orientation underscores the need for examination of influential primary institutions in modern society and establishes the centrality of questions such as: How do primary institutions influence emotional and personality development? How are these impactful systems modified; and What is the relationship between institutional change and optimal psychological development?" (pp. 48-49).

If we view colleges as primary institutions, it is only natural to speculate about their influence on student mental health and to search for broader etiological concepts of health and disease. The need for a broader context for mental health was underscored by Hobbs in his project ReED. Hobbs (1968) views the disturbed child ". . . as a manifestation of the 'breakdown of an ecological system composed of child, family, neighborhood, school, and community." The goal of mental health services for children would then not be to cure the child or to prepare him to cope with all possible life roles but to restore to effective operation the small social system of which the child is an integral part" (p. 13).

Extrapolating from Hobbs's work, we might imagine a mental health center restoring to effective operation the small campus social system of which the disturbed student is a part. The mental health center would view the administration, faculty, and students as an ecosystem where the action in any part of the system affects all parts in the system.

Kahn (1968) discusses modification of the social environment as an engineering problem. He states: "Community mental health is not the whole of social engineering, but it is one of the major fields of such application, and application involves both repairing the effects of present environments and attempting to identify and modify the sources of damage" (p. 73).

Kelly (1968), in a pioneering work on ecologically-based mental health interventions in high schools, delineates four main variables used in his investigations: (1) the diversity of student coping styles,

(2) adaptive roles that fit particular school environments, (3) the concept of setting as a way to define the school's environmental structure, and (4) the effect of immigration and emigration on the school's environment. A restatement of these variables makes them applicable to campus design, namely the campus designer:

- recognize individual differences among students
- see the possibility of creating diverse school environments
- be able to ascertain the structure of a school environment
- be able to fit the campus environment to the student

From these fundamental notions, a set of assumptions can be set forth which will form the basis of a philosophy of environmental design.

A DESIGN PHILOSPHY FOR CAMPUS ENVIRONMENTS

Such a set was developed by Kaiser (1971) for the design of new towns. Placed in the context of campus design, these assumptions may be restated as follows:

1. A transactional relationship exists between college students and their campus environment, i.e., the students shape the environment and are shaped by it.

2. For the purposes of environmental design, the shaping properties of the campus environment are focused upon; however, the students are still viewed as active, choice-making agents who may resist, transform, or nullify environmental influences.

3. The campus environment consists of all the stimuli that impinge upon the students' sensory modalities and includes physical, chemical, biological, and social stimulation.

4. Every student possesses a wide spectrum of possible behaviors. A campus environment may be designed to facilitate or inhibit any one of these behaviors. The campus may be intentionally designed to provide opportunities, incentives, and reinforcements for growth and development.

5. The students will attempt to cope with any educational environment in which they are placed. If the environment is not compatible with the students, the students may react negatively or fail to develop desirable qualities.

6. Because of the wide range of individual differences among students, fitting the campus environment to the students requires the creation of a variety of campus sub-environments. There is an attempt to design not only for the normative students but also for the deviant students.

7. Every campus has a design, even if the administration, faculty, and students have not planned it or are not consciously aware of it. A design technology for campus environments, therefore, is useful both for the analysis s of existing campus environments and the design of new ones.

A design philosophy must be paralleled with a design methodology before the construction of intentional campus environments is a reality.

Appendix A

DESIGN METHODOLOGY FOR CAMPUS ENVIRONMENTS

Essentially, the question is: How do you "fit" a campus environment to a student? In this view, optimal fit is equated with mental health of the student. Two methods arc possible:

8. <u>Method A – Self Selection Method</u>: The designer creates diverse campus environments structured to appeal to different kinds of students. Students are allowed on the basis of preference to select the environment of choice. The student is responsible for the goodness of fit.

<u>Method B – Matching Method</u>: Each student is studied individually, and individual profiles of personality, interests, attitudes, etc., are constructed. A range of campus environments is created, each with clear-cut design features to appeal only to students with certain profiles. Students and environments are then matched on the basis of similarity. Goodness of fit is the responsibility of someone other than the student.

Either Methodology A or Methodology B depend upon how well campus designers can:

- determine what the campus environment actually is

- determine how the campus environment is viewed by the majority of students (normative view)

- determine how the campus environment is viewed by the minority of students (deviant view)

- relate the perceptions of the campus environment to structural features of the environment, i.e., administrative policies, curriculum, faculty-student relations, etc.

- design environments with structural features known to produce given student perceptions

- determine the environmental perceptions and preferences of the individual student and relate these to a particular campus environment.

The state of the art is not well developed, yet enough is known to begin designing campus environments. A good place to begin is with the elimination of noxious environmental stimulation—what students don't like about the campus (what causes them distress). From this negative viewpoint can emerge a concern with providing growth environments for student fulfillment.

A TYPOLOGY OF ENVIRONMENTS

A typology of environments is suggested by Kaiser (1971). He describes compensating environments, facilitating environments, and potentiating environments. A compensating environment "makes up for deficits in individual functioning. It supports the disability in such a way that it does not become a handicap." A facilitating environment "provides opportunity for the expression of existing individual capabilities." A potentiating environment "stimulates the development of dormant abilities possessed only a behavior potential by the individual." Campus environments then may be designed to support student disabilities, facilitate expression of existing interests and abilities, and potentiate dormant aptitudes or traits.

USE OF BEHAVIOR MODIFICATION IN ENVIRONMENTAL SHAPING

As Tharp and Wetzel (1969) suggest: "The learning theories, which underlie behavior modification, attempt to specify the relationship between an organism's behavior and his environment. As the environment changes according to the several laws of learning, so with behavior. Thus, behavior modification assumes the appropriate locus for intervention in effecting behavior change in the individual's environment" (p. 2).

A campus designer may use behavior modification to reinforce desirable student behaviors through appropriate rewards placed in the campus structure. This extension of behavior modification, from the laboratory to the natural environment, is anticipated by Tharp and Wetzel (1969) when they state: "Thus it may be seen that the potent 'reinforcers' for an individual ordinarily lie within his natural environment and these reinforcers are controlled by those people to whom he is naturally related. The task of contingency management comes to us through the reorganization of the patterns of reinforcement control exercised by the people of an individual's environment."

If the prospect of deliberate contingency management is awesome, it should be remembered that every environment has a payoff structure, chaotic though it may be. Some behaviors are encouraged, others are discouraged. In the design of campus environments, the effort is deliberate and organized, and an attempt is made not to reward destructive behaviors and reward constructive ones.

SUMMARY

Campus ecology is the study of student/environment transactions. Campus design is an attempt to create healthy campus environments for student growth and development. An attempt is made to reduce student emotional disorders, not through treatment of the student, but treatment of the environment which shapes the student behavior. Behavior modification offers a powerful tool for analyzing existing environments for their reward structure and for building new ones. Mental health is viewed as an optimal student-environmental fit. The range of individual differences among students requires a range of campus environments. Every environment has an identifiable structure that may be related to student perception. Change the structure and the student perceptions change. Although the state of the art is young, a review of the literature reveals a growing body of knowledge that may be utilized to build better campus environments for our students.

(Please note: Prior to the above summary, Kaiser reviewed a substantial body of literature, but due to length, it is not included in this presentation of his paper. In addition, the references noted in the paper are not available.)

www.ingramcontent.com/pod-product-compliance
Lightning Source LLC
Chambersburg PA
CBHW071805300426
44116CB00009B/1206